D1742963

WHAT DO I KNOW?

*What Montaigne Might Have Made
Of The Modern World*

WHAT DO I KNOW?

What Montaigne Might Have Made
Of The Modern World

Paul Kent

Beautiful
Books

First published 2011

Beautiful Books Limited
36-38 Glasshouse Street
London W1B 5DL

www.beautiful-books.co.uk

ISBN 9781907616112

9 8 7 6 5 4 3 2 1

Cover design by Ian Pickard.
Printed in and bound in the UK by CPI MacKays, Chatham ME5 8TD.

This book is dedicated to the memory of Christine—uxor carissima

INTRODUCTION

'I have never seen greater monster or miracle in the world than myself.' (Book 3, Chapter 11: 'Of Cripples')

'Dost thou, then, old man, collect food for others' ears?' (Perseus, Satires, i. 22., quoted in Book 1, Chapter 38: 'Of Solitude')

It's often claimed that Michel de Montaigne (1533-1592) invented the essay form. Which is true—up to a point.

He was almost certainly the first person to *describe* his work as '*essais*', although the practice of composing short philosophical excursions can be traced back to classical antiquity and writers like the younger Pliny. But what sets Montaigne's 107 essays apart from any others past or present is their creator's open-mindedness, and the breadth of subject matter he addresses. This ranges from fatherhood to flatulence, cowardice to cannibals, Socrates to smells: 'I enter into discussion and argument with great freedom and ease,' he writes, 'No propositions astonish me, no belief offends me, whatever contrast it offers to my own. There is no fancy so frivolous and so extravagant that it does not seem to me quite suitable to the production of the human mind.'

And for the most part, he upholds this claim—which is no mean feat, given that modern editions can run to almost 1500 pages. As such, his work is the perfect embodiment of Aldous Huxley's definition of the essay, which he describes as 'a literary device for saying almost everything about almost anything.'

But most of what Montaigne is saying concerns Montaigne himself. He sits right at the front, centre stage while performing his one-man show, brilliantly lit by the unforgiving spotlight he trains on every aspect of his thought and behaviour. By the end, it feels like we know him inside out; literally so, as he provides us with regular updates on the state of his bowels. Not to mention several peeks within the confining trouser.

Montaigne's famous fans are said to have included William Shakespeare: *Hamlet, King Lear* and particularly *The Tempest* have been shown to bear his influence, and a copy of John Florio's 1603 English translation, currently in the British Library, is graced with the playwright's signature.[1] Balzac claimed that Montaigne had carried human reason as far and as high as it could go, both in politics and in morals. Blaise Pascal and Ralph Waldo Emerson both reckoned he taught them a thing or two. Virginia Woolf acknowledged him as her mentor.[2] Even *übermensch* Friedrich Nietzsche, a man as temperamentally opposite from Montaigne as it's possible to get, gave him a glowing press: 'That such a man has written,

---

1. However, whether the signature is *genuine* remains a controversial subject.

2. 'Movement and change are the essence of our being', Woolf writes, '...Let us say what comes into our heads, repeat ourselves, contradict ourselves, fling out the wildest nonsense, and follow the most fantastic fancies without caring what the world does or thinks or says.' It's a slightly ditzy version of Montaigne's approach, but not a million miles away.

joy on earth has truly increased... if my task were to make this earth a home, I would attach myself to him.' As have 5,632 followers on Facebook.[3] And the former French President, Francois Mitterand, whose official photo shows him standing in a library gripping an open copy of the *Essays*.

Montaigne's writings are also a rich source of aphorisms. Here's ten completely random samples:

- *One should always have one's boots on, and be ready to leave*

- *Fame and tranquillity can never be bedfellows.*

- *Man is quite insane. He wouldn't know how to create a maggot, and he creates gods by the dozen.*

- *Every man's shit smells good in his own nostrils.*

- *When seated upon the most elevated throne in the world, we are but seated upon our own bottoms.*

- *A man must have courage to fear.*

- *Age imprints more wrinkles in the mind than it does on the face.*

- *He was become a fool by too much wisdom.*

- *I see no people so sick as those that take physic.*

And so on. And on, literally by the hundreds, bulked out with illustrative quotations from the greatest minds of antiquity like Cicero, Plato and Seneca. Yet amid all the wit and erudition, Montaigne plays down his role as author, preferring to cast himself as a simple compiler: 'I have gathered a garland of other men's flowers', he claims, 'and nothing is mine but the cord that binds them.' Which is, of course, complete tosh; the flowers are mainly his own, and they're a dazzling display of rare blooms.

---

3. As of July 2010, Nietzsche has only 3,171 fans.

Yet that typical example of Montaigne's modesty is part of the reason, I suspect, why 17 of the 20 individuals who bothered to review the latest English translation on amazon.com have given *The Complete Essays* five stars out of five. They are drawn to him *as a man* and not simply for what he has written. They like the fact that he freely admits his memory is bad; he bolts his dinner; his boots are always dirty; he waters down his wine and won't put on his glasses. He certainly refuses to conform to the traditional images of the philosopher: he's not some remote white-bearded ancient in a toga spouting metaphysics to an audience of adoring neophytes in the *agora*; a black-gowned academic skulking in the stacks of a musty Oxford library; or even a be-denimed philosophy tutor puffing a thoughtful spliff on a '70s campus. He's neither Plato, nor Francis Bacon, nor Umberto Eco—and thank God for that. Instead, he cultivates the role of the gifted amateur, while actually being phenomenally well-read. He could almost be one of us, which for me at least, makes his observations that much more compelling. Montaigne's philosophy isn't abstract; it's not some academic exercise—he actually lived it. And, should we choose, we can live it too.

This is far from being a terribly scientific evaluation—but that's entirely deliberate. I'm using Amazon recommendations as my evidence precisely because they're not written by the usual eggheads or reviewers quoted on book jackets—they are genuine endorsements from members of the reading public who want to encourage those who don't yet own a copy of the *Essays* to dive in and enjoy them. Which, if you haven't already, is what I want, too. One web commentator was moved to write this:

There is in Montaigne a sanity, a balance, an affability, and a modesty and tolerance that is found in no other European thinker.

And here's my particular favourite:

There's a lifetime's reading in here. For such a big fat classic of a book it reads like it was written yesterday... Wisdom is maybe underrated these days, but Montaigne isn't just spouting off. This is not a 16th century 'Evening with Morrie' [sic]. *You can see him thinking. He encourages you. (What a great word 'encourage' is.)*

And I'm not going to argue with a syllable of either, because embedded within those comments are the reasons I'm writing this book.

Here's the pitch:

Of all the great thinkers, certainly in the Western tradition, none is more appropriate for a 21st-century audience than Montaigne. Philosophy, when most of us think about it at all, is too often viewed as something too difficult or abstruse for the modern age: its reputation isn't helped by comments like this one from Karl Marx, who judged it to be 'To the real world what masturbation is to sex.' Which is, of course, utter tripe, because philosophy lies at the heart of everything we are, whether we acknowledge it or not. Our personal philosophies are continuously, and often unconsciously, moulded by countless factors in our past and present that influence and ultimately govern how we think, feel and behave. Yes, in the real world.

Montaigne's essays constitute the story of one man's philosophy, written simply and directly for anyone to understand. As we read we can indeed 'see him thinking', so we not only get the philosophy, but the process that grows and shapes it as well. It's a process which, as our first reviewer notes, is influenced by Montaigne's 'sanity', 'affability' and, most importantly of all, 'balance'. For he weighs everything carefully, sifting the knowledge and wisdom in an ongoing process of trying to understand who he is. Then, as our second reviewer comments, by leading from the front, '[h]e encourages you' to do some thinking of your own. If a philosopher is traditionally viewed as 'someone with a problem for everyone solution', Montaigne is the exact opposite; the *Essays* don't tell us *what* to think, but quietly urge us *how* to think—and think *well*.

The only problem is that most of us don't have the time to think anything meaningful *at all*. So we turn, like magpies, to opinion columns, TV, blogs—anywhere—for quick fixes of someone else's thinking, a bit here, a bit there, which very often lack any of the redeeming qualities of Montaigne's writings— least of all sanity, balance, affability, modesty and tolerance. It's a process ably reported in Nick Hornby's novel *How To Be Good* in which doctor and mother Katie Carr describes *her* experience of self-realization, or rather, her frustrated attempts at it:

I wanted someone wise to teach me things I needed to know to survive the rest of my life. And I know it's pathetic that it should have been a children's science fiction film telling me this—it should have been George Eliot, or Wordsworth, or Virginia Woolf. But then that's precisely the point, isn't it? There is no time or energy for Virginia Woolf, which means that I am forced to look for meaning and comfort in my son's Star Wars *video.*

Look no further. Montaigne's your man; he wrote the ultimate in self-help books without necessarily intending to.[4] It's a weighty volume that may seem daunting at first, but doesn't demand to be finished in one sitting, one year, or even one lifetime. But it's my contention that even a nodding acquaintance with Montaigne will produce more tangible and more enduring results than anything currently available in the mushrooming self-help genre. And the *Essays* will continue to be a

---

4. Sarah Bakewell's recent (excellent) biography of Montaigne is called *How To Live*, and she rightly claims that 'Readers come to him in search of companionship, wisdom and entertainment—and in search of themselves.'

force for the good long after John Gray and his ilk have been consigned to the dump bin of history.[5]

And so in *this* book I'm going to try and address a number of subjects, many (but by no means all) prompted by my reading of Montaigne, in a manner as close to Montaigne's as I can possibly manage, to serve as an introduction for a 21st-century reader of the *Essays;* to speculate how Montaigne might have dealt with some contemporary themes; and, at the end, to sum up why he's more relevant than ever.

End of pitch.

Unfortunately, there's a slight drawback: I'm not Montaigne, and I can't compete with him on any level, least of all in classical erudition—you're as likely to find Tom and Jerry in here as quotes from Thomas Aquinas. Temperamentally, I'm way less phlegmatic, and far more private—unlike my hero, I'm unlikely to tell you how often I shit, or how long I spend in the bathroom while doing it. Being spared those essential details would, I hope, occasion gratitude and not censure.

But what I *can* claim to share with Montaigne is an often annoying level of curiosity and a reluctance to think I know the answers to everything. Or, indeed, that answers to anything are necessarily knowable *at all.* Because this is an issue I've had to confront on many occasions both in my personal and professional life when I've not been ready or able to deliver conclusive answers to questions I don't feel have instant resolutions. And, as you'll discover, I've found this both annoying and troubling. There's a good deal of doubt beneath the veneer of certainty I feel I have to show the world, and ever since I first

---

5. As of summer 2010, there are almost 200,000 self-help books in print. In the United States alone, the market is said to be worth over \$10bn per annum. That's a lot of people wanting to help themselves.

read his work, I've envied Montaigne's easy ability to admit to ignorance and irresolution—and by doing so turning them from negatives to positives. I think the following paragraph from his essay 'On Repentance' sums up the ebb and flow of Montaigne's thought—and mine too:

I cannot fix my object; 'tis always tottering and reeling by a natural giddiness; I take it as it is at the instant I consider it; I do not paint its being, I paint its passage; not a passing from one age to another, or, as the people say, from seven to seven years, but from day to day, from minute to minute, I must accommodate my history to the hour: I may presently change, not only by fortune, but also by intention. "Tis a counterpart of various and changeable accidents, and of irresolute imaginations, and, as it falls out, sometimes contrary: whether it be that I am then another self, or that I take subjects by other circumstances and considerations: so it is that I may peradventure contradict myself, but... I never contradict the truth. Could my soul once take footing, I would not essay but resolve: but it is always learning and making trial.

So if you're questing after certainty, read no further—these essays won't provide you with that, because it's not mine to give. But with any luck they will leave you with the comforting thought that there's nothing amiss if the answers we all seek don't always present themselves on demand, on a plate and in Technicolor vividness.

So as you read these ramblings, please bear in mind Laurence Sterne's admonition, taken from the preface to *Tristram Shandy*: 'As we jog on, either laugh with me or at me, or in short do anything—only keep your temper.'

And also this, from the great man himself: 'Titles of my chapters do not always comprehend the whole matter.'

And we will see what we can see.

★ ★ ★

Before we go any further, however, I thought it might be an idea to devote three short essays to subjects that underpin everything that follows: I've already briefly stated why I reckon Montaigne's philosophy is an antidote to modern ways of thinking, so I'd better expand a little on that claim; second, I'd like to elaborate on why I feel he's a kindred spirit; and finally, in a piece ostensibly about autobiography, I need to address my own doubts about Montaigne's motivations in putting pen to paper, and why he chose himself as his subject.

One final item of housekeeping: I have used Charles Cotton's elegant 1685/6 translation of the *Essais* throughout, which I have freely adapted in places where the language or syntax might not be clear to modern readers. It's available for free internet download on a number of sites. Other excellent complete translations are those by M.A. Screech (Penguin Classics, 2004) and Donald M. Frame (Stanford University Press, 1958). A lively selection by J.M. Cohen (Penguin Classics, 1958) is widely available in second-hand bookshops and on the internet.

Chapter One

Opinions with Bowels

'We take other men's knowledge and opinions upon trust; which is an idle and superficial learning. We must make it our own. We are in this very like him, who having need of fire, went to a neighbour's house to fetch it, and finding a very good one there, sat down to warm himself without remembering to carry any with him home. What good does it do us to have the stomach full of meat, if it do not digest, if it be not incorporated with us, if it does not nourish and support us?' (Book 1, Chapter 24: 'Of Pedantry')

'I examine myself even to the very bowels.' (Book 3, Chapter 5: 'Upon Some Verses Of Vergil')

Reading the above quotation from 'Of Pedantry', we can probably take it for granted that Montaigne wouldn't take much notice of the opinion mongers that have colonized the world's media like a pernicious infestation of woodlice.

He favoured quiet statement over clangorous hectoring, observing that someone with knee-jerk opinions on everything is nothing more than an 'incorrigible coxcomb.' His description of gossipy writers is wonderfully prescient of the 21st-century's mass media: these people, he writes, 'pretend…to nothing but babble, not to be very solicitous of any part but that, and so, with a fine jingle of words, prepare us a pretty contexture of reports they pick up in the streets.' Much later in life, the following maxim appears: 'Affirmation and obstinacy are express signs of want of wit.' Which indicates to me that 'the louder the noise, the emptier the vessel' was as true five hundred years ago as it is now. And that it consistently got on his wick. In one of his darker moods, he declares, 'The world is nothing but babble; and I hardly ever yet saw that man who did not rather prate too much, than speak too little.'

Too true. These days, like it or not, bite-size opinions have become the new philosophy of the time-poor, and they're thrust at us everywhere we look. As I write, a 60-foot LED billboard near my flat proudly proclaims that the star columnists of the UK's bestselling tabloid deliver a daily dose of 'OPINIONS WITH BALLS.' A headshot and a by-line are all you need to start what our Amazon reviewer calls 'spouting off'—no previous experience or qualifications seemingly necessary.

This elephantiasis of media-generated opinion had to start somewhere, and in journalistic histories, the finger tends to point, perhaps unfairly, at just one man—Herbert Bayard Swope of the New York *Evening World* who decided, in the 1920s, to print a selection of miscellaneous content on the page opposite his newspaper's editorial. He later proudly commented on his invention:

It occurred to me that nothing is more interesting than opinion when opinion is interesting, so I devised a method of cleaning off the page opposite the editorial, which became the most important in America… and thereon I decided to print opinions, ignoring facts.[6]

---

6. Swope was a fascinating figure: not only did he coin the phrase, 'The Cold War', he won a Pulitzer Prize for reporting in 1917 and, allegedly,

These fact-free opinions certainly made for a snappy alternative to the staid and anonymous editorial copy, and the so-called 'Op Ed' ('Opposite the Editorial') page rose in popularity and rapidly expanded. And expanded, to the point where we can all self-publish our opinions by micro-blogging in 140 characters or less. Were he alive now, Montaigne could syndicate his essays using any number of digital platforms. 'OPINIONS WITH BOWELS' might be a catchy title for his musings. Particularly on a 60-foot LED billboard overlooking West London.

Anyway, not only is my local tower of babble a blight on the visual landscape, it's yet another depressing symbol of our taste for disposable subjectivity. Depressing because opinion is to knowledge what bulimia is to healthy eating: in go the raw materials and out they come again scarcely digested. When the London *Times* recently relaunched its website, did the ad campaign focus on the quality of its journalism? No, it led with its opinion columns, which are apparently stuffed with 'views you can't afford to miss.'

Well, I beg to differ: I can solicit all the fatuous opinion I'll ever need down the pub; and second, as Montaigne's fellow countryman Voltaire noted almost 300 years ago:

Les opinions ont plus causé de maux sur ce petit globe que la peste et les tremblements de terre. ('Opinions have caused more ills than the plague or earthquakes on this little globe of ours').

Very true: the huffing and humbug of the op columns are usually intended to work their readers into a righteous lather about something or other. But Voltaire might have refined his statement slightly by adding that *unsubstantiated* opinion

---

$470,000 in a single poker game.

is the real culprit. He once famously declared that he would defend to the death a person's right to spout tedious bollocks, as would I; that's one of the prices we pay for freedom of speech. Unfortunately, having the *entitlement* to an opinion is very often confused with the *value* of that opinion.

Voltaire again: '*Le préjugé est une opinion sans jugement.*' ('Prejudice is opinion minus judgement'). Which implies, correctly, that judgement is an essential component of opinion. Robbed of judgement, opinion has no lasting value, or general application. Quite simply, it doesn't come *with* balls—it *is* balls and should be consigned to the litter tray of history. Because we all know what devastation can be caused by prejudice. Or at least we should by this point in our little globe's development.

So with an opinion come certain responsibilities that are not automatically conferred by entitlement. Not terribly onerous ones, but ones that are often trampled underfoot in the rush to say something desperately novel or controversial. JFK acknowledged this when he noted: 'Too often we…enjoy the comfort of opinion without the discomfort of thought'; and, here's a surprise, Kurt Cobain said much the same thing: 'We have no right to express an opinion until we know all of the answers.'

So our opinions reveal something of the way we understand the world and, like everything else we do or say, they reflect back on us. Someone who changes his opinion as often as his underpants is either deeply insecure, badly confused, a moral casuist, or a pathological liar. In any case, you wouldn't necessarily want to trust their judgement, let alone be influenced by it.

But why get worked up about this? After all, Montaigne's *Essays* are still in print 500 years on, while a nation's cats defecate on yesterday's shredded rentagobbery which is, of course, the way it should be. And besides, in a democracy we can usually exercise our right to disagree.

No, what alarms me is not just the empty vehemence with which opinions are currently expressed; it's the sheer speed and turnover of opinion that is unique to our time, courtesy of advancing technology. I'm no Luddite, in fact I adore living in an age where so much is instantly available, because I can remember a time when it wasn't. Yet although many of us have fully integrated the new digital gizmos into our lives, the instant access they provide has elevated opinion to being the keystone of our intellectual grammar, simply because it's faster and more immediate than other slower options that require actual thought, or the application of prior knowledge and experience. A recent example:

During the 2010 UK General Election campaign, the British public was treated, for the first time ever, to a series of TV debates between the leaders of the three main political parties. No problem with that—at base, it's a worthwhile attempt to re-engage a generation of voters lost to democracy through apathy or disgust. But then came THE WORM, beloved of US TV punditry for years, yet brand new to Britain. A panel of twenty floating voters each turned the dial on a handheld device to indicate if they liked or disliked what the politician was currently saying. The aggregate result was displayed in the form of a moving on-screen wiggly line for the benefit of viewers: a wiggle of the cursor upwards indicated overall approval, a wiggle downwards general disagreement. During pauses in the proceedings, the Tigger-like anchorman thrust his microphone in the faces of the guinea pigs, chanting 'instantreaction, instantreaction' and read out viewers' Tweets.

Of course, there's always been opinion polls, but the sheer speed at which opinion now travels is mind-blowing—from synapse to syndication in a millisecond. *This...is...GOLD

DUST!' squawked Tigger as the Worm peaked.[7]

Diverting, I grant you. Interesting? Perhaps. But in the end, Tigger me old mate, it was only REACTION, and it's dangerous to confuse instant reaction with anything of meaning, substance or value. Which is what's increasingly happening, and *that's* why I'm concerned. Speed + Stridency = Superficiality. Sworn enemies of knowledge and understanding. On this occasion, the Worm merely caused an over-excitable presenter to come dangerously close to voiding his bowels live on air— which would have proved about as enlightening as the views of twenty don't-knows on tax reform, only more entertaining. Because speed is no substitute for comprehension; stridency no surrogate for authority.[8] And anything superficial lacks a necessary context. Like a Tweet removed from its torrent, it just doesn't make sense.

But holding back your views until you've even had the chance to formulate them—let alone contextualize them—is a rare luxury in our era of instant everything. People tend to grow impatient and even suspicious if you keep your opinions to yourself. Very often, it seems preferable to blurt out *anything* no matter how contingent just as long as you say *something*. Only 'I'll have to give some thought to that' or 'I don't know—let's kick that about a bit' are becoming less acceptable responses, no matter how accurately they reflect your current state of comprehension. You need to KNOW. NOW. Or else you're a BIG FAT PUSSY who's either dumb, ill-briefed or shifty. Just watch Prime Minister's Questions live from the British

---

7. Miles Kington's spot-on definition of an opinion poll: 'a survey which claims to show what voters are thinking, but which only succeeds in changing their minds.'

8. My favourite ever headline came from the lead item in a BBC radio news bulletin. It began, 'Speculation is expected to continue today.' Speculating about speculation represented a new low point in my experience of news coverage.

Parliament if you want to witness the sorry level of debate this attitude fosters.

And the antidote to frenzy and superficiality described in the last few pages? A bit of quality time curled up with Montaigne and a cold drink of one's choice. Sanity, affability, erudition, wisdom, entertainment...and room to breathe and think. Bliss. For as we'll see in the next essay, Montaigne's conception of what knowledge is, how we get it and what we do with it exists at 180° to our contemporary value system.

What's not to like?

Chapter Two

Skepticism, Montaigne and Me

'Solum certum nihil esse certi, et homine nihil miserius ant superbius.'

'It is only certain that there is nothing certain, and that nothing is more miserable or more proud than man.'— **(Pliny the Elder, Naturalis Historia., ii. 7) quoted in Book 2, Chapter 14: 'That Our Mind Hinders Itself'**

In 1576, at the age of 42, Montaigne ordered a medal to be struck bearing the inscription 'Que sçais-je?' (literally, 'What do I know?'). On the reverse, was the single Greek word 'ἀπέχω' ('I abstain'). Two sides of the same coin, literally and metaphorically. As the title of this book might indicate, I wouldn't mind one of these to remind me of a worthwhile intellectual principle.

Why did he have it made? Well, five years into writing the *Essays*, those that know these things argue that Montaigne was undergoing an 'epistemological crisis'—in other words, he wasn't sure he could believe or trust in anything, and that 'knowledge' was not actually knowable, having no basis in truth or reality. Which is, of course, pretty bewildering—if

the only conclusion you can come to is that there are no conclusions, you may to end up confused, or at worst insane.[9] The
medal has been widely interpreted as the physical embodiment
of this impasse. A 21st-century man of a similar vintage would
have considered buying a Harley or perhaps making a fool of
himself with a younger woman.

But *was* it a crisis? Those in favour attribute Montaigne's confusion to the dizzying speed of intellectual progress in the 16th-
century: Galileo and Copernicus were turning astronomy,
religion and philosophy on their heads, and the discovery of
the New World meant that Europe was no longer (geographi-
cally at least) at the heart of Civilization. All of which were
radical ideas that took a lot of getting used to, and Montaigne
would not have been alone in having difficulty assimilating
them into his personal philosophy.

But let's look at it another way: the four words on that medal
are deliberately riddled with ambiguity, and it's quite possible
to interpret them as the reverse of the intellectual paralysis with
which they've come to be associated—namely, that an inability
(or a refusal) to draw conclusions is actually healthy, and that
Montaigne was reminding himself not that knowledge and the
truth are ultimately unknowable, but that they are to be celebrated as rich and complex. In that context, he's basically saying
'Who am I to judge?' Being thoroughly familiar with the philosophy of Socrates, he will have remembered the paradox
ἓν οἶδα ὅτι οὐδὲν οἶδα ('I know that I know nothing', or perhaps
the more confident 'I know through knowing nothing') and
maybe taken his lead from that. The medal could just as easily
celebrate his triumph over doubt as represent a guilty reminder
of it.

---

9. Or a Deconstructionist, who believes that one opinion is just as good
as any other, and that any unification of these opinions is impossible.
Chief deconstructionist was Jacques Derrida—also a Frenchman.

Whether or not this dovetails with the details of Montaigne's biography, I'm convinced it is closer to the guiding principle of the *Essays*, and furthermore I think that their continuing relevance (and popularity) are directly attributable to Montaigne's refusal to nail his colours to the mast in any dogmatic way. You can't help but be won over by the guy's modesty, honesty and abiding curiosity at an age when intellectual arteries tend to start hardening. And yet he reveals just enough of his inner Grumpy Old Man to stop his fair-mindedness from becoming routine and irritating. He's perpetually in the state of 'becoming' who he is—and he'll never arrive. Deliberately.

Nevertheless, it's crucial to acknowledge that this was not the case 100% of the time. As we'll see in a future essay, this lack of certainty could unsettle and even depress him; the waywardness of reality made it seem that resolution was beyond his grasp, and in those periods he longed for a single, defining truth, unadulterated by choice and possibility. But for the most part, he shows himself content with his lot, and sufficiently self-confident not to be downhearted when just about everything presented itself in a multiple aspect.

In addition, it's important to distinguish between Montaigne and the columnists I was slagging off earlier whose opinions lack judgement. Because if I'm *praising* Montaigne for withholding judgement, surely that represents a contradiction in my own thinking. Or favouritism. So, briefly, here are the four ways they're different:

First, as I've just noted, Montaigne doesn't *lack* judgement, he *withholds* it. Which is not to say he doesn't *make* judgements, because he does in almost every sentence. Rather, he doesn't view his judgements as the final word on the matter—his view is not *the* view, and he doesn't usually speak for anyone but himself. As such, his judgement is always *conditional*; he's not going for closure, since judgement is a staging post on the road to knowledge, not the destination.

Second, he isn't afraid to question himself in public;

Third, he'll routinely examine an issue from different angles, and;

Fourth, as I hope to demonstrate by the end of this book, the two decades or so it took him to write the *Essays* were characterized by the steady accretion of a core of stable philosophy. For underpinning all Montaigne's writings is a fundamental fairness and decency, so decent in fact, it's perfectly possible to call it a code of ethics, or even morality. It's seldom po-faced, and almost never self-righteous, but it represents something much more grounded in truth than the spoutings of those who are paid for their ability to temporarily stir, irritate or shock their readers.

And that's why I reckon we need him now more than ever. It's going to be difficult, perhaps even impossible, to break the hegemony of those whose conception of knowledge is embodied by the three Esses (see page 16), but by conscripting Montaigne, we stand a slightly better chance than the proverbial mosquito on the elephant's arse of remembering that there *is* an alternative.

* * *

So what kind of philosopher *was* Montaigne? Well, for a start, his uniqueness confuses the hell out of those who like to pigeonhole their thinkers, and it's been severally argued that Montaigne is a Stoic, a Humanist or a Skeptic. But inasmuch as any label is helpful, these are all in the correct ballpark.

Unfortunately, however, they're all wrong. Or, perhaps more accurately, incomplete, for at different times, Montaigne shows symptoms of being all three: he's certainly a Humanist, in his insistent focusing on human-scale values, and his concern to increase the variety of the created world; he's often (but not always) a Stoic, believing that Reason (and not the emotions) should govern our thinking. Most often, although this is only my opinion, he's a card-carrying Skeptic, in that he has an excellent onboard bullshit detector and questions everything. Perhaps his best known quotation, 'When I play with my cat, who knows whether she is not amusing herself with me more than I with her?', succinctly demonstrates the Skeptical technique of inverting a subject to look at it from both ends.

So it's probably helpful before we venture any further to define Skepticism—and who better for our purposes than a member of a contemporary group of Skeptics from Merseyside, a bunch of people I really like the sound of:

Skepticism is a method for discerning truth from fiction. When presented with a claim, a skeptic reserves his or her right to reject that claim until such time as the claimant produces sufficient evidence to back up that claim. If the skeptic finds the evidence is compelling, then we will provisionally accept the claim as true; provisionally because we may see more evidence tomorrow that proves the claim to be false. The quality and quantity of evidence required will vary from claim-to-claim and skeptic-to-skeptic. If you tell me that you have a pet dog, well, I'll probably accept that claim just on your word. You're not likely to get anything out of making up stories about owning a dog and I know that dogs are kept as pets by many people. If you tell me that you have a pet dragon, on the other hand, I'm probably going to want to at least see the dragon before I believe you.[10]

Which neatly sums it up: a Skeptic never says 'That's total

---

10. For further information on The Merseyside Skeptics Society, visit their excellent website at http://www.merseysideskeptics.org.uk. They meet regularly in a pub, which also endears them to me. Beer and skepticism—bliss!

bollocks!', preferring the more conditional, 'That *sounds* like total bollocks,' until he's researched the full picture. And even then, he will not completely discount the possibility that circumstances may change, forcing him to reconsider his position.

Montaigne's view of how history should be written neatly sums this up: some historians, he says, are partisan, biased and therefore misleading; some simply report what happened with no bias one way or another; but the best historians (like Plutarch and Livy) 'have judgement to pick out what is most worthy to be known; and, of two reports, to examine which is the most likely to be true...such have title to assume the authority of regulating our belief to what they themselves believe; but certainly, this privilege belongs to very few.'

'Most likely' are the key words here. Montaigne doesn't categorically state there's no such thing as Truth; simply that it can never be taken for granted, and that it's our duty to continually re-evaluate it. As such, true knowledge is composed of a cloud of considered, contingent opinions which have been shot through the prism of judgement.

In short, we *earn* the right to hold our opinions because we've taken time to formulate them. And *that's* the responsibility that comes with mouthing off. Unfortunately, says Montaigne, not many historians have earned the right to be trusted.

God knows what he'd make of modern journalism. But looking on the bright side, all of this makes Kurt Cobain, whom I quoted earlier, a Skeptic. Who knew?

★ ★ ★

So what's all this skepticism got to do with me, and why am I drawn to Montaigne to the point where I'm writing a book about him? As you'll already have gathered, I'm no philosopher; I have no background in philosophy; in fact, I'm not sure if I even *have* a workable philosophy. It's more a sort of motley quilt that I'm continually working on, patching it where holes have developed, sewing up where it's unravelling and generally trying to stop it from looking too shabby. So I'll try and explain—as much for my benefit as yours…

The seeds of this book were first sown when I was 17, as three schoolmates and I went to stay in a log cabin in Scotland for a weekend of illicit drinking and smoking. The ringleader had, a few days before, passed his driving test, and his extremely generous and/or stupid father had lent him his brand-new 3-litre Ford Capri. And it was in the back seat of this car that I had the mother of all arguments with my friend Frank, which forced me to think for the first time in my short life about what it was to 'know' something. He asked me if I 'knew' what I was going to do with my life once I'd left college. I replied that I hadn't a clue (I still haven't, incidentally), at which point, fuelled perhaps by a few tins of lager, he got quite shirty. He knew *exactly* what his life held in store, and, stone me, thirty-odd years and a bit of internet surfing later, I've discovered that's *exactly* how his life *did* pan out (he's a hot-shot legal in the defence industry). And all credit to him—he *knew* what he wanted to do and went ahead and did it. To the letter. Moreover, he opined, it was our duty to *know* this, and anyone who hadn't cast their *curriculum vitae* in tablets of stone by the age of 17 was, in his view, weak in the head and a BIG FAT PUSSY. It was on this point that our opinions necessarily divided.

I confess to having been quite upset at first; the more I tried to argue with him, the more he dug his heels in. He was not to be moved. Total conviction, Thatcherite in its intensity.[11] His vehemence made me begin to feel he was right and I was

11. And indicative of his own political leanings.

mistaken—and it's still something I occasionally ponder in my less self-confident moments. Which are many, and growing more frequent the older I get.

As we approach our half-century, Frank appears to be considerably richer and more successful than me. And good luck to him. His foreknowledge served him well. I just hope he's moved on from being the insufferably smug little prick he was back then, and that he's started standing his round in the pub.

Any road... I soon began to regroup, and to actually argue the case against Frank's brand of dogmatism. After all, hadn't that magnificent poet Keats, the hero of all us English students, posited that one of the *sine qua non*s of creativity was to suspend judgement, to deliberately and consistently curtail that leap from feeling and appreciation into certainty? He called it 'negative capability.' The thirst for absolute truth, he implies, closes doors that are best left open. And didn't that other hopeless romantic (and Keats fan) F. Scott Fitzgerald say much the same thing in 1936?

[T]he test of a first-rate intelligence is the ability to hold two opposed ideas in the mind at the same time, and still retain the ability to function.

Certainly, at 17, my less than first-rate intelligence felt it was way too early to be drawing conclusions about a life I'd hardly begun living. After all, what did I actually *know*? Bugger all, if I was brutally honest with myself. Even my appreciation of English Literature, which I was aiming to study at university, was confined to a detailed reading of eight 'A'-Level set texts. Laughable, really. I simply didn't feel myself *equipped* to formulate my own opinions.

And so, for the most part, I began to abstain from the teenage habit of making pronouncements as if I was in touch with the wisdom of ages. This got me the reputation for being intellectually wishy-washy among my teachers who were looking for taut, muscular arguments drenched in the testosterone of certainty to get me through the Oxbridge entrance exam. One correctly remarked that my train of thought was constantly being derailed by a tendency to focus on small shiny things glinting in the scrub by the side of the track. How right he was. And indeed still is. I've always admired the saying coined during the California Gold Rush of the 1850's: 'If you only search for one thing, you will only find one thing.' And what's the fun in that?

This is one reason I prefer to read Montaigne's *Essays*, and not those of his contemporary Francis Bacon. For Bacon, (who of course famously tossed off Shakespeare's plays in his lunch breaks), produced some of the driest, dullest, self-satisfied lectures in the English language. It was he who famously noted *Nam et ipsa scientia potestas est*, ('Knowledge is power').[12]

For Montaigne, by contrast, the pursuit of knowledge is not rooted in utilitarianism. It does not exist to be owned, manip-ulated, traded, quantified or displayed—it is not a commodity; rather it should be appreciated and nurtured as an enabling and enriching quality on its own terms and for its own sake. Montaigne, I feel, simply couldn't be *bothered* playing power games with what he knew; his reverence for knowledge was such that he probably would have considered such behaviour banal or even vulgar—although to be fair I nowhere remember him saying as much.

So when reading Bacon, I tend to admire his brilliant but rather frigid lecturing style from a distance: but with Montaigne, I want to buy him a pint. Or indeed several. He's like me, only far better read, complete with all the weaknesses flesh is heir to.

One last proof that Montaigne had his skepticism under control:

---

12. Which he half-inched from the *Book of Proverbs*.

he was the first writer to describe his writings as '*Essais*'. In the original French, *essai* translates as 'attempt', implying that any knowledge gained thereby was simply a single version of the truth in a multiverse of truths. Like the contents of the lava lamp on my desk, truth and knowledge will keep recasting themselves in interesting, unpredictable shapes. And if you think that's the copping-out of a relativist who can't reach a proper conclusion you're probably right. You can call me a BIG FAT PUSSY if you want, but I've got a pretty wonderful ally in Montaigne.

But then, Frank *does* have a Roller...

Chapter Three

The Doings

'If you belittle yourself, you are believed; if you praise yourself, you are disbelieved.' (Book 3, Chapter 8: 'Of the Art of Conference')

Autobiographies are among the publishing industry's biggest earners: it seems the reading public loves a bit of curtain-twitching. From the rich, famous and powerful down to the vulnerable and abused who satisfy the current demand for 'misery lit' (my local bookshop has created a separate 'Painful Lives' shelf, so swollen have their ranks become), anyone's life seems grist to the mill.

But why would Montaigne want to join this endless procession of self-publicists by writing such a nakedly autobiographical work as the *Essays?* Wouldn't he be too modest? Or simply above all that?

Well, seemingly not. Only to think of Montaigne as a rampant egotist ruins the fond image I have of him and, in a way, demeans the value I place on the book's philosophical content. So I guess I'm going to have to look into the matter to set my mind at rest.

It could be argued that you have to have a grossly over-developed ego to even contemplate foisting the details of your earthly existence on an unsuspecting world. Of course, a large cheque from a publisher will offer an incentive, as will the simple desire to be noticed among those who feel they have no voice (hello, bloggers everywhere). And then there's the politician's desire to 'set matters straight' by placing a spurious sheen on the catalogue of screw-ups that constitutes his 'legacy.'

But aside from the obvious motivations of money and notoriety, it's actually a big step from, say, writing a diary or personal letters, to fashioning these primary sources into an account of your life and having it made available to people you've never met in places you've never visited. Not to mention what your Mum's going to say when she finds out what you've been up to. The Puritan in me considers it an act of overweening pride—but obviously I don't take much notice of him, or I wouldn't be writing this book which, following the example of its inspiration, contains a fair few personal anecdotes.

We could begin this brief inquiry with one of Montaigne's contemporaries, the sculptor and goldsmith Benvenuto Cellini, who wrote in his own snappily-titled autobiography *Vita ('Life')*, that 'No matter what sort he is, everyone who has to his credit what are or really seem great achievements, if he cares for truth and goodness, ought to write the story of his own life in his own hand.' So, the great and the good (of whom he considers himself a representative) are almost honour bound to disseminate details of their fine fine superfine careers for the benefit of those of us who don't scale the heights of wonderfulness they have.

Inevitably, there's a certain amount of automatic selection in this category; indeed, we'd begin to wonder if an autobiography of, say, Tony Blair *hadn't* appeared. It's expected—not necessarily because we take for granted that all the world's premiers have voracious appetites for self-publicity, but because they are often at the cutting edge of events that impinge on all our lives. Worst luck.

Which is OK—we all occasionally need moral and behavioural beacons to inspire, or indeed caution us—but it's the idea of setting *yourself* up as one that really sticks in my craw.

Then again, back in Cellini and Montaigne's era, you could get away with that sort of thing: as Renaissance man emerged blinking into the light from beneath the all-enveloping shadow of a vengeful God, the notion that you could 'build' or 'invent' yourself first gained currency. Hence the phrase 'Renaissance Man', still applied to those who have the time, the means and the ability to cultivate a 'rounded' understanding of themselves and the world they live in. So, by writing an account of your successes and failures—whether they be intellectual, spiritual, mercantile or whatever—you could claim to be performing a public service, particularly if your life was in any way exemplary.

Some autobiographies of this kind had appeared way before the Renaissance—St. Augustine's *Confessiones* were written at the turn of the 5th century, in which he warns his readers not to imitate the 'past foulnesses and carnal corruptions' of his youth, when he was heavily into acts of sordid frightfulness and had an 11 year-old fiancée. His famous prayer '*da mihi castitatem et continentiam, sed noli modo*' ('Grant me chastity and continence, but not yet') has been paraphrased by those other noteworthy philosophers, James Bond and Robbie Williams.

Then there's the harrowing life story of the 11th-century medieval scholar Peter Abelard, whose *Historia Calamitatum* expresses the hope that 'in comparing your sorrows with mine, you may discover that yours are in truth nought, or at the most but of small account, and so shall you come to bear them more easily.' But then he had been castrated for knocking up his girlfriend, which is a calamity in anyone's book.

Montaigne's successful career as a high-up courted by the great and the good certainly fits the Cellinian model for autobiography, which also stipulates that these accounts of a life well lived argue a minimum level of age, experience and acquired wisdom. Cellini notes that 'no one should venture on such a splendid undertaking before he is over forty.' Well, Montaigne began writing the *Essays* on his 38th birthday, on which he retired to his vast personal library of 1500 books and began scratching away. He commemorated his near-total retreat from worldly affairs with the following declaration, which he had inscribed in view of his desk.

In the year of Christ 1571, at the age of thirty-eight, on the last day of February, his birthday, Michel de Montaigne, long weary of the servitude of the court and of public employments, while still entire, retired to the bosom of the learned virgins, where in calm and freedom from all cares he will spend what little remains of his life, now more than half run out. If the fates permit, he will complete this abode, this sweet ancestral retreat; and he has consecrated it to his freedom, tranquillity, and leisure.

In his prefatory remarks to the *Essays*, written no doubt while reclining on the busty substances of these learned virgins, Montaigne notes that his editorial approach is just to be 'honest': in fact, it's to be so free from 'strain or artifice' that, were it not unmannerly, he would parade stark bollock naked in front of his audience. The resulting book, he continues, is intended as a simple and artless self-portrait, warts and all.

And in so thinking, without perhaps fully realizing it, he penned a unique, genre-busting autobiography. Rather than a record of what he achieved, Montaigne actually wrote a biography [sic] of his mind.

The best description I've come across arrives courtesy of the English essayist William Hazlitt, who noted:

Of all egotists, Montaigne, if not the greatest, was the most fascinating, because, perhaps, he was the least affected and most truthful. What he did, and what he had professed to do, was to dissect his mind, and show us, as best he could, how it was made, and what relation it bore to external objects. He investigated his mental structure as a schoolboy pulls his watch to pieces, to examine the mechanism of the works[.]

Which is exactly right. The autobiographical element arrives not in any kind of chronological or thematic structure, but dressed in his choice of subject and illustrative anecdote. From receiving the king to the waywardness of his penis, there seems almost no subject he will not address.[13]

And why shouldn't he write about himself? If, as I've already noted, Montaigne's skepticism posited that the world was ultimately unknowable, one thing he *could* write about with some degree of certainty was his own intellect—and, of course, by extension, himself:

I dare not only speak of myself, but to speak only of myself: when I write of anything else, I miss my way and wander from my subject.

Fair enough on the surface of things. But at this point we can go all postmodern and demand whether the 'Montaigne' of the *Essays* bears any resemblance to the real one. In the era of unreliable and multiple narrators, Yeatsian masks and literally dozens of other narrative strategies that allow writers to hide behind different *personae*, how do we know we're getting

---

13. Except perhaps Mrs Montaigne. More of whom later.

the real thing? How accurate is Montaigne's depiction of Montaigne, particularly bearing in mind Iris Chase's observation in Margaret Atwood's novel *The Blind Assassin*:

The only way you can write the truth is to assume that what you set down will never be read. Not by any other person, and not even by yourself at some later date. Otherwise you begin excusing yourself.

On go the rose-tinted spectacles, building the public image you wish to present to the world. The minute you suspect you have an audience, the perception of yourself can change radically. And once again, we can only speculate whether this occurred when Montaigne put pen to paper—and once again, it's his extraordinary candour which lets him off the hook: the *Essays* seem to contain few of the personality-building techniques beloved of autobiographers. There's almost no trace of self-justification, no hint of revisionism, and no imposition of an artificial intellectual consistency or progression as the *Essays* ramble on. He shows and doesn't tell—and so the 'true' Montaigne, the core of the man, can only exist in the reader's head after he has finished the book. As such, it's a rather modern work—a collaboration between the writer and his readers culled from a large body of random and often conflicting evidence.

But what of those readers? If we could tease out who (and how many) Montaigne thought they might be, perhaps we could get a better handle on his motivations for setting pen to paper. In the Introduction, he claims that his account is simply intended as a memento of his character and disposition for his friends and family:

I have dedicated it to the particular commodity of my kinsfolk and friends, so that, having lost me (which they must do shortly), they may therein recover some traits of my conditions and humours, and by that means preserve more whole, and more life-like, the knowledge they had of me.

But Montaigne's work has turned out to be much more than the exercise in vanity publishing that quotation suggests. Did he know in advance it would be read by an audience that extended far outside his circle of familiars? Hazlitt again helps us with his thoughts on the matter, speculating that yes, he probably did:

It was reasonable enough that Montaigne should expect for his work a certain share of celebrity in Gascony, and even, as time went on, throughout France; but it is scarcely probable that he foresaw how his renown was to become world-wide; how he was to occupy an almost unique position as a man of letters and a moralist; how the Essays would be read, in all the principal languages of Europe, by millions of intelligent human beings, who never heard of Périgord or the League, and who are in doubt, if they are questioned, whether the author lived in the sixteenth or the eighteenth century. This is true fame. A man of genius belongs to no period and no country. He speaks the language of nature, which is always everywhere the same.

Brilliant—and coming from a brain the size of Hazlitt's, we really ought to sit up and take notice. Montaigne could never, as he jotted down the opening sentences, have any idea that you or I would be reading them in the 21st century. But he would surely have anticipated *some* local interest, particularly since he was a prominent public figure. After all, we all like a bit of goss, don't we? It's interesting to conjecture how Montaigne's conception of his readers might have influenced the deeply personal material he ended up including, particularly the more scatological stuff. Does this make him an honest man or a shameless exhibitionist? Discuss—because, quite frankly, I don't know.

In trying to resolve the issue, up pops my Inner Puritan again, insisting that Montaigne's modest ambition for his work and its future reception is so much eyewash. We've all come across that very British kind of understatement, such as 'I was only doing my job', or 'it was really nothing' when the speaker has jumped in front of a speeding bullet to save the life of a nursing mother. Would Michelangelo describe the roof of the Sistine Chapel as 'just one of my daubs'? Could Mahler say of his Second Symphony, 'Hey, I was just sitting at the keyboard trying a few things and Bang!' In certain circumstances, this Pavlovian modesty can come over as desperately rehearsed and self-satisfied—the very opposite, in fact, of modest. In many ways, it's worse than those rampant self-publicists who parade their monstrous egos in public—they're at least being true to themselves and their code.

So when Montaigne describes himself as a 'frivolous and un-rewarding subject', one is tempted to ask what purpose this evident self-libel is serving. And when, in his essay 'On Giving the Lie', he comments that 'the subject is so poor and sterile that I cannot be suspected of ostentation', surely this is an excellent example of what my college tutor use to describe as 'ironic self-deprecation'? I mean, a bottom-feeder like Katie Price fits those descriptions rather better, as the slow-motion car-crash that is *her* autobiography unfolds volume by weary ghost-written volume.[14] But the god-like genius that is Montaigne?

Well, right at the start of the pivotal Essay 'On Presumption' (Book 2, Chapter 17), Montaigne addresses the issue head-on:

There is another sort of glory, which is the having too good an opinion of our own worth. ''Tis an inconsiderate affection with which we flatter ourselves, and that represents us to ourselves other than we truly are: like the passion of love, that lends beauties and graces to the object, and makes those who are caught by it, with a depraved and corrupt judgement, consider the thing which they love other and more perfect than it is. I would not, nevertheless, for fear of failing on this side, that a man

---

14. A.k.a. Jordan—a brilliant woman who has built a multi-million pound industry off the back of her stupidity.

should not know himself aright, or think himself less than he is; the judgement ought in all things to maintain its rights; 'tis all the reason in the world he should discern in himself, as well as in others, what truth sets before him; if it be Caesar, let him boldly think himself the greatest captain in the world. We are nothing but ceremony: ceremony carries us away, and we leave the substance of things.

So, it is our duty to be realistic. We mustn't a) flatter ourselves or b) play down our achievements to *avoid* flattering ourselves. Yet Montaigne is perpetually guilty of the latter. He will not call a spade a spade when discussing himself. His excuse? 'Ceremony'—by which he means 'convention'.

And, to be fair, he was not alone. Just about everyone at that time, Shakespeare included, practised the most cringeworthy self-abasement when dedicating their work to its intended audience—or, more usually, to the patron who had helped bankroll it. It was the done thing, and compared to some, Montaigne's is positively dignified. John Florio's English translation of the *Essays,* published in 1603, is described by their author as 'defective' and 'worthlesse', and he accounts himself so 'insufficient' to the rigours of the job, you wonder why he bothered in the first place. Of course, he didn't mean a word of it—self-flagellatory hyperbole (or is it litotes?) was the name of the game, and Florio ably proves himself—to modern tastes— the ultimate in fawning lickspittles. Yet for all his aristocratic arselicking, he still died in abject poverty—so a fat lot of good it did *him.*

There is nevertheless one piece of evidence that clinches the argument for me, although, once again, it is far from conclusive. In his essays 'Of Solitude' and its continuation 'A Consideration Upon Cicero', Montaigne contrasts the attitudes of two pairs of writers to their vocation: Caesar and Xenophon; Cicero and Pliny the Younger. Montaigne holds the latter pair in lower esteem, for they both express the wish that their writings should confer immortality on them; the former, Montaigne implies, were content to let their actions, not their words speak to posterity. By a man's deeds shall ye know him, not by his scribblings. It is 'vanity', and 'testimony of an over-ambitious nature' to think otherwise, he says. Which in his own case is somewhat ironic; many of his readers are completely unfamiliar with the history of his civic duties, yet adore the *Essays*. But unlike Cicero and Pliny, he doesn't seem to have wished it to happen that way. Writing came a poor second to any other kind of useful and productive activity. It's like praising a king for being good at painting—there's no earthly reason why he should be a fine artist because his real job is ruling, and ruling well. Montaigne notes that as far as he's concerned, he's retired, and writing is something he's doing to stop himself getting bored. It's his equivalent of an allotment, a model train set or restoring a vintage car. His writing is basically a highly sophisticated form of pottering. A hobby, even.

The clarity and vehemence with which Montaigne argues the toss on this occasion, coupled with the frequent attacks on human vanity scattered throughout the *Essays*, lead me to think that this is his considered view on the subject, free from the influence of 'Ceremony'. So my own imagined portrait of Montaigne is of a man so at ease with himself, so self-possessed, that his stated intentions ring completely true, no matter what conventions they are cloaked in. And that calm is a philosophic calm, not the smug, complacently assumed pose of a wealthy and privileged man like Cellini. I can't of course prove Montaigne means what he writes, but then again at a remove of five hundred years, nor can anyone else. It's just a hunch, but it is comforting to my Inner Puritan to feel that maybe there is no necessary contradiction when an inherently modest individual, who has nothing whatever to be modest about, writes his autobiography. So now I feel rotten for having doubted him.

In fact, this motto from Seneca, which Montaigne quotes in Book 1, Essay 25 'Of the Education of Children', could have been written for him: '*Licet sapere sine pompa, sine invidia.*' ['Let us be wise without ostentation, without envy.'] Indeed.

Chapter Four

Heaven Knows I'm Miserable Now

'All the opinions of the world agree in this, that pleasure is our end...for who would give ear to him that should propose affliction and misery for his end?' (**Book 1, Chapter 19: 'That To Study Philosophy Is To Learn To Die'**)

Like the rest of us, Montaigne had his moods. But whether good or bad, he refused to take them for granted. In particular, when he enjoyed periods of happiness or prosperity, he embraced them with keen gratitude:

Do I find myself in any calm composedness? Is there any pleasure that tickles me? I do not suffer it to dally with my senses only; I associate my soul to it too: not there to engage itself, but therein to take delight; not there to lose itself, but to be present there; and I employ it, on its part, to view itself in this prosperous state, to weigh and appreciate its happiness and to amplify it.

Happiness was not some superficial levity; Montaigne 'associates [his] soul to it', feeling an almost visceral gratitude for the inner calm it brought to him. He senses that he is being 'protected' by it; 'No desire, no fear, no doubt, troubles the air; no difficulty, past, present or to come' can hurt him.

He reserves pity for those who are unable to share that deep contentment, or who are suspicious of happiness, for they 'negligently and incuriously receive their good fortune'. I can only agree; we're put on this earth for seventy or so summers, and we'd better make the best of them. But whereas Montaigne more usually felt pity or concern for the Jeremiahs of this world, I'm rather more ambivalent, and find a rather selfish impatience creeping into my reactions. Happiness is fleeting and precarious enough without people trying to deliberately rain on my parade, so I find myself angered by those who, for no good reason, try and manufacture gloom in the most unlikely circumstances...

Last Friday, I was lucky enough to see a retrospective of Henry Moore sculptures and drawings at one of London's major galleries. It was one of those shows that makes you feel refreshed and uplifted as you emerge blinking into the daylight. My attempts to analyse that uplift usually descend into the trite and sentimental, so generally I don't bother; instead, I'm content to wallow in this heightened sense of well-being for as long as I can make it last.

But on this occasion I felt that impatience return, having belatedly read the exhibition catalogue which claimed that I'd got it all wrong. No, the life-enhancing show I'd just seen was designed to draw out 'a dark and erotically charged dimension' to Moore. It further suggested that 'the artist as a young man was a more brooding, rebellious figure than the gentleman he became as success made him respectable and rich.' Which was almost enough to burst the bubble of my joyous little reverie. So I felt like composing a reply to those who put forward this banal and badly-argued thesis.

First of all it would be a miracle if Moore *wasn't* more brooding and rebellious when he was younger. Isn't everyone, irrespective of their choice of career and material circumstances? And there's nothing like success, wealth and acclaim to knock the edges off your curmudgeonliness.

But what made me *really* impatient was the frequently-rehearsed implication that enduring art can only emerge from darkness, despair and misery. What usually sets off the alarm bells is this claim to have discovered a 'darker side' to an artist's personality, as if this confers greater significance on his work—and just as importantly, that this 'new' bleaker perspective will make it more attractive to punters. In order to be taken seriously, every artist now has to have their 'darker side.' It's the default position of reviewers, biographers, journalists and now, it seems, museum curators. If, as an artist, you're happy, well-balanced and free from wild erotic urges you can kiss your dreams of immortality goodbye. On the dark side, every comedian weeps the tears of a clown, and every children's writer is tormented by deep psychological wounds.[15]

Now look. It's impossible to keep the dark side out of any balanced account of human life, which is the stuff of art, because we live in its shadow every day of our lives. Sometimes, of course, we are more susceptible to its influence than others, and any attempt to deny this will quickly have you sounding like the brainwashed victim of a religious cult. But the routine search for a dark side reinforces the view that art and misery walk hand in hand. Which I don't deny for a second—but it's far from being the whole picture, or even, in my view, a vaguely representative one.

Of course, when Van Gogh mutilated his ear, this was not evidence that he was possessed of a sunny disposition. And

---

15. On an idle afternoon, I tried to find someone connected with artistic endeavour who resolutely refused to acknowledge the existence of a dark side to their personality. I found one…Kylie Minogue. Having hitherto been indifferent to her music, I now regard her in a whole new light. And I've forgiven her for giving me the 'flu in 1999.

reading *Pollyanna* or any other relentlessly optimistic work is not likely to contribute to any rounded assessment of the human condition. But then *Pollyanna* isn't exactly as popular among the arts *cognoscenti* as routinely miserable gits like say, Ingmar Bergman, Leonard Cohen, Thomas Hardy or Nick Cave. No, to be deep you've got to be melancholic. Or, perhaps more accurately, your *art* has to be. Or, refining this observation still further, *has to be seen to be.* Henry Moore is, by anyone's standards, a great artist, so somewhere in his biography and/or his art must lurk that seed of gloom common to all his ilk. And so a circle of despair is created and perpetuated.

One of the set texts I studied for 'A'-Level at the age of 17 was *Waiting For Godot*, Beckett's absurdist masterpiece which was perfect fodder for a bunch of teenagers who felt the world would not and indeed could not understand them. How we empathized with the alienation of Estragon and Vladimir, completely by-passing the comedy and slapstick that give Beckett's vision greater depth and richness than he's often credited with. Even back then, I was disturbed by the partiality of this interpretation, and I was feeling it again now, thirty-odd years later: here was a bunch of eejits misrepresenting an artist's vision to fit their own modish agenda.

Back to the catalogue, which asserts that the holes in a Henry Moore sculpture speak of wounds, of absence, of incompleteness. However, if you're a Pollyanna like me, you consider the holes give a lightness to what would otherwise be a great fat clumsy monolith; they're a series of passages through which air and light can flow. Which is why they work so well in outdoor settings. When I look at many of Moore's reclining figures, the words that first spring to mind are calm, poise, balance, serenity—which are so at odds with the Tate curator's vision that I threw all the interpretive literature in the bin.

OK, let's try and be charitable. For all I know, he may well have been right—that dark vision may also have been shared by Moore himself. But I don't have to share it, do I? Any art that instructs you how it should be interpreted surely isn't art at all—it's straying into a mindset more commonly associated with propaganda.

And then I read this the following day in a newspaper review: one of the Moore galleries contained six or seven 'mother and child ensembles'—ladies breastfeeding—an image, we are needlessly told, Moore was often drawn to. What could be lovelier? But oh no, there's all kinds of Freudian subtexts flying around the room for those who want to find them. Notice, wrote our guide, that none of the mothers are looking at their children as they suckle them. And this speaks of the modern alienation between the generations.

Now I don't know if the writer of that piece had examined any *real* mothers breastfeeding (perhaps he feels it too rude to stare), but in my experience at least, once she's made sure the docking procedure has taken place correctly, the mother's gaze is usually focused somewhere in the middle distance, snatching whatever 'me-time' she can get, planning what Junior's next demands will be, or running down a mental list of chores. I may be guessing here, but alienation isn't top of her list of priorities. Alienation's for those who've too much leisure time, like Jean Paul Sartre. So Moore's sculptures, in my view at any rate, are for the most part innocent of the gloomy agenda that is being foisted on them. And that's why I found that particular gallery so affecting—these were no idealized infant/ Madonna couplings of the kind that were repeated *ad infinitum* in Renaissance art—these were the real thing. But if you want to find misery in *everything*, then that's your lookout.

I'm starting to work up a head of steam here, so let's try and regain Montaigne's composure and even-handedness by confessing that I've never been one for the great tragic set-pieces of literature and film—Anna Karenina diving under a train,

Emma Bovary swallowing arsenic, Oedipus putting out his eyes with a brooch, that kind of thing. I remember, in an otherwise gripping production of *The Duchess of Malfi* at the National Theatre, I drew attention to myself during Act 4 by inappropriate laughter during a moment of high emotion: the Duchess amazingly comes back to life after being strangled, only to utter two words before returning to the shadows. At which point, the hapless actor playing Bosola had to deliver the line 'Oh, she's gone again!', which I think is one of the biggest asks in English drama.

Shakespeare ran Webster a close second in *Cymbeline* when poor old Imogen wakes up next to a headless corpse which happens to be wearing her husband's clothes: what the audience knows but Imogen doesn't, is that it's not her husband but the doltish would-be rapist Cloten who's had his head removed—but grief is blind, and Imogen, parading her proof, is forced to exclaim, 'I know the shape of his leg!' Even the most gifted actresses must dread the stifled titters that often accompany this revelation.

I can't resist a third example of tragic bathos: in *Jude the Obscure*, I actually laughed helplessly when I first read the passage in which the eldest of Jude's children kills the other two then hangs himself 'because we are too menny [sic]'. That spelling error's the clincher: the novel received a hostile reception from its Victorian reviewers on the grounds of its immorality, not because some of its plot elements were melodramatic crap. On the other hand, some good did come out of it—Hardy never wrote another novel and went on to compose some of the most wonderful poetry in the English language. Things are never *all* bad.

Jokey interludes aside, there are, of course, utterly harrowing accounts of the dark side in every branch of artistic endeavour. But what's always puzzled me is that in the critical pecking order, 'happy' always scores way below 'sad', and that somehow happiness is portrayed as shallow whereas misery is deep. Artists seem to find wallowing in *taedium vitae* easier than raising a laugh. Take Tolstoy—the opening line of *Anna Karenina* goes, 'Happy families are all alike; every unhappy family is unhappy in its own way,' as if happiness is rather bovine and boring, whereas there's countless more satisfying artistic possibilities lurking in the shadows. P.G. Wodehouse took the odd swipe at the classics of Russian literature through his fictional mouthpiece Vladimir Brusiloff, who 'specialized in grey studies of hopeless misery, where nothing happened till page three hundred and eighty, when the moujik decided to commit suicide.' And, I have to say, I share his distaste for this type of writing, which has found its modern expression in 'misery lit', those harrowing accounts of cruelty and abuse which often read like the lyrics to a bad blues song.

When I was the commissioning editor of book serializations at the BBC, I was handed the manuscript of a forthcoming memoir entitled *Angela's Ashes*, which, having read a few pages, I summarily threw in the bin. This act, I think, hastened my departure from the Corporation, as the subsequent book went on to win a Pulitzer and launch a lucrative new literary genre. Didn't see that coming.

Ten years later, I met the book's author Frank McCourt, and marvelled that such a lovely, funny, well-adjusted guy could have written such a pile of manure—even if it was all true. Well, now he's left his misery to posterity, bless him, and we have to suffer excrescences called *Daddy, Please Don't, Don't Tell Mummy, Betrayed, Daddy's Little Girl* and countless other squalid cash-ins.

So amid all the pain and despair, when a classic of comic narrative does emerge, it ought to be cherished—and, to be fair, it usually is. At the time of writing, the uniform edition of Mr Wodehouse's novels is 72 titles strong—all of which are still in print, which must be some kind of record. Yet for all his mastery of language and plotting, and the fact that he has brought happiness to hundreds of thousands of readers on several continents in many different languages, Wodehouse cannot be mentioned in the same breath as, say, Kafka. Different order of creativity altogether, apparently. Which is why, in the old days at the Beeb, any radio comedy (including Wodehouse adaptations) was made by a department patronizingly called 'Light Entertainment'. On duller studio days, we used to fantasize about creating a 'Heavy Entertainment' production unit that would specialize in the work of Ibsen, Lorca, Dostoievsky and Strindberg. But then a casual glimpse at the 'Future Productions' schedule made us realize that such a department wasn't necessary. British playwright Howard Barker has argued strenuously for the rebirth of tragedy in the contemporary theatre, most notably in his volume, *Arguments for a Theatre*. 'You emerge from tragedy equipped against lies. After the musical, you're anybody's fool,' he insists. Looks like I'm anybody's fool, if I emerge from the Tate with a grin on my face—like most of my fellow attendees were doing last Friday.

I guess comedy just isn't serious enough, in the same way that for the journalist, good news is no news. I wish I had an answer for this. But all we can do as individuals is cling to the belief, in the teeth of all the evidence we are fed to the contrary, that the world isn't such a vale of tears, and is simply the victim of a media hate campaign. And even if Henry Moore isn't as miserable as he's painted, he's every bit as much of a genius.

Chapter Five

The Wrath of Grapes

'Every one overrates the offence of his companions, but extenuates his own.' (Book 2, Chapter 2: 'On Drunkenness')

I like a drink. To the point where I have to lie to my doctor. Which is not to say I drink to excess; it's more that medical profession keeps redefining the limits it's safe to consume, and I get confused. At least, that's what I tell myself—because there's a clearly a game of double bluff going on here; they're steadily lowering the number of units because they know we're lying to them, and we're drinking more than they recommend because we know they're lying to us.

Montaigne too is doubtful that medical advice on alcohol intake is sound:

If your physician does not think it good for you...to drink wine... never trouble yourself; I will find you another that shall not be of his opinion; the diversity of medical arguments and opinions embraces all sorts and forms.

But alcohol is one of the issues on which Montaigne is somewhat inconsistent, and we can witness his philosophy evolving the older and sicker he gets. Certainly, by the time of his final essay 'Of Experience', written in his fifties and when he was suffering from prolonged renal colic, he'd thrown caution to the winds. Having observed that 'wine is hurtful to sick people', he continues:

I drink pretty well for a man of my pitch: in summer, and at a relishing meal, I do not only exceed the limits of Augustus, who drank but thrice precisely; but not to offend Democritus' rule, who forbade that men should stop at four times as an unlucky number, I proceed at need to the fifth glass, about three half-pints; for the little glasses are my favourites, and I like to drink them off, which other people avoid as an unbecoming thing.

So this particular invalid can knock back a pint and a half of wine at a sitting. Now, we've no way of knowing precisely how Cotton's translation correlates to modern measurements, but if we tot up Montaigne's intake in current metric values, that would equate to a little over a standard 75cl bottle of wine. He would only have to drink that amount on two days a week for him to be in the upper recommended levels of intake (assuming the wine's low to medium strength).

Every week would total 63 units, exactly three times the recommended intake of 21 units for men. In Montaigne's favour, however, is his habit of watering down his tipple, which might win him back some sympathy from his physician, although we now know that the consumption of red wine would particularly exacerbate his condition.[16]

---

16. Here's what a modern dietician would recommend for Montaigne: 'Consumption of oxalic acid in foods such as rhubarb, asparagus, spinach, peanuts, chocolate, tea and coffee should be restricted, and intake of purines (found in organ meats, sardines, beans, beer and red wine) should also be reduced. Increasing dietary consumption of fibre, cereal, fruit and vegetables can increase citrate excretion, which inhibits stone formation. Conversely, refined carbohydrates, sugar and sodium increase

Amid all the recent UK press hysteria about binge-drinking, and how the deleterious effects of alcohol swallow between 1-6% of the average country's GDP, it's quite instructive to put the statistics we're routinely bombarded with into some kind of historical context. Here's three examples I've dug out that stretch credulity to breaking point:

- In the 1690s, the garden fountain of an anonymous English country house was used as a giant punch bowl. Into this receptacle was poured and stirred 560 gallons of brandy, 1200 pounds of sugar, 25,000 lemons, 20 gallons of lime juice, and five pounds of nutmeg. The barman rowed around in a small boat, filling up guests' cups.

- Again in the 1690s, the British government deemed it unpatriotic to drink French brandy, and actively encouraged the switch to gin. In 1743, a staggering 13.2 million gallons were consumed by a UK population of a little over 6 million—most of it in London (in the country they stuck to beer and cider).

- The bill for the celebration party for the 55 compilers of the United States constitution—who one traditionally imagines to have been relatively sober individuals—itemizes 54 bottles of Madeira, 60 bottles of claret, 8 bottles of whisky, 22 bottles of port, 8 bottles of cider, 12 beers and seven bowls of punch large enough that 'ducks could swim in them.' In the 1780s, Thomas Jefferson alone spent a staggering $3,000 annually on wine. God knows how many units that is.

So maybe we shouldn't be too hard on ourselves, given what our ancestors managed to put away. Of course, alcoholism has never been any fun either for those individuals concerned, their friends and families, and the people who have to clear up the

---

calcium excretion and increase the risk of recurrent stone formation.'

mess afterwards. In fact, this essay was prompted by a recent report on the alarming rise in bladder explosions in the UK; apparently, there's a growing trend among drinkers to get so pissed, they forget to relieve themselves, and like any bag that's overfull, the bladder pops like a balloon. Thankfully, it's a far from common condition, but you might bear it in might next time you have a big night out. Like the brewers and distillers admonish us, as they slaver over their profit forecasts, 'Please drink responsibly.'

But what does philosophy have to say? Can it contribute anything towards our understanding, which these days at least, seems to be exclusively influenced by statistics emanating from the medical profession and the social services?

In his younger days, there's no doubt that Montaigne was a card-carrying Stoic, although even then he was gently bending the philosophy's central tenets to suit himself. Stoicism originated in Ancient Greece, but in the absence of any complete texts from that period, most of our knowledge is derived from its Roman adherents like Epictetus and Seneca[17], the latter being one of Montaigne's firm favourites. For a Stoic, drinking was problematic: there's nothing really wrong with it, but getting pissed tends to deprive the Stoic of his chief weapon—Reason. So a true Stoic would be, at the very least, wary of letting a thief into his mouth. Seneca, for example, called drunkenness 'voluntary madness'[18], and this has been echoed by philosophers down the ages: Plato, that old killjoy, reckons that in his ideal state, the law wouldn't allow you to get pissed until the age of forty; and in modern times, Bertrand Russell

17. Seneca is mentioned or quoted a staggering 149 times throughout the *Essays*. Third only to Cicero (215) and Plato (161).

18. There is apparently a cocktail called a 'Falling Seneca', made with apple juice, tomato juice, Tabasco and vodka, served over ice with a cinnamon stick.

branded it 'temporary suicide'.

Clearly, they'd had unfortunate experiences—perhaps, as philosophers, they felt, when in their cups, they'd been granted unparalleled insight *de natura rerum* only to discover on sobering up that they'd borrowed their brilliant *bon mots* from a Paulo Coelho novel ('Love can consign us to hell or to paradise, but it always takes us somewhere'; 'no heart has ever suffered when it goes in search of its dream', and so on). And the world has quite enough Hallmark philosophy already without tipsy *savants* adding to its stock. Not only that, it's nigh on impossible to even *say* the word 'philosophy' when you've had a skinful. Try it.

To some philosophers, however, booze was a necessary lubricant. Socrates was, apparently, the king of preaching drunkenly from his chair (according, at least, to the Roman orator Cornelius Gallus); in the *Odes,* Horace notes that Cato the Elder (a stern critic of drunkenness) was often 'warmed with wine.' And of course in 'The Philosophers' Song', the wags from Monty Python manage to rhyme Emmanuel Kant with 'pissant'; Heidegger with 'boozy beggar', Wittgenstein with 'beery swine' and Rene Descartes with 'drunken fart', once again reinforcing the link between alcohol and intelligence repeatedly noted in learned journals. No, really. For example, according to a Japanese study published in 2000, a moderate intake of saki raises the average male IQ by 3.3. But then, that only constitutes a 3.3% rise in a human of average intelligence, which isn't that impressive. Then again, it would represent a spectacular leap forward for a regular viewer of Fox News, boosting his brain power a staggering 330%.

So at the opening of the essay 'On Drunkenness', Montaigne the Stoic comes out with statements like: 'drunkenness is a grim and brutish vice,' which overthrows reason and 'renders the body stupid'. He concludes by saying 'The worst state of man is that wherein he loses the knowledge and government of himself.' In mitigation, he does remark that he's never really developed a taste for it and doesn't enjoy the physical consequences of a night on the lash. He backs up his argument with a quote from Lucretius:

> *Cum vini vis penetravit…*
> *Consequitur gravitas membrorum, praepediuntur*
> *Crura vacillanti, tardescit lingua, madet mens,*
> *Nant oculi; clamor, singultus, jurgia, gliscunt.*

['When the power of wine has penetrated us, a heaviness of the limbs follows, the legs of the tottering person are impeded; the tongue grows torpid, the mind is dimmed, the eyes swim; noise, hiccup, and quarrels arise.']

One might add to this list, which studiously ignores other, less delicate side effects: after all, it's not only the tongue that grows torpid; and what seemed beautiful and fascinating the previous evening is often revealed to be quite the opposite in the cold light of day. As the Porter in *Macbeth* correctly observes, drink may be a great provoker of 'nose-painting, sleep and urine,' but it's in amatory issues where it wreaks greatest havoc:

> *Lechery, sir, it provokes, and unprovokes;*
> *it provokes the desire, but it takes*
> *away the performance: therefore, much drink*
> *may be said to be an equivocator with lechery:*
> *it makes him, and it mars him; it sets*
> *him on, and it takes him off; it persuades him,*
> *and disheartens him; makes him stand to, and*
> *not stand to; in conclusion, equivocates him*
> *in a sleep, and, giving him the lie, leaves him.*

Montaigne adds that drink loosens our tongues, not only encouraging indiscretion, but dredging up grimness from the depths of our souls which would be best kept hidden. But in the course of the essay, he manages to wander quite spectacularly off his opening thesis, even at one stage musing whether his father was a virgin when he married aged 38, before getting back on track with a lovely paragraph on how booze keeps your feet warm in old age. The ebb and flow of the argument from hearty approval to utter intolerance via guarded acceptance seems worthy of…well…a man who's had a few.

But then in the midst of all this, you get the impression he's moved on to taking the piss out of the more doctrinal Stoic philosophers, like Cato, who 'set up an express profession of scornful superiority', and who are dead against all artificial stimulants. Having stated that 'the rudest nation this day in Europe is that alone where [drinking] is in fashion', Montaigne goes on to actually *praise* the Germans, who will drink practically anything and lots of it, while berating his fellow Frenchmen for being parsimonious and undervaluing this wonderful gift from the gods. Those Ancients could teach us a thing or two about the benefits of Bacchanalian bunk-ups, he says, warming to his theme, and complaining that alcohol consumption has regrettably fallen in recent times.

The pleasure we hold in esteem for the course of our lives ought to have a greater share of our time dedicated to it; we should, like shopboys and labourers, refuse no occasion nor omit any opportunity of drinking, and always have it in our minds. Methinks we every day abridge and curtail the use of wine, and that the after breakfasts, dinner snatches, and collations I used to see in my father's house, when I was a boy, were more usual and frequent then than now.

Is this another side of our great man? The real side, perhaps? In less time than it takes to scratch our heads and wonder, he's noting that as vices go, drinking is 'less malicious and hurtful' than others, and agreeing with Plato that being pissed over 40 is OK as long as:

- you aren't a magistrate with an important caseload the following day;

- you aren't a soldier on a military campaign;

- you don't drink all day to the exclusion of useful activities; and

- you aren't planning on making overtures to the wife.

And then we hit the nub of the argument: in the battle for the soul of a wise man, will booze or sobriety win? Montaigne notes that it's not so great being wise, and that anyone whose ambition is to be wise *all* the time is proud and not a little delusional. And anyway, booze is only one of thousands of things that can knock your soul off-kilter—so why single it out for special attention? He concludes, 'It is sufficient for a man to curb and moderate his inclinations, for totally to suppress them is not in him to do.' And indulging your tastes a little will set you up for the privations of old age, when there aren't many other pleasures left. And as we've seen, it wasn't too many years before Montaigne's kidney stones would force him to put this theory into practice.

Now illness was practically a gift made for the Stoic, because he could use it as proof that reason can conquer anything, even intense physical pain. Montaigne quotes Epicurus, who, 'playing' with his gout and refusing treatment, cried out for a greater affliction that would be a sterner test of his philosophy. Such weirdness, Montaigne mischievously hints, may have been stimulated by drink—after all, only a nutter actively courts suffering. And how did Epicurus develop gout in the first place? A surfeit of red wine, perhaps? He certainly lent his name to those of us who live for pleasure alone.

So, on balance, it seems that in Montaigne's world view, a little of what you fancy does you good. Time after time in the *Essays*, he makes statements like 'Let the philosophers say what they will, the thing at which we all aim, even in virtue is pleasure,' or words to that effect. Philosophy, he implies, should not set the philosopher apart from humanity, one of the chief complaints against Stoicism. So, well...cheers!

Which liberality, as I noted earlier, aligns him with the Skeptical axis—that other branch of philosophy, less doctrinal and more forgiving than Stoicism, which doubts that true knowledge and certainty is possible. Montaigne can certainly see both sides of the argument—just like Homer Simpson, that other great Skeptic thinker, who once noted that beer is 'the cause of and the solution to all of life's problems'. And as if to prove his successor correct, Montaigne includes this slightly racy anecdote in his 'Drunkenness' essay, giving weight to the unlikely theory that an enduring relationship can result from being totally off your face:

I have been further told by a lady whom I highly honour and esteem, that near Bordeaux and about Castres where she lives, a country woman, a widow of chaste repute, perceiving in herself the first symptoms of breeding, innocently told her neighbours that if she had a husband she should think herself with child; but the causes of suspicion every day more and more increasing, and at last growing up to a manifest proof, the poor woman was reduced to the necessity of causing it to be proclaimed in her parish church, that whoever had done that deed and would frankly confess it, she did not only promise to forgive, but moreover to marry him, if he liked the motion; whereupon a young fellow that served her in the quality of a labourer, encouraged by this proclamation, declared that he had one holiday found her, having taken too much of the bottle, so fast asleep by the chimney and in so indecent a posture, that he could conveniently do his business without waking her; and they yet live together man and wife.

So, no harm done. But then again, we must ask ourselves if rape is the most satisfactory route to wedded bliss…and we must also bear in mind the unfortunate fate of Pausanias, who, Montaigne tells us, plied with drink by his enemy Attalus, 'abandon[ed] his beauty, as of a hedge strumpet, to the muleteers and servants of the basest office in the house.'

So the next time I go to the doctor, I'm not sure whether I'm going to come clean. I don't want to enter the surgery a well man and emerge a few minutes later as a sick one—but I certainly wouldn't want to be anyone's hedge strumpet either.

Chapter Six

Do the Stupidity

'We *should rather examine, who is* better *learned, than who is* more *learned.*' (Book 1, Chapter 24: 'Of Pedantry')

'*Miserable and senseless men, who strive to be worse than they can!*' (Book 2, Chapter 12: 'Apology for Raimond de Sebonde')

Montaigne loathed stupidity. And stupid people. It's one of the rare subjects where he's quicker to condemn than to understand. For stupidity, he says, is not just about ignorance; it encourages vices of every complexion. It's a fertile breeding ground for many of the evils that beset humanity and must be fought against at all costs. Everyone, whether predisposed to intelligence or not, is prey to it, and one of the deadliest sins in Montaigne's philosophy is to squander knowledge and/or education. Those who do, he describes as 'mongrels'.

As far as I can make out, every period of history has in varying degrees been ashamed of its ignorance, but it was not until the 20th-century that stupidity began to be studied in any depth. And it's a huge subject, for stupidity embraces not only a lack of knowledge, but the misapplication of knowledge. One of the earliest books on the subject was published in 1934, and has remained a standard text. *A Short Introduction to the History of Human Stupidity* by Professor Walter B. Pitkin of Columbia University opined that four people out of five are stupid enough to be labelled 'stupid'.[19] And, of course, being stupid, most of them don't realize they're stupid. Apparently, one of the benchmarks of intelligence is having an inkling of how stupid you are.

Disturbing though that statistic may be, it's not going to be the main concern of this essay: rather it's those people who insist upon making a stigma of intelligence. Which, in my book and Montaigne's, is *really* stupid, but doesn't stop me from doing it.

When I was a cub producer at the BBC, I noticed that one of my colleagues had booked Brian Eno to come into the studio to be interviewed, not just for a ten-minute promo session, but for a whole three hours. As a fan, I just had to take the afternoon off and sit in—and I wasn't disappointed. His answers ranged far and wide over an incredible array of subjects, way beyond the brief of the programme of which they were to become a part. And this from a rock star noted for wearing feather boas and generally queening around as Roxy Music's 'treatments' man.

At one point, the interviewer asked Eno about his reputation as an intellectual. The question went something like, 'You've been accused of being too clever by half...' At which point Eno giggled, and noted that only in England would anyone have invented that particular phrase.[20] In France, he said, intelligence

19. Professor Pitkin's 'short introduction' is in fact around 300 pages long.

20. Jonathan Miller, the doctor, opera director and all-round egghead, was once accused of being 'too clever by three-quarters'.

and intellectual curiosity are celebrated, and you end up being awarded the Legion d'Honneur; back home, you're a pretentious git with ideas above your station. Warming to his theme, he added that just about everywhere else in the world, polymaths are respected; in Britain, you're branded a jack of all trades, or at best a dilettante if you demonstrate any kind of expertise or knowledge in more than one field. Which reminded me of my school—the last place you'd expect (or hope) intelligence to be treated with suspicion.

I remember once being asked what I thought about a poem, and, being the pretentious teenager, opined that it was full of clichés. The teacher then grew red in the face, accusing me of using words I didn't understand. When I demonstrated that I actually did, he threw a large hardback book at my head.[21]

Which naturally set me thinking whether there was such a phenomenon as being 'too clever'…and so back I went to Montaigne…

The nature of what constitutes true intelligence is an issue Montaigne addresses in his essay 'On Pedantry', which opens with a quote from Rabelais (*via* Chaucer and an old saw or two), 'The greatest clerks are not always the wisest men.' With knowledge, says Montaigne, should come the wisdom to put that knowledge to good use, otherwise, what's the use in accumulating it? As usual, he casts the first stone at himself: what else is this book, he asks, but a collection of apposite quotations from minds greater than my own? How can anyone learn anything from this? If all you do is regurgitate gobbets

---

21. I dodged it, by the way. 'Everard', as we knew this irascible master, was no stranger to violence, despite being pudgy, chinless and foppish with a predilection for burgundy velvet suits. He occasioned the best teacher put-down I ever witnessed; having belted 'Sandie' Shaw in the stomach for some trifling misdemeanour, he was informed 'You punch like a girl.'

of second-hand wisdom without understanding, internalising and, ultimately, applying them, you might as well be a parrot. Your memory may be full enough, he says, but your judgement will be 'totally void and empty.' Knowledge can be a highly addictive drug, but if its accumulation is unaccompanied by wisdom then all you've effectively done is swallow a reference library. Still, he notes in mitigation, having the facility to quote freely from the ancients means you're always a welcome guest at dinner parties. At least the conversation won't flag, even as your fellow diners quietly despise your showy displays of knowledge.

The formalities over, Montaigne then lets his inner Grumpy Old Man out of the cage:

I hate our people, who can worse endure an ill contrived robe than an ill-contrived mind, and take their measure by the leg a man makes, by his behaviour, and so much as the very fashion of his boots, what kind of man he is.

'Never mind his brain, what's he wearing?' seems to have been the popular cry then as now; most newspaper columnists would rather discuss culture guru Melvyn Bragg's brand of hair dye than the enormous brain that pulses beneath that subtly-tinted barnet.

So, in Montaigne's view, we're probably going to get the intelligentsia we deserve—the sort that traffics in life's superficialities, unwilling or unable to immerse itself in deeper currents of thought. Then factor in our widespread discomfort with public displays of intelligence, and there's little wonder that, on the surface at least, there's an incredible confusion as to what learning is *for*, how and why we acquire knowledge, and how to make best use of it.

But then, you can't really blame those who confuse education with the simple process of fact-cramming; our appreciation of intelligence seems to be based on the evident falsehood that the getting of knowledge can be measured both qualitatively and quantatively. Hence IQs, invented in 1912, and used over the years by a variety of dubious philosophies to help them discriminate against groups of people they didn't like.[22]

And IQs begat MENSA ('Anyone with an IQ in the top 2% can join MENSA'), simply so that 100,000 smug bastards around the world can prove to anyone who cares to know (i.e. nobody) that they're DEAD BRAINY; as if working out how many men it takes to dig a hole has got anything to do with wisdom.

And then there was the introduction of school and university league tables, principally compiled from exam results and published in the UK since 1992—the premise being that a student with 15 GCSE passes is more intelligent than one with 14. And other such idiocies that encourage envy, snobbery and division. Which tendency doesn't argue a high level of intelligence among those who have faith in them.

Then again, there is a lot of fun to be had taking the piss out of those who parade their knowledge ostentatiously beyond their capacity to actually understand or engage with it—and this harmless pursuit was not unknown in Montaigne's era.

Po-faced Francis Bacon, who we've encountered already, complained in his *Of the Proficience and Advancement of Learning, Divine and Human* that 'It hath been ordinary with politic men to extenuate and disable learned men by name of pedants.' Which precisely sums up the character of Holofernes, the schoolmaster in Shakespeare's *Love's Labour's Lost*, proving once

---

22. IQs in England among the bottom 50% scorers were actually rising in the UK—until Mrs Thatcher's educational reforms took hold. Fact.

again that he and Bacon weren't one and the same. Holofernes loves showing off, usually by reeling off strings of superfluous synonyms, Latinisms and definitions of words he's just used:

> *Most barbarous intimation! yet a kind of*
> *insinuation, as it were,* in via, *in way, of*
> *explication;* facere, *as it were, replication, or*
> *rather,* ostentare, *to show, as it were, his*
> *inclination, after his undressed, unpolished,*
> *uneducated, unpruned, untrained, or rather,*
> *unlettered, or ratherest, unconfirmed fashion, to*
> *insert again my* haud credo *for a deer.*

Holofernes uses his knowledge (which itself is sometimes faulty) to big himself up while making others look small. But whereas Bacon implies that respect should be routinely accorded to those with learning, Shakespeare is more concerned with how the intake of knowledge influences personality. All Holofernes can do is preen—which ultimately earns him nothing but contempt.

In fact, the whole of *Love's Labour's Lost* is a keen satire on learning—King Ferdinand and his three friends plan to study uninterrupted for three years and so create 'a little Academe' which shall be 'the wonder of the world'. All proud and scholarly, until the King of France's daughter arrives with three highly pneumatic ladies-in-waiting, whose beauty instantly makes them neglect their vow and take up wooing instead. Learning is but vanity, implies Shakespeare—but then, unlike Bacon, he wasn't an infant prodigy who was sent to Cambridge University at the age of 12, so maybe he had a chip on his shoulder.

Yet despite our tendency to poke fun at them, just about all of us have felt the need to impress teacher. Which reminds me of another rock star encounter, this time with Sting, the former schoolmaster who once famously rhymed 'cough' with 'Nabokov' in a song lyric, and as a result got the reputation for being rock's foremost intellectual.

A certain BBC Radio 1 DJ and I had been given a brief to interview the great man, and the DJ really wanted to impress upon his subject that he wasn't as dumb as many of his colleagues are traditionally thought to be. And so, once we'd settled down in the studio, he put his serious face on, and prefaced the first question with, 'I was reading through Kant last night...' at which point I corpsed, completely wrecking the atmosphere and, of course, embarrassing the DJ not a little. I just couldn't stop laughing. To be fair, I don't remember Sting being particularly pretentious once the interview had got back on track (although he did mention that his children were 'geopolitically aware from a very early age'), but it was the disjunction between Kant, the bloke who wrote 'De-do-do-do-da-da-da-da' and a DJ who cuddled up in bed with the *Critique of Pure Reason* which probably set me off.

But then, I asked myself, why should I be amused by that incident and not by Eno's pontifications? After all, he too makes a living from popular entertainment and is no stranger to pomposity—and then I started feeling guilty.

It's all too easy to fall into the habit of lampooning those who go public with their intelligence or abilities—particularly rock stars (and DJs), who aren't supposed to *be* intelligent, and who therefore set themselves up as easy targets should they dare to venture outside what is deemed suitable for a rock star to talk about. And I'm not immune. I remember once hearing an interview with Debbie Harry, during which she referred to herself as an 'artist'—not an 'artiste', but an artist—like Matisse or Beethoven or Marcel Proust. Now I was greatly enamoured of old Debs (even though she once kicked me in the face), but I still felt a *frisson* of annoyance at her presumption—and, subsequently, at my own irritation, since I had momentarily fallen into a pattern of thinking I've always despised. Which goes as follows:

There is among the British (and certain other English-speaking nations) a marked predisposition towards Philistinism that originates—paradoxically—in modesty. We have an onboard squeamishness of those who parade their learning or expertise as if it were aberrant behaviour—even if they are genuinely talented or gifted. On a personal level, we err on the side of caution before coming out with anything too clever in case someone takes the piss out of us. Intelligence is something to be hidden away, and we in our turn despise or ridicule those who are unwise enough to let their lights shine out from under their bushels. It's a vicious circle that has contributed, among other things, to the 'dumbing down' of the British media, and the daily spectacle of people who are actually quite intelligent pretending they're not. Jonathan Swift, had he lived three hundred years later, could have had Jeremy Clarkson of *Top Gear*, or any number of other well-educated middle-class media types in mind when he wrote this, from *A Tale of a Tub:*

For, to speak a bold truth, it is a fatal miscarriage so ill to order affairs as to pass for a fool in one company, when in another you might be treated as a philosopher; which I desire some certain gentlemen of my acquaintance to lay up in their hearts as a very seasonable innuendo.

In other words, if an intelligent man acts as if he's stupid then perhaps on balance he actually *is* stupid, for all his intelligence and/or education. He's guilty of failing to put the precious commodity he's been given to its best possible use. And he's a great big wuss for worrying what people will think if he outs himself as smarter than the average bear.

The main problem, particularly with this issue of so-called 'dumbing down', is that it's often confused with what meejah students term 'the democratization of knowledge'—or in plain

English, communicating with as broad a range of the public as possible. You have to use words of one syllable so that people who haven't reached the level of tertiary education won't get left behind. A laudable ambition of course, but one that in practice often degenerates into the worst kind of patronizing drivel.

Whereas in the past, you'd have brilliant TV academics like AJP Taylor ('the grand-daddy of all TV historians'[23]) lecturing directly to a pair of static cameras, modern factual programming now resembles an extended pop video, complete with cameramen with *delirium tremens*, a director with ADHD, flash graphics, unexplained lapses into black and white and a narrator whose sing-song modulation sounds like a someone addressing a dead baby in a pram.[24] Last night, I almost got an attack of vertigo as a camera whirled around a presenter who was introducing a piece on the harmful side-effects of certain drugs used to treat diabetes. And the point of all this production whizz-bangery exactly? Is it simply, like the dog licking its balls, because it's possible? Or are they scared that without extraneous visual stimuli the subject is so boring we'll all switch off?

The tendency to infantilize knowledge, no matter how well-meaning its 'democratic' intentions ain't good—and you don't have to take my word for it. Professor Susan Greenfield, who's no slouch in matters psychological (and is something of a media don herself), has remarked on the threefold increase in UK prescriptions for the drug methylphenidate, which is used to treat hyperactivity, and has controversially linked this observation with the way we take in knowledge, particularly from on-screen sources. She argues that streams of 'instant new screen

---

23. © Simon Schama, the dutiful grandchild of TV historians.

24. It reminded me of another wonderful Python moment: a be-suited John Cleese is asked by an elderly lady (played by Terry Jones) 'Ooooooooooo, can he talk? Can he talk then, eh, coochie poo?' To which he replies, 'Yes, Mother, I'm Minister for Overseas Development.'

images' deny the brain the chance to create coherent narratives from them, which in turn reduce the significance, meaning—call it what you will—of everything we ingest through those media. So the more we watch, the less we get out of it. Nothing grips the heart or mind. And we get bored and ultimately depressed. Then hey presto we reach for mother's little helper.

It's a neat argument that makes logical sense. Unfortunately, I'm told, it has yet to be scientifically proven, which has got Professor Greenfield's colleagues rather exercised. But I reckon she may have a point. Pop videos aren't meant to be understood—even Sting's. Documentaries, presumably, are. So in that context zappy visuals are actually counter-productive. So the sooner the Prof puts some flesh on the bones of her theory, maybe TV execs will take notice and we'll once more be able to stylistically differentiate between a Police video and a documentary on law and order.

But then, reading back what I've just written makes me sound like George Orwell ranting about 'prolefeed' as supplied by the Ministry of Truth in *1984*, which is not the impression I wish to convey at all. I really don't want to add my voice to the chorus of those commentators like Richard Hoggart who, as far back as the mid-1950s, suspected that the sole purpose of the popular media (which they snobbishly despised) is to administer a drug-free anaesthetic on the general population to stop us misbehaving. Because it isn't—at least not *all* the time.[25] And at the other end of the political spectrum, I refuse to believe that culture and a mass audience are mutually exclusive, so you might as well commission and schedule using the

---

25. I've got a bet with myself that I'm going to contradict this view before the book's finished. The troubling paradox at the heart of Hoggart's thesis is that he considers TV audiences are too thick to notice this happening—which maybe isn't good coming from a left-leaning academic.

bread-and-circuses principle of providing programming that's deliberately crap.

As theories go, I usually favour cock-up over conspiracy, and in this case I think it's definitely true. Far from deliberately trying to amuse us all to death, I rather think there's an unfortunate misconception among the more serious broadcasting organizations about how far you can challenge a mass audience, which represents an abject failure of nerve—and we end up with the spectacle of intelligent people who clearly should know better (but don't) talking down at us. Or, in the case of some male presenters, channelling their inner troglodyte. OK, explaining the Higgs Boson particle's always going to be a tough sell, and pitching it at the right level and using the appropriate tone is hugely problematic, but there's no harm giving it your best shot.

Once, as an experiment, my friend Rhys 'The Brilliant Physicist' did it for this non-scientist in words of one syllable... but then again, I've always said he should be on TV.[26] He certainly made a better job of it than the BBC's science correspondent, who kept using the word 'special' with massive overemphasis, gurning and waving his arms whenever he reached a complicated bit. And he got some of it wrong, apparently.

So after all that, if we don't wish to drown in a sea of babyspeak, perhaps it *is* our civic duty to mock, or at least forcibly explain the error of their ways to both the smartarses and those embarrassed by their knowledge who equally, but in very different ways, do intelligence a great disservice. That is, as long as we choose our targets carefully and appropriately—and we

26. At the National Physical Laboratory, Rhys's job title used to be 'Head of Time and Space'. Fortunately, it didn't go to his head and he hasn't, thus far, made a bid to take over the world from an uninhabited island in the Caribbean.

don't make the crass (but very British) mistake of confusing popularity with stupidity, and/or versatility with shallowness.

After all, we wouldn't have been aware that Brian May had gained a PhD in 'Radial Velocities in the Zodiacal Dust Cloud' had he not been better known as Queen's guitarist, but the fact that he's sold tens of millions of albums should take nothing away from his academic credentials—sickening overachiever that he is. By way of recompense, we can always poke fun at his hair.

And although his intellectual mobility and fashion sense may have branded him as a lightweight in some quarters, Eno's role as a cultural catalyst and stimulant should never be underestimated, as even a cursory glance through his CV will attest.

Which makes me wonder why he hasn't been made a member of the French *Ordre Des Arts Et Des Lettres* alongside his fellow artist…Kylie Minogue, whose election had nothing whatever to do with her penchant for gold sequinned hot pants.

Chapter Seven

There's More To Life Than Books, You Know—But Not Much More

'I seek, in the reading of books, only to please myself by an honest diversion; or, if I study, 'tis for no other science than what treats of the knowledge of myself, and instructs me how to die and how to live well.' (Book 2, Chapter 10: 'Of Books')

'Books are pleasant, but if, by being over-studious, we impair our health and spoil our good humour, the best pieces we have, let us give it over; I, for my part, am one of those who think, that no fruit derived from them can recompense so great a loss.' (Book 1, Chapter 38: 'Of Solitude')

One of Montaigne's longer essays concerns Books and, with a reported 1500 of them in his personal library (a phenomenal collection for the time in which he lived), there's no denying his status as one of history's most celebrated bibliophiles. He also extols the habit of reading in 'Of Three Commerces' (Book 3, Chapter 3), and indeed throughout his writings, Montaigne leaves us in no doubt that he is a hopeless bookworm.

Montaigne's library, which can still be visited down in the Périgord region east of Bordeaux, was also his den, from which he excluded his wife, children, servants and friends whenever feasible. The rafters of the circular room are inscribed with sixty or so apposite classical quotations, making this as convivial a place as possible to exercise the little grey cells:

There without order, without method, and by piece-meales I turn over and ransack, now one book and now another. Sometimes I muse and rave; and walking up and downe I endite and enregister these my humours, these my conceits.

And of course these vigorous cerebral workouts ended up producing the *Essays*, so he must have spent a fair old time up there on the third floor of his tower. Apparently, over 100 of the original books still survive in one collection or another, at least ten of them being bought by Gilbert de Botton (father of bestselling author and TV presenter Alain), and bequeathed to Cambridge University Library.

Montaigne divided his personal favourites into entertainment and edification, favouring Boccaccio, Rabelais and Johannes Secundus in the first category and Plutarch, Seneca and some of Cicero in the second. He says he's grown out of Ariosto and Ovid (he probably means the naughty stuff), and no longer has a taste for tales of knight-errantry like *Amadis of Gaul*, which was so heavily satirized in *Don Quixote*. History is almost certainly his favourite genre, indicating that he has, to a large extent, put away childish things.

As to what he accomplishes by reading such a lot, Montaigne has two important points to make:

The principal use of reading to me is, that by various objects it rouses my reason, and employs my judgement, not my memory.

In other words, it sets him thinking. Reading is the catalyst that gets the cogs whirring. And there's this:

Every day I spend time reading my authors, not caring about their learning, looking not for their subject matter, but how they handle it.

So really, he's not looking at content, but rather the writers' thought processes and how they influence what eventually appears on the printed page. A reasonable synonym might be 'style', but there's more than a little emphasis on personality too, with Montaigne continually asking himself *what kind of person could have written this?* Which is, of course, entirely consistent with the way we read the *Essays;* the personality of the writer being at least as memorable and attractive as the gist of what he's saying.

Clearly, Montaigne got a lot out of his reading which, filtered through his consciousness, he's sharing with us. And then it struck me that I had no ready-formulated answers for why *I* bother to read—after all, no-one's forcing me. It's something that takes up a lot of my time and, other than habit and simple pleasure, I can't really account for why I continue to do it. Unlike Montaigne, I'm not really trying to educate or better myself, certainly not in any systematic way. I query many other aspects of what I do, so why this unquestioning, seemingly hard-wired loyalty to the printed word?

Cue harp glissando and the picture dissolving into wavy lines as we travel back…back…back…to around 1963.

I can just about remember the moment when I learned to read on my own. It must have been what walking unassisted first felt like: utterly elating. Being teachers, both my parents had made strenuous efforts to ensure I could read before I went to school. Immediately prior to the big day, we moved from London to Lancashire, where there was a completely different curriculum in operation. This involved me un-learning everything they'd taught me, and being instructed in the mysteries of the dreaded 'ITA' or 'Initial Training Alphabet'. This was essentially a baby language for 5-7 year-olds which replaced words with groups of phonetic squiggles. Its alphabet had 40 letters and no capitals. Which modish bollocks completely mucked up the spelling of an entire generation and handed the lovely Lynne Truss a career on a plate. It also made Pitman's, the publishers, a huge amount of money.

Anyway, reading, as the cliché goes, opened up an entire new world that enabled me to communicate without the need for speech or gesture. With complete strangers. From anywhere on the planet. We all like to feel that our personal experiences are somehow unique, but it's quite clear that Alberto Manguel, author of the excellent *A History of Reading* felt exactly the same rush I did:

Then one day, from the window of a car...I saw a billboard by the side of the road. The sight could not have lasted very long; perhaps the car stopped for a moment, perhaps it just slowed down long enough for me to see, large and looming, shapes similar to those in my book, but shapes that I had never seen before. And yet, all of a sudden, I knew what they were. I heard them in my head, they metamorphosed from black lines into a solid, sonorous, meaningful reality... I and the shapes were alone together, revealing ourselves in a silent respectful dialogue. Since I could turn bare lines into living reality, I was all-powerful. I could read...It was like acquiring an entirely new sense...

And so, I hope, it was with you. It's a hugely significant moment in anyone's life to learn how to decipher text. From that milestone onwards, we become part of the huge family who are privileged to possess the gift of reading, the ability to turn written or printed symbols into something meaningful to us. And don't just take my word for it: Virginia Woolf once imagined God and St. Peter having a conversation on the Day of Judgement wondering what benefits they could bestow on those who had been gathered up into heaven. 'We have nothing to give them,' says God ruefully, 'They have loved reading'.

Which is a bit arch, but the general drift just about saves it.

And old Ginny knew a thing or two about why we mortals read, and the manner in which we digest literature. Not only, of course, was she a novelist and critic, she also co-founded the Hogarth Press in 1917 with her husband Leonard which signed up TS Eliot, Katherine Mansfield, Sigmund Freud and Maxim Gorky, among others—not a bad little roster for an indie publisher. In her collections of essays, *The Common Reader*, two volumes of which were published (by Hogarth) in 1925 and 1932, she makes the following observations, which I think are worth quoting in full:

There is a sentence in Dr. Johnson's Life of Gray *which might well be written up in all those rooms, too humble to be called libraries, yet full of books, where the pursuit of reading is carried on by private people. '...I rejoice to concur with the common reader; for by the common sense of readers, uncorrupted by literary prejudices, after all the refinements of subtlety and the dogmatism of learning, must be finally decided all claim to poetical honours.' It defines their qualities; it dignifies their aims; it bestows upon a pursuit which devours a great deal of time, and is yet apt to leave behind it nothing very substantial, the sanction of the great man's approval. The common reader, as Dr. Johnson implies, differs from the critic and the scholar. He is worse educated, and nature has not gifted him so generously. He reads for his own pleasure rather than to impart knowledge or correct the opinions of others. Above all, he is guided by an instinct to create for himself, out of whatever odds and ends he can come by, some kind of whole—a portrait of a man, a sketch of an age, a theory of the art of writing. He never ceases, as he reads, to run up some rickety and ramshackle fabric which shall give him the temporary satisfaction of looking sufficiently like the real object to allow of affection, laughter, and argument. Hasty, inaccurate, and superficial, snatching now this poem, now that scrap of old furniture, without caring where he finds it or of what nature it may be so long as it serves his purpose and rounds his structure, his deficiencies as a critic are too obvious to be pointed out; but if he has, as Dr. Johnson maintained, some say in the final distribution of poetical honours, then, perhaps, it may be worth while to write down a few of the ideas and opinions which, insignificant in themselves, yet contribute to so mighty a result.*

In an uncharacteristic act of intellectual generosity, Old Virginia makes some excellent points about the way most of us organize our reading (or don't):

1) Our consumption is mainly random; very few of us have a 'programme' for exploring different avenues in literature, even assuming that's an ambition we've set ourselves. We're like the silver ball in the pinball table, careening off the buffers and being randomly propelled from one side of the machine to the other as we search for new stuff that might interest us. We either lack the initiative or knowledge to make many structured decisions about what we buy or borrow. So we're not likely to have a full grasp of what's available, and hence, what we might enjoy. And this lack of science is reflected in a set of official statistics from the UK: 40% of us Brits regularly rely on friends' recommendations for our choices, and 16% get tips on what to read from their work colleagues. 24% place our trust in reviewers and 14% of selections are governed by what adverts we chance to see. 8% don't even know why they read, which brings us to Miss Woolf's second point;[27]

2) While we might claim to read for a purpose beyond simple pleasure, at best we're only dimly aware what that purpose is. We don't, for example, approach or read a text in the way an academic would; usually, the level of time and attention we're able to routinely invest in our reading doesn't stretch to what might be termed a considered interpretation. More of us, according to figures originating from the UK's National Literacy

---

27. I presume, because these figures add up to more than 100%, that respondents were allowed to put their ticks in more than one box. Or maybe government statisticians can't count to 100.

Trust, apparently read for 'information' rather than 'entertainment'—just like Montaigne with his bias towards history; but in the absence of a definition for either of those two terms in their survey, I would take this to mean that we expect to get something tangible or expressible from our reading labours, something meaningful we can take away and perhaps communicate to others. This would help make sense of the fact that 'interest' in the subject matter is most regularly cited as the reason we pick up a book (71%); that kind of involvement is felt to be more satisfying than simply wallowing in a text and not being able to justify the investment of time to ourselves. Of course, we mustn't forget that people tend to be on their best behaviour when taking part in cultural surveys: most of us, naturally watch TV exclusively for the documentaries, and most men turn straight to the short story in *Playboy*, by-passing the centrefold. Don't we? Anyway:

3) Although the voice of 'The Common Reader' is seldom heard in the media, it's our patterns of attention and consumption, and not those of literary professionals, that ultimately validate a book and, yes, give it meaning. But whereas Virginia Woolf (and Dr Johnson) had the good fortune to be able to dedicate that most precious (and increasingly rare) of commodities, time, to their experience of reading, the majority of us unfortunately don't. And it is a time-consuming habit, as well as being an essentially selfish one which, if pursued single-mindedly, excludes pretty much all other outside factors— wives, boyfriends, children, the ironing, driving, TV, anything practical or social. And because it monopolizes the attention to such a degree, it's not always easy to find space for it.

Good points all, but now slightly showing their age. For the last fifteen years in particular have witnessed a revolution in the way books are sold to us—and the way we 'consume' them, which, I and many others would argue, has irretrievably altered how we conceive of them. For a start, these days books are not such much the clay tablets Moses brought down from Mount Sinai; they're gradually assuming the status of a commodity, bought, sold and valued like any other, whether it be DVDs, TVs or tins of baked beans. Not only are there many more books available than ever before (a staggering 133,000-plus appear every year in the UK alone), they're being marketed using techniques that make traditionalists shudder.[28] Heavens, we've now got book charts, just as pop music's are dying. And, in the UK, following the abolition of the Net Book Agreement in 1995, booksellers were actually able to offer *discount*s on books—a practice common in just about every other corner of retailing but previously denied to booksellers.

Add all this together, and maybe books aren't as special as they used to be. Perhaps the only privilege they still enjoy over other leisure consumables is that they remain free of VAT (the UK's version of Sales Tax).

Bearing all this in mind, I reckon it's time to update our conception of 'The Common Reader', and his experience of this activity. In fact, let's construct a whole new biography both for him, and the books he reads, starting from scratch.[29]

I think we'll start by giving him a new name, since, being brought up in Lancashire, I'm acutely aware that 'common' may bring pejorative overtones into the discussion (as in 'not out of the top drawer'). Let's call him/her 'The Recreational Reader', since that represents more accurately that type of reading that usually ends up with the book thudding to the bedroom floor as he falls asleep mid way through a sentence he's already scanned five times because he's too tired to concentrate.

---

28. Compare that with the 1800s, when an average of only 95 titles per year were published in the UK—or the early 1900s, when the number had risen to 600.

29. For 'him', please read 'him/her' throughout what follows.

So let's join our Recreational Reader as he stands by the door of the bookshop one Saturday morning, wondering what he's going to buy with his hard-earned disposable income. First, he's got to find a bookshop. As of the close of 2009, independent booksellers were closing in the UK at the rate of 2 per week, leaving only 1,289 still trading... Maybe we should imagine him browsing on Amazon instead.

For a start, why does the Recreational Reader want to spend money on another book and not a new T-shirt? Well, let's go back to Katie Carr, Nick Hornby's fictional character we met earlier; she looks to literature to 'teach me the things I needed to know to survive the rest of my life'—which is not uncommon among readers who look on literature as a branch of white magic. Many of us feel we're almost duty bound to read books. They're somehow good for us.

Back in the glory days of the 'Everyman' imprint, the inside front cover of every title carried the famous quote from John Milton's *Areopagitica* which states that 'a *good* book [italics mine] is the precious life-blood of a master spirit embalmed and treasured up on purpose to a life beyond life.' And he was far from alone in thinking this; to the essayist Charles Lamb, quality books were 'spiritual repasts', to Thomas Carlyle 'a University' and 'the purest essence of a human soul'—an attitude that dates back to the era when many of those who were privileged enough to be literate considered themselves duty bound not to squander their skills by reading rubbish or composing trifles.

As such, books, or the best of them at any rate were, and still are, a distillation of what goes on inside the brains of mankind's most eminent thinkers and creative artists. Montaigne's *Essays* are an integral component of Humanity's Greatest Hits, a physical repository of all that is worthwhile about *homo sapiens*. So by reading 'good' books, we're engaging in an act of self improvement, connecting ourselves to this ongoing tradition of defining endeavour. As such, books embody an *aspirational* quality, and we often hope that by opening ourselves up to their influence, we'll somehow be the better for it. It's an utterly compelling ambition, but one whose origins are often difficult to pinpoint. It's as if we're hard-wired into believing it.

In Philip Larkin's well-anthologized poem, 'A Study of Reading Habits', the narrator equates the gradual loss of his love of reading with the general absence of spirituality in his life, which leads him to famously conclude that 'Books are a load of crap'. As his sense of wonder dims with age, so his tastes coarsen, and his opinion of the value of literature diminishes. It's as if he's voluntarily (and perversely) giving up his birth-right, and if the guy wasn't such an obvious arsehole you might even feel sorry for him.

But if you're after less ambiguous testimony to the esteem in which reading is held, look up practically any child-develop-ment book or website, and there's a wealth of unimpeachable and seemingly incontrovertible evidence, both academic and anecdotal, that spiritual impoverishment will inevitably ac-company a bookless childhood. To quote a random example, reading 'sharpens children's brains. It helps develop their ability to concentrate at length, to solve problems logically, and to express themselves more easily and clearly.' And who wouldn't wish that for their child? Whether you're a linguistic philosopher like Noam Chomsky or a helper in a kindergar-ten, you'll have arrived at the conclusion, albeit by very differ-ent paths, that books are good for kids. And with most of us, that's pushing against an open door because we somehow *know* it's true, not least because many of us who now love reading caught the bug when we were young.

And this sense of Value is further reinforced by the fact that books are bound up with ideas of free speech and the dissemi-nation of knowledge, so they tend to be a priority target for those who aren't enamoured of those two fundamental human rights, or those fearful for the souls of the morally vulnerable. And we have a long and sometimes bloody history of censorship in this country that stretches from the dawning of the English language right through to the present day, which lends books even *more* meaning; people have actually *died* that we might continue to read them.

In the 1530s, William Tyndale was repeatedly lambasted by Sir (now Saint) Thomas More for daring to print and distribute Bibles in English, then strangled and burned at the stake when he wouldn't recant. The reason usually cited for this act of barbarity is Tyndale's inclination towards Lutheranism, a heretical creed outlawed by the church in England at the time. And this was the ground of More's challenge. But there was, of course, a far more fundamental principle at stake: at the root of the clergy's objections was the fact that they no longer had the monopoly on translating, interpreting and explaining the Bible's meaning now it was available in the *lingua franca*. Even though very few people could at that point in history read the new vernacular translation, the church knew its exclusive franchise had been broken, and that this represented the thin end of a very fat wedge which might eventually do them out of a job. Heaven forbid that people should be able to think for themselves and start challenging the *status quo*.

And so it's continued up until 1960, when the last big homegrown stink over literary censorship was convincingly deodorized by the *Lady Chatterley's Lover* trial, with the law once again proving that when it comes to guessing the public mood concerning literature, it is indeed an ass. I know it's familiar, but I can't resist quoting the often misquoted prosecuting council, Mervyn Griffith-Jones, who effectively lost the case when he rose to his feet and instructed the jury:

Ask yourselves the question: would you approve of your young sons, young daughters—because girls can read as well as boys—reading this book? Is it a book that you would have lying around the house? Is it a book you would wish your wife or servants to read?

The astonishing revelation that young girls could read, and, what's more, that their fathers had the casting vote not just in *their* reading matter, but that of their wives and staff, was only marginally less ludicrous in 1960 than it is now. But what is perhaps not so well known is that *Lady Chatterley* wasn't the first of DH Lawrence's novels to attract the censorious attentions of British law. Back in 1915, when his novel *The Rainbow* first appeared, it was (rightly, this time) interpreted as not being entirely supportive of the Great War, and the police seized and burned 1,011 copies (as so often in British history, moronic acts are accompanied by scrupulous paperwork).

And of course, there was the sex: the book was banned by Bow Street magistrates after the police solicitor told them that the obscenity in the book 'was wrapped up in language which I suppose will be regarded in some quarters as artistic and intellectual effort' [sic]. The readers in those 'quarters' eventually won the day and, after the publication of *Lady Chatterley* by Penguin (which sold nearly 2 million copies in its first year), it was only a matter of time before the position of the 'official' British censor, the Lord Chamberlain, was abolished in 1968 for being both outdated and unsustainable.[30]

---

30. Of course, the law still has to participate in the banning of any form of art if it's judged to transgress the laws governing public decency, which still includes the charges of blasphemy and blasphemous libel. James Kirkup's poem, 'The Love That Dares To Speak Its Name' (1976) was found guilty of blasphemous libel in the UK. It describes a Roman centurion's sex with Christ's corpse and asserts that Jesus had group sex with his disciples. It has been briefly quoted on a few occasions, though it remains an illegal text.

Elsewhere in the world, the symbolic and empirical value of books was clearly understood by those who set fire to entire libraries.

Library burning has long been a favourite tactic for those dictators, demagogues and oligarchs who wish to demoralize or destroy entire cultures, and, as with everything else, the Chinese got there first, during the reign of Shih Huang-ti in the third century BC.

At an imperial banquet in 213 BC, a Confucian scholar decided he wanted to talk about historical continuity, and offered his opinion that only by studying the past could China move forward. The emperor's grand councilor Li Ssu angrily responded, 'There are some men of letters who do not model themselves on the present, but study the past in order to criticize the present age. They confuse and excite the ordinary people. If such conditions are not prohibited, the imperial power will decline above and partisanship will form below.' He was so enamoured of this idea, he ordered that all books in the empire be burned, with the exception of those that dealt with agriculture, medicine, and fortune telling. On top of that, it was decreed that even to discuss the forbidden works was punishable by death.

Then there was the notorious destruction of the greatest library of Western antiquity in Alexandria. No one seems to know exactly whose fault it was, not even Tom Stoppard, who marks the event in his 1993 play *Arcadia*, during which the budding (and rather theatrical) genius Thomasina says to her tutor, 'Oh, Septimus!—can you bear it? All the lost plays of the Athenians! Two hundred at least by Aeschylus, Sophocles, Euripides— thousands of poems—Aristotle's own library! How can we sleep for grief?' Whoever *was* responsible owes posterity—and Western culture—an explanation.

And on into the twentieth century. The desire to eradicate the past inspired Hitler's book-burning ceremonies of May 1933. The Nazi propaganda minister, Joseph Goebbels, told the students at the bonfires, as they hurled the forbidden works into the conflagration, 'These flames not only illuminate the final end of an old era, they also light up the new.' So that's alright then. All in a good cause.

And it's still happening. In August 1992, in Bosnia, Serb forces targeted Sarajevo's multi-cultural National and University Library with a bombardment of incendiary grenades. Bosnia's written heritage was consumed—a million and a half volumes, one hundred and fifty-five thousand of them rare books and manuscripts. The library's director said that the Bosnian Serbs 'knew that if they wanted to destroy this multi-ethnic society, they would have to destroy the library'. So they did.

And at the time I'm writing this, the occupying forces in Iraq have determined that one of their top priorities is to restore the looted treasures of the Baghdad Library, alongside the rein-statement of essential services such as water and electricity.

But it's not just under dictatorships or in areas of the globe ravaged by war that books and reading are stigmatized. In 1953, during the McCarthyite witch-hunts that sought to root out all real or imagined Communist subversives within the United States, the American Library Association was moved to issue its seminal document, *The Freedom To Read* in response to what they considered was the threat to freedom of expression posed by the Cold War. Here's an inspiring digest of it:

The freedom to read is essential to our democracy. It is continuously under attack. Private groups and public authorities in various parts of the country are working to remove or limit access to reading materials, to censor content in schools, to label 'controversial' views, to distribute lists of 'objectionable' books or authors, and to purge libraries. These actions apparently rise from a view that our national tradition of free expression is no longer valid; that censorship and suppression are needed to avoid the subversion of politics and the corruption of morals. We, as citizens devoted to reading and as librarians and publishers responsible for disseminating ideas, wish to assert the public interest in the preservation of the freedom to read.

Most attempts at suppression rest on a denial of the fundamental premise of democracy: that the ordinary citizen, by exercising critical judgement, will accept the good and reject the bad. The censors, public and private, assume that they should determine what is good and what is bad for their fellow citizens.

We trust Americans to recognize propaganda and misinformation, and to make their own decisions about what they read and believe. Such pressure toward conformity is perhaps natural to a time of accelerated change. And yet suppression is never more dangerous than in such a time of social tension. Freedom has given the United States the elasticity to endure strain. Freedom keeps open the path of novel and creative solutions, and enables change to come by choice. Every silencing of a heresy, every enforcement of an orthodoxy, diminishes the toughness and resilience of our society and leaves it the less able to deal with controversy and difference.

Now as always in our history, reading is among our greatest freedoms. The freedom to read and write is almost the only means for making generally available ideas or manners of expression that can initially command only a small audience. The written word is the natural medium for the new idea and the untried voice from which come the original contributions to social growth. It is essential to the extended discussion that serious thought requires, and to the accumulation of knowledge and ideas into organized collections.

To which one can only add, 'Spot on'. But the depressing thing is, the ALA are still having to revise and update the document

50-odd years after it was first issued.[31] So even those of us living in (nominal) democracies need to be constantly on our guard. As the hawks on the American Right tend to say, 'the price of freedom is eternal vigilance'. Just read the introduction to the UK edition of Michael Moore's *Stupid White Men*, and you'll see how insidious forms of censorship are very much with us in the 21st century—and how in this particular case, the suppression of Moore's book was foiled by a group of militant librarians who took on the combined strength of Rupert Murdoch and the then US Government. I know Moore over-eggs his puddings and is profoundly smug and annoying, but even if half of what he claims here is true, it still makes for disturbing reading.

So the struggles that writers, publishers and librarians have faced down the centuries and are still facing, all contribute to the special place books continue to hold in our own democratic culture as repositories for man's creative and intellectual endeavours. It's the bedrock of what books can subliminally mean to us, and that history's thrown in with the cover price of every book we buy. They've had a long journey to get here, of which the above is a necessarily small sample of the trials they've undergone.[32]

---

31. Section 215 of the USA Patriot Act of 2001 currently threatens bookshop and library privacy following the catastrophic events of 9/11. FBI agents do not need to prove they have 'probable cause' before searching bookshop or library records: they can get access to the records of anyone whom they believe to have information that may be relevant to a terrorism investigation, including people who are not suspected of committing a crime or of having any knowledge of a crime. The request for an order authorizing the search is heard by a secret court in a closed proceeding, making it impossible for a bookseller or librarian to have the opportunity to object on First Amendment grounds prior to the execution of the order.

32. And just look at *this* list: these are all the books that have either been 'banned, expurgated or challenged' in the last 50 years in America (I can find no equivalent list in the UK, although we're as guilty as

But that's not the end of the story. Printed books now face a whole new threat—from digital technology. If you read this

---

many. Maybe we just keep quiet about it): Dorothy Allison—*Bastard Out of Carolina, American Heritage Dictionary, The Anarchist Cookbook*, Maya Angelou—*I Know Why the Caged Bird Sings*, Anonymous—*Go Ask Alice*, James Baldwin—*If Beale Street Could Talk*, Frank L. Baum— *The Wizard of Oz*, Judy Blume—*Deenie; Forever; Tiger Eyes; Blubber; Wifey*, Boston Women's Health Book Collective—*Our Bodies, Ourselves*, Ray Bradbury—*Fahrenheit 451*, Edgar Rice Burroughs—*Tarzan*, William Burroughs—*Naked Lunch*, Robert Cormier—*The Chocolate War*, Roald Dahl—*Charlie and the Chocolate Factory; Witches*, Charles Darwin—*On the Origin of Species*, Ralph Ellison—*Invisible Man*, William Faulkner—*As I Lay Dying; Mosquitoes*, F. Scott Fitzgerald—*The Great Gatsby*, Gustave Flaubert—*Madame Bovary*, E.M. Forster—*Maurice*, Anne Frank—*The Diary of a Young Girl*, Gabriel Garcia Marquez—*One Hundred Years of Solitude*, Nancy Garden—*Annie on My Mind*, Allen Ginsberg—*Howl and Other Poems*, Nikki Giovanni—*My House*, William Golding—*Lord of the Flies*, Bette Green—*The Drowning of Stephan Jones*, Judith Guest—*Ordinary People*, Alex Haley and Malcolm X—*The Autobiography of Malcolm X*, Joseph Heller—*Catch-22*, Langston Hughes, ed.—*Best Short Stories by Negro Writers*, Aldous Huxley—*Brave New World*, James Joyce—*Ulysses*, Norton Juster—*The Phantom Tollbooth*, Stephen King—*Cujo; The Shining*, John Knowles—*A Separate Peace*, D.H. Lawrence—*Lady Chatterley's Lover*, Harper Lee—*To Kill a Mockingbird*, Henry Miller—*Tropic of Cancer*, Toni Morrison—*The Bluest Eye; Song of Solomon*, Leslea Newman— *Heather Has Two Mommies*, Eugene O'Neill—*Desire Under the Elms; Strange Interlude*, George Orwell—*1984*, Katherine Paterson—*Bridge to Terabithia*, Sylvia Plath—*The Bell Jar*, Pauline Reage—*The Story of O*, Luis Rodriguez—*Always Running*, JK Rowling—the Harry Potter series, Salman Rushdie—*The Satanic Verses*, J.D. Salinger—*The Catcher in the Rye*, Hubert Selby Jr.—*Last Exit to Brooklyn*, Maurice Sendak—*In the Night Kitchen*, William Shakespeare—*The Merchant of Venice; Romeo and Juliet*, Jane Smiley—*A Thousand Acres*, John Steinbeck—*The Grapes of Wrath; Of Mice and Men; The Red Pony*, Mark Twain—*Huckleberry Finn*, Kurt Vonnegut, Jr.—*Slaughterhouse-Five*, Alice Walker—*The Color Purple; In Love and Trouble*, Walt Whitman—*Leaves of Grass*, Michael Willhoite— *Daddy's Roommate*, Edmund Wilson—*Memoirs of Hecate County*, Richard Wright—*Native Son; Black Boy*. Some you can just about understand— but 'The Great Gatsby'?

in even five years' time, you'll probably wonder what all the fuss was about—the printed book will still be very much the preferred vehicle of our reading habits, with the Kindles and iPads and e-readers relegated to useful adjuncts which have complemented but not replaced a medium that has been with us for over 600 years. At least I hope that's what we'll all be thinking.

But media-fuelled panic is inevitable at this stage in the game, and so far the discussion has tended to take place in three separate arenas: the ideological; the mercantile and the technological.

Ideologically, as we've already noted, getting rid of books is a bad thing. No question. Yet the threats to the dissemination of knowledge we've looked at so far in this essay have been primarily Orwellian—books being banned or burned for political reasons. But then there's the less well-known but equally disturbing Huxleyan model of censorship, in which culture in general is relegated to the level of amusement and is therefore ultimately ignorable. I'm by no means immune to this fear, since this kind of self-censorship is slow, cumulative and insidious. And it doesn't take dictators to do it—although, of course, they and their media whores can oil the wheels. No, we, the consumers do it *ourselves* without necessarily realizing that we're part of the problem. So the next time you're channel-surfing and select the fifteenth re-run of *Die Hard 4* over a documentary on Saul Bellow, just be aware of the implications of your choice for the future of culture and free speech. I am—and then flip to *Die Hard 4* anyway.

Now I'm all for the popularization of Culture, but I draw the line at trivializing it. And the argument goes that by reducing books to the level of a commodity, to be bought alongside your inexpensive music downloads, that's precisely what's happening. The significance of books will evaporate as they morph from objects you can touch, hold and feel into electronic downloadable texts. Don't laugh—I'm just rehearsing the arguments, which I know can sound incredibly Luddite and pompous. But there is a grain of truth in all of them, so please bear with me.

At this point, the mercantile argument clicks in: digital distribution does away with the need for a physical product, so downloads can be sold more cheaply. Publishers don't have to buy paper, ink and binding and they have to pay far fewer middlemen to distribute and sell them. So the spiritual value of books is undermined by the cheaper pricing structure and instant availability. Buying a book is no longer a special event; you haven't had to earn as much to get it, and you haven't had to travel to a bookstore or wait for the postman—it's there in your computer or netbook or smartphone at the click of a mouse. It doesn't stand proudly collecting dust on your shelf; it's lost somewhere in that shiny entertainment gizmo along with all the other digital media you consume.

So much for the articles themselves—now let's look at the human factor. By making texts cheaper, you're robbing large numbers of people of their livelihoods—the mail workers, truck drivers, publishers, printers and—gulp—writers. None of these groups will survive intact if the cover price of a book keeps being driven down, which, in short, will mean that any title that isn't likely to ship huge quantities simply won't see the light of day. Which will reduce the choice available to the reader: anything remotely challenging or niche will disappear, and all we'll have to read are the ghost-written 'autobiographies' of celebrity nobodies.

Lastly, there's the simple technological argument: digitizing books makes them easier to pirate which will kill off the book trade even if everything else doesn't.

And here concludes the threat to books posed by the evils of technology—which I'm not going to bother refuting as some of them are thinly-disguised propaganda pumped out by publishers, retailers, snobs and recidivists. However, in an optimistic spirit almost entirely contrary to my nature, I will make the following general observations:

- Most of these issues are already being successfully addressed by the music industry;[33]

- If authors cut out book publishers and deal directly with distributors, they can earn far higher royalties —up to 70% in some cases, as against 7-15% through traditional outlets;

- Book sales are currently higher than ever in the UK despite the decimation of the independent bookselling trade;

- Charge consumers a reasonable amount for a product and they're less likely to indulge in acts of piracy;

- The content of books is far more important than the means by which it is distributed, and the format it arrives in;

- It is impossible to trivialize quality content;

- Everything evolves or dies.

Now I'm not kidding—the following is absolutely true. I've just this second read those last few paragraphs back, thinking I've made a reasonable case for refusing to panic about the future of books and reading—and then this pops into my mailbox, and my carefully-nurtured optimism is blown to smithereens:

---

33. Which is shifting from what they call 'an acquisitive culture' to an 'access culture'—i.e. we pay for access to centrally-held libraries of music rather than buying our own copies.

✶✶✶ PRESS RELEASE—PETER ANDRÉ:
MY WORLD IN PICTURES AND WORDS[34] ✶✶✶

Michael Joseph (an imprint of Penguin Books) is delighted to have bought world rights to Peter André's illustrated memoir... In 2009, Peter André's profile exploded, making him one of the biggest male celebrities in the UK. His upcoming Revelation tour, his TV projects and now his book will further catapult him to stardom—2010 will cement his reputation as the sexy and extremely loveable heart-throb the nation has taken under its wing.

Packed with approximately 150-200 gorgeous photographs, most of which have never been seen before, the book will focus on Peter's amazing journey so far. This is a celebration of his life, from aspiring singer to celebrity popstar. It charts the rise of his success, the trials and tribulations he had to endure along the way, his newfound maturity. And of course it focuses on what it means to be a father—and a single parent too.

My considered reaction is to lose it completely.

OK, calm, calm. Breathe deeply... What would Montaigne think were he here to witness this parade of the witless?

In all probability he'd correctly argue that without shite like Peter André's illustrated memoir, Penguin could not produce their peerless series of Classics—which includes, incidentally, *two* translations of Montaigne's *Essays.* Then he'd smile a knowing smile and continue reading the digital edition of Plutarch's *Lives* on his iPad. He probably wouldn't be overly concerned, choosing to believe that quality will triumph. I have to believe that too, but my faith is sorely shaken by buffets like that one.

---

34. I don't know how widespread Peter André's fame is, nor how the foreign rights of this book will sell, so here's a summary: he's a pop singer, and one of Jordan's former consorts (see above). Errrr...that's it. Except that the British media is obsessed with him.

Chapter Eight

Mmmmmmmmmmmmmmmmmm. *Nice.*

'*Dionysius laughed at... musicians, who were so exact in tuning their instruments, and never tuned their manners.*' (Book 1, Chapter 24: 'Of Pedantry')

Montaigne doesn't have a great deal to say about music—which disappoints me slightly. As it's such a central feature in my own life (and career), I'd like to have known his thoughts on the subject. As a child, his father—rather oversolicitously—employed a musician to wake him gently from his slumbers; later in life, he admits, 'In music or singing, for which I have a very unfit voice, or to play on any sort of instrument, they could never teach me anything.' But there's precious little else on the subject, forcing this reader to reluctantly conclude that like many whose lives are spent in cerebration or immersed in public duties, Montaigne had neither the time nor inclination to pursue any musical interests. He quotes the Athenian statesman Alcibiades, who banished all music from his home, preferring instead the stimulation afforded by good conversation. As did George Bernard Shaw, who labelled music 'the brandy of the damned', probably because he preferred the sound of his own voice.

Over the years, I've noticed that I tend not to click with people who don't have a taste for music. Likewise when travelling—I'll always choose to visit somewhere that has a rich musical heritage over a place that doesn't. I haven't the faintest idea why this might be, other than to speculate that as an art form, music adds another dimension to my life which I miss on those occasions when it's absent.

Yet there are certain types of music that just don't register when I'm listening to them—not many, but the ones I don't 'get' enjoy such widespread popularity that I have managed to convince myself that either my taste or education is failing me. True, I don't lose any sleep over my loathing of German brass bands or anything featuring the Scottish pipes; but my total inability to listen to opera and certain forms of jazz strangely exercises my inner guilt—as if somehow I'm not trying hard enough.

Opera I can dismiss with very little difficulty; two quotes will serve to sum up its sheer ludicrousness and utter tedium—both from renowned orchestral conductors: there's Edward Gardner ('Opera is when a guy gets stabbed in the back, and instead of bleeding, he sings') and David Randolph ('*Parsifal* is the kind of opera that starts at 6 o'clock. After it has been going on for three hours you look at your watch and it says 6.20').

And then there's the 200lb gorilla in my particular music room—jazz.[35] Does anyone *really,* in their heart of hearts, *like* jazz—except, perhaps, as a lifestyle accessory? I know, I know—the answer is yes, but if that 'yes' is to remain unchallenged, how do you account for these two phenomena?

---

35. I've often wondered why proverbially it's a 200lb gorilla, which would make it a very small gorilla indeed. Even young females weigh in at around 300lbs. If you're going to have a gorilla in the room, it might as well be a big one.

First, nobody in the UK, despite several attempts, has managed to make a jazz radio station pay. The good folks behind Classic FM know a thing or two about popularizing 'difficult' classical music—they've got 6 million-odd listeners to prove it. But when they applied the formula to jazz—the station collapsed within a year. Similarly, the various incarnations of Jazz FM only play jazz late at night to audiences that are scarcely measurable; the rest of the time they spin soul or Norah Jones-style dinner-party jazz.[36] Even in the U.S.A., most jazz stations are small, local, run mainly by volunteers, and cover their running costs with a mix of subscriptions, private donations and begathons.

Second, I've been lucky enough to attend the 'New Orleans Jazz and Heritage Festival', a mammoth event held every year in the city generally acknowledged to be the crucible of jazz. It takes place at a giant horseracing track that can accommodate tens of thousands of spectators. And guess what? There's very little jazz played there. In fact, the so-called 'Jazz Tent' is a comparatively small affair stuck in a remote corner of the site and for the most part is three-quarters empty. And having stuck my head round the flaps a few times, it wasn't difficult to hear why.

But is this failure to hook a mass audience a fault of the music, or us listeners who won't go that extra mile? Is it essential to 'work' at liking jazz? And if that's the case, doesn't it argue that you're forcing yourself to enjoy it? Shouldn't the pleasure engendered by music involve joy and spontaneity rather than a dogged determination? Should you have to do your homework before you can 'understand' the music? And should you have to understand music at all? With the words of Satchmo playing on my mind, ('Man, if you have to ask what it [jazz] is, you'll

---

36. Wonderfully accurate headline from *The Onion* in 2007: 'Norah Jones releases debut album for the third time.'

never know'), I thought a bit of homework might be in order if I was to get to the root of my ambivalence.

Last year in New Orleans, I picked up a giant poster entitled 'Highlights of the Jazz Story', a labour of love compiled and drawn by Peter von Bartkowski. It depicts a huge tree—one central trunk with countless boughs, branches and twigs flying off it, demonstrating how one form of music evolved into others. I've spent many idle hours staring at the 920 musicians depicted on it and trying to make sense of it all. And Peter's done a fantastic job, revealing many unfamiliar artists: I'd love to pick up some recordings by Stale Bread Lacoume's Spasm Band simply on account of the name, but he never made it into a studio, probably because studios hadn't been invented in 1890. Looking agape at the chart, it becomes quickly apparent that jazz has a breathtaking pedigree, right up from King Oliver, Louis Armstrong and Fats Waller through to swing, Duke Ellington, Count Basie—but then the trouble starts just over half way up the main trunk, some time after the end of World War Two, with two giant obstacles to the amateur jazz consumer like me—'Bop' and 'Cool', not to mention their offspring 'Hard Bop', 'Fusion' and 'Free Jazz'.

Briefly (for this is a familiar argument), bop actively encouraged the kind of instrumental virtuosity that poses huge challenges for the musician and listener alike. Lengthy free-form improvisation, tricksy time signatures and a gradual abandonment of the traditional song form together constituted a wilful plunge into musical obscurity that many jazz fans couldn't—or wouldn't—follow, and won the genre few new friends. Spike Milligan, no mean jazz musician himself, described this approach as 'farting into a trumpet.' In the course of an insightful interview in 1970, he said this:

Sure, music has to be a means of communication. But it's turned inwards now—and they turn their backs on the audience. It has become masturbation instead of love-making with an audience... They're so insecure, they've got to baffle you with technique—and they don't say anything.

Succinctly put.[37] It's all about the inexplicable urge to feel superior to someone else, which, after all, is what Cool's all about. Or rather that affected, self-mythologizing brand of *faux* cool beloved of the Beats, who adored the freedom the new forms of jazz represented. In his book *Venice West*, bohemian biographer John Arthur Maynard writes:

Jazz served as the ultimate point of reference, even though, or perhaps even because, few among them played it. From it they adopted the mythos of the brooding, tortured, solitary artist, performing with others but always alone.

In his only successful book *Go,* Beat author John Clellon Holmes supported this view:

In this modern jazz, they heard something rebel and nameless that spoke for them, and their lives knew a gospel for the first time. It was more than a music; it became an attitude toward life, a way of walking, a language and a costume; and these introverted kids...now felt somewhere at last.

Those who dug the new breed happily became an embattled freemasonry, rejoicing in their coolness and repeating the same cyclical formula: play (or listen to) difficult music; alienate the squares; feel cool. By 1960, Duke Ellington, who knew a thing or two about music (and that kind of effortless cool that's so cool it doesn't even know it's cool), could write:

---

37. Spike produced another priceless musical observation: a certain tenor's vibrato sounded like 'he was driving a tractor over ploughed fields with weights tied to his scrotum.'

Jazz has developed into one of those intellectual art forms that scare people away... People will not come into places where jazz enthusiasts congregate if they are going to be made to feel ignorant...if the man next to them might look down his nose at them, so to speak, with a flatted fifth. Nothing can be worse than to have somebody look down his nose with a flatted fifth, believe me.

Ellington also noted that bop was like 'playing Scrabble with all the vowels missing'. Record man Syd Nathan, who championed just about every musical form under the sun on his 'King' label, was also having difficulties with jazz:

I still can't get this bop and I've really tried. They go around talking of flatted fifths, and sometimes it seems it's just people with inferiority complexes just boosting their egos.

And so things have remained for the last half-century. While the sharper edges of jazz may have been rounded off a little, there's still plenty of rectal hornplay going on (a mate who records the jazz gigs for BBC Radio 3 assures me of this); or there's the kind of gig where the musicians establish a theme, take turns to riff around it in strict rotation, then repeat this sequence and structure on every tune till closing time. Rock music went through a similar period of obligatory virtuosity, improvisation and noodling—you remember—concept albums you couldn't dance to. My favourite relic of that era was the sleeve note from 'progressive' band Gentle Giant's first album, in which the group set out its manifesto to 'expand the frontiers of contemporary popular music at the risk of becoming very unpopular.' An ambition they quickly fulfilled.

But rock (and Gentle Giant) grew out of this adolescent posturing within a decade, and punk finally left it a barely twitching corpse;[38] yet noodling is still such an integral feature of

---

38. Until the dreaded 'jam bands'—low rent copies of the Grateful

jazz performance that the need to be 'difficult' seems permanently hard-wired into the music—and the brains—of its practitioners.

It's regularly argued that a discomfort with ground-breaking, experimental art is the sure sign of a bourgeois mindset—but I'm not suggesting for a moment that jazz should stick within the territory defined by the impeccably tasteful but utterly yawnsome Diana Krall, the sub-Sinatra cocktail slickness of Michael 'Bloody' Bublé, or even the neutered rebelliousness of Jamie Cullum. All music must evolve, and in the 20th-century, just about every art form pushed boundaries and definitions to their limits—it was almost a rite of passage to see how far you could go whether you were writing, painting, dancing—whatever. And jazz was no exception—it would have been utterly strange if it hadn't. Some artists just managed it with better grace and good humour than others. At base, as Spike says, the writing and performing of music is at least in part about communication, and art of any type that sets out to deliberately exclude participation isn't destined to succeed on any level.

And, as in every other branch of the arts, there's a boredom threshold beyond which experimentation quickly outs itself as self-indulgence. So I adore the weirdness of Captain Beefheart, because his sense of humour doesn't leave me with the suspicion his music is a gigantic mind-wank. By contrast, when Miles Davis started literally turning his back on his paying audiences around the time of *Bitches Brew*, he was just being a humourless nobhead. Or, if you prefer, an 'artist'. It's no secret that he entertained high aspirations for his work—and nothing wrong with that—but Miles's understanding of his role in the evolution of jazz verged on the Messianic, as this extract from John Swzed's fair-minded biography makes clear:

Dead—brought it all back again. Let's hope they never make it past cult acceptance.

At Juilliard, he had learned what an artist could demand of an audience, and it was he who would correct the music, who would purify it of its brothel and tent show origins, and present it as the art it was… [T]his had the weight of a mission.

It's the word 'correct' that speaks volumes to me. Davis was a troubled man prone to bouts of substance abuse, but no amount of special pleading can excuse the arrogance, however delusional, of someone who sets out to 'correct' Louis Armstrong, Duke Ellington, and the other ground-breaking musicians on the bottom half of my wall chart. Swzed makes an excellent case that Davis's perceived arrogance was the result of acute shyness, but it's still difficult to ignore the fierce contempt that seems to lie behind, and indeed at the root of, much of his behaviour, both musical and otherwise. He even quotes the joke of the old guy sitting looking miserable in a jazz club in heaven; 'Who's that?' a punter asks the bartender. 'Oh, that's God,' comes the reply. 'He thinks he's Miles Davis.'

Who knows, maybe I could be considered terminally bourgeois. But it's a small price to pay for not feeling obliged to dig Miles's later experiments. That said, *Bitches Brew* did sell over half a million copies… yet I continue to wonder how many of its owners were drawn to the album for the cool it represents rather than the music it contains. When I was at college, it was one of those trophy albums that blokes who couldn't get a girlfriend used to own—those two facts not being entirely unconnected. That aside, I did try. I bought *Sketches of Spain* and *Kind of Blue* and thoroughly enjoyed them. I still do. But then Miles jammed his trumpet up his arse and left me behind.

To conclude, I recently went to a Van Morrison gig in which he showcased his 'jazzier' side. Brilliant. Note perfect. But at its heart there was an emptiness caused by the paradox that while Morrison obviously takes great care to put on a slick show, his sullen demeanour and stubborn refusal to acknowledge his audience *at all* grated somewhat. And then he finished his set early. After which, the fulsome onstage tribute by the MC, informing us that Van is a 'genius' and we had 'just witnessed true greatness' rang rather hollow. No, I screamed, he's a miserable old nob. A nob who, paradoxically, could write both the beautiful and sensitive lyrics of 'And It Stoned Me' and the truly pathetic whining of 'Why Do I Always Have To Explain' which justifies, in his mind at least, why he's a miserable old nob.

Although I'll try to discount it, his behaviour at that gig will doubtless colour my appreciation of his music when I listen to it in future. Which is a pity.

So maybe that's why I don't like certain sorts of jazz—and other music that demonstrates a similar detachment—that much. After all, as in life, so in art: why bother trying to like somebody who doesn't like you?

Chapter Nine

The Eeeeeuuuuuwwww Factor

'Stercus cuique suum bene olet.'

'*To every man his own excrements smell well.*' (Erasmus, quoted in Book 3, Chapter 8: 'Of the Art of Conference')

Montaigne wasn't a great fan of scent, possibly because it made his nose itch. Besides, he entertained the suspicion that perfume is more about concealment than attraction:

[S]*uch as make use of fine exotic perfumes are with good reason to be suspected of some natural imperfection which they endeavour by these odours to conceal.*

Which of course 500 years ago was all too true, and not a great point in history to be blessed with an alert and sensitive nose. He continues:

I am nevertheless a great lover of good smells, and as much abominate the ill ones, which also I scent at a greater distance, I think, than other men:

> *Namque sagacius unus odoror,*

Polypus, an gravis hirsutis cubet hircus in aliis
Quam canis acer, ubi latest sus.

[*'My nose is quicker to scent a fetid sore or a rank armpit, than a dog to smell out the hidden sow.'*—Horace, Epodes, xii. 4.]

Delicately put, since in Montaigne's time, the ratio of good smells to bad would be heavily weighted towards the latter, as it's only in the immediate past that the general population has made a fetish of personal cleanliness. One of the most evocative descriptions of the combination of human secretions with perfume was concocted by Scottish surgeon Tobias Smollett in his novel *Humphry Clinker*, published in 1771, in which the narrator, Matthew Bramble is quite overcome:

I no sooner got home, than I sent for Doctor Ch—, who assured me I need not be alarmed, for my swooning was entirely occasioned by an accidental impression of fetid effluvia upon nerves of uncommon sensibility. I know not how other people's nerves are constructed; but one would imagine they must be made of very coarse materials, to stand the shock of such a horrid assault. It was, indeed, a compound of villainous smells, in which the most violent stinks, and the most powerful perfumes, contended for the mastery. Imagine to yourself a high exalted essence of mingled odours, arising from putrid gums, imposthumated lungs, sour flatulencies, rank armpits, sweating feet, running sores and issues, plasters, ointments, and embrocations, hungry-water, spirit of lavender, assafoetida *drops, musk, hartshorn, and* sal volatile*; besides a thousand frowzy steams, which I could not analyse. Such, O Dick! is the fragrant aether we breathe in the polite assemblies of Bath.*

And those were the smells of the rich. We can laugh, but it was only in the early 20th-century that the widespread installations of baths and toilets with S- or U-shaped traps (to keep sewer gases from backing up into the home) made bathing the routine affair it is now. And when I was at college, one of the older dons remembered that when he was first appointed a junior lecturer in the 1950s, one of the crustier dons at New College Oxford was shocked, when returning from vacation, to see that the authorities had installed bathrooms for the students; 'What do they need those for?' he ranted. 'They're only here for eight weeks at a time!'

So it's only in the last half century or so that anointing our bodies with perfume has ceased to be an entirely diversionary tactic. Only we seem to have replaced one set of smells with another, substituting the human for the chemical, which is often equally retch-inducing. Having showered or bathed in a product made with raspberry essence, we'll moisturize with something containing extracts of mandarin and beech wood, then splash around a third set of whiffs as we add the finishing touches of perfume or aftershave. In fact, it's getting increasingly difficult to keep clean and *not* trail some weird acrid cocktail in your wake, since in the UK at least, unperfumed brands cost more than stinky ones. If you ask for additive-free soap in my local chain chemist, they assume you have some kind of embarrassing skin complaint that's contact-spread and back away.

Montaigne suspects that for men at least, it's a bit effeminate to be over-assiduous in the matter of personal grooming. In an otherwise flattering portrait of Julius Caesar he remarks:

...one testimony is the peculiar care he had of his person, to such a degree, as to make use of the most lascivious means to that end then in use, as to have all the hairs of his body twitched off, and to wipe all over with perfumes with the extremest nicety.

One gets the feeling that in Montaigne's eyes (or perhaps nose), vanity ill became the great military campaigner. In the same way that after a session at the hairdresser's, I reckon Montaigne would prefer to be asked if he wanted 'something for the weekend' and a nostril trim, rather than 'Do you use any waxes or gels at all?'

He concludes his short essay on the subject by noting that *'To smell, though well, is to stink'*. And I must say, I agree. Why is it necessary to smell *of* something? Smell-neutral would be my ideal. For the following reason:

If you were to construct my own personal Ninth Circle of Hell, it would closely resemble the perfume section of a department store. Wherever I've travelled in the world, they look identical, probably because the brands they peddle are international. To me, they represent an unwelcome assault on all five senses, and the way they've evolved seems just plain *weird,* being a sort of hybrid between an operating theatre and a night club. The blinding white light and shiny décor are symbolic, I suppose of technology and cleanliness; the pounding techno indicates energy, fun and youth; the sales staff, faces resembling lurid orange death masks, smile those creepy rictus grins. Then there's the mildly erotic product names courtesy of some marketing man's wet dream—'Obsession', 'Besotted', 'Sensuelle', 'Forbidden' and, er, 'Wang' (oddly enough for women). Or they may be celebrity brands—did you know that long-dead surrealist Salvador Dali has his own fragrance? Or country star Tim McGraw? And the weirdest of all...Donald Trump.

And to cap it all there's THE SMELL—dozens of frowzy steams leeching together to create one great olfactory nightmare; the mists from a hundred atomisers forming a viscous cloud that hangs in the air, irritating both eyes and skin. And because the perfume sales area is usually situated on the ground floor between the store entrance and the escalators, you have to run the gauntlet of the aerosol samplers like some psychedelic re-enactment of Gunfight At The OK Corral. So. Deep breath, shoulders down and...CHARGE!!

If my life were a movie, at this point I'd wake up sweaty and palpitating. But I'm not, and this is for real. God help the poor buggers who have to work in these hell-holes eight hours or more a day. But when you manage to get through them un-squirted there's that massive sense of achievement accompanied by the relief you won't smell of a guilty afternoon in a suburban brothel. Or Donald Trump. It's something to celebrate. Usually with a prolonged sneezing fit and a nosebleed.

Just one word: why?

Dumb question—to get a mate, stupid. To get you noticed by a prospective partner and, these days, to prove that you're clean. Perfume practically dates back to the time man crawled out of the fetid swamp he called home. Like the dog rolling in the rotting corpse of some dead animal to increase the chances of getting his end away with that hot labrador bitch over there, we want to be attractive. We may not be animals now, well most of us anyway, but the perfume industry still insists on plundering glands and secretions from the animal kingdom to concoct scents to make us smell better; among its victims are sperm whales, beavers, the mongoose, the rock hyrax, bees and the Asian musk deer. It's always intrigued me—who first got the idea to rub the oxidised fatty compounds of some un-suspecting marine mammal onto their skin? Not an obvious thing to do, surely? But it gave birth to an industry. I rang up Selfridge's just now, and their PR lady told me their perfume department stocks around 600 brands.

Perhaps my hostility to honky smells lies in the fact that I as-sociate these acrid scents with sexual desperation. The other day I was reminiscing with my niece, who used to attend a Catholic boarding school in the north of England. Thirty years ago, my school (all boys) used to bus in a coachload of young ladies from that very same establishment for an annual summer orgy of…ballroom dancing. For just one evening out of 365, it was possible for the boarders to get up close and personal with a female of the opposite sex with the blessing of the school authorities. The very same authorities that forbade pin-ups of Faye Dunaway lest they aroused unsuitable but perfectly natural desires. Two whole hours of heaven holding on to that soft, white, alien flesh as the assembly hall's crackly PA system played the bossa novas, tangos and waltzes no-one had been taught to dance.

On the Saturday afternoon prior to the event, long-lost suits were exhumed from wherever they'd last been flung to be pressed into something resembling smartness. Smells were everywhere; the sensitive organ could distinguish a heady miasma of coal tar soap, cheap shampoo, stain remover, shoe wax, silver polish and...after shave. Gallons of it. Poured, sprayed or slapped on to every possible square inch of available flesh. The stench was unimagineable—and given that most of this went on in the sports changing rooms which had its own perfume of fermenting kit, not unlike what caused Matthew Bramble to faint two centuries before.

Of course, us day pupils were thankfully not invited, so we did what any mature teenagers would do in the situation and poked fun at these would-be David Cassidys. Before, that is, going home and performing exactly the same ritual to try and pull at Trader Jack's disco that night.

Aramis, Cedar Wood, Aqua Manda, Hai Karate, Old Spice, evocative brands all, most long since vanished.

Once again I can hear Montaigne laughing at human folly. As did my niece.

I'm not sure she even believed me.

Chapter Ten

Peeping Toms at the Keyhole of Eternity

'...all I write here are but the idle reveries of a man that has only nibbled upon the outward crust of sciences in his nonage, and only retained a general and formless image of them; who has got a little snatch of everything and nothing of the whole.' (Book 1, Chapter 25: 'Of the Education of Children')

Montaigne wasn't a scientist as such, but the way his thought processes worked wasn't that far removed from those regularly employed in scientific pursuits, particularly if you agree with Pierre Émile Duclaux, the French biochemist who noted that science is 'a series of judgments, revised without ceasing'—a skeptical position if ever I heard one. Had experimental science been more highly developed in the 16th-century, I reckon Montaigne would have drawn to it by his all-embracing curiosity, yet, like H.L. Mencken, would have stopped short of declaring that science can provide us with answers to everything:

Penetrating so many secrets, we cease to believe in the unknowable. But there it sits nevertheless, calmly licking its chops.

From the perspective of 21st-century science, I think he would be intrigued by the frequent collisions between certainty and doubt, hypothesis and proof; and that he would take enormous pleasure in the prodigious displays of imagination involved at the outer reaches of scientific conjecture. But then again, he wasn't educated at my school, which was rubbish at teaching science. The teachers couldn't have made it more dull if they'd tried.

In Biology, the taboos of sexual reproduction were addressed by examining the mating habits of dogfish and, get this, pond weed; in Chemistry, instead of creating fabulous bangs and smells, we were taught to balance equations; in Physics, we wanted to learn about space flight and computers and how transistor radios worked—and we did experiments to prove that things accelerate if you shove them down a hill. Important, but dull, dull, dull. And in the last case, utterly obvious, as anyone whose Dad had made them a home-made go-kart would attest.

Just about everyone in my class felt that science was fascinating. It was the era of the Apollo moon landings; Jacques Cousteau was on TV filming the depths of the ocean in his submarine; new species of fearsome dinosaurs were being dug up; Concorde made its early test flights; the first heart transplant was carried out in South Africa; skyscrapers grew ever taller. All around us, scientists from every discipline were demonstrating new and exciting possibilities for the future while uncovering tantalising glimpses of mankind's evolution. This was much more fun than cissy poetry or boring novels by dead guys. We wanted—we needed—to learn about these things.

In the science block at my school, however, it was as if none of these amazing developments was happening. There was absolutely no attempt to exploit the almost visceral enthusiasm us schoolboys experienced when we looked at the world outside those gale-blown, salt-smeared windows. All that childhood wonder was recklessly squandered. Faced with things like this scrawled across the blackboard,[39]

$$\ln(\gamma_i) = -\frac{z_i^2 q^2 \kappa}{8\pi\varepsilon_r\varepsilon_0 k_B T} = -\frac{z_i^2 q^3 N_A^{1/2}}{4\pi(\varepsilon_r\varepsilon_0 k_B T)^{3/2}}\sqrt{\frac{I}{2}} = -A z_i^2 \sqrt{I}$$

many of us jettisoned every science subject we could prior to taking our 'O' Levels—a course of action, I've since found out, adopted by a large percentage of my generation. Paradoxically, at a time when science had so much to offer the questing mind, pupils like me were turning our backs on it in droves. Was the odd explosion too much to ask?

The most damaging legacy of this failure to engage young minds was twofold: first, it reinforced the idea that the arts and sciences were mutually hostile; and second, it encouraged us to believe that what we learned of science from the TV and picture books was the flashy, 'easy' kind of science—'real' science was a painful, tedious, empirical methodology carried out by socially inept people with leaky biros sticking out of their top pockets.

The stereotype persisted well into my college days: how clever we arty types thought ourselves when compared to the scientists with their pints of lager, greasy hair and almost total absence of fashion sense. In the Junior Common Room at St. Catherine's, two worlds eyed one another suspiciously across the pool table; the ones destined to lead us into the technological future, and those, like me, trying to recreate *Brideshead Revisited*. How smug and arrogant we were.

Because, of course, the arts and sciences were originally conjoined twins, if we'd bothered to find out. And Philosophy was the father.

---

39. It's the Debye–Hückel equation, dummy.

Both sets of disciplines had their origins in classical antiquity in the work of such polymaths as Aristotle and Pliny the Elder, both of whose influence in the field of science extended right through the Renaissance to the Scientific Revolution of the 16th and 17th-centuries (and in the case of some of their work, even beyond that).

Aristotle's inquiries extended beyond the parameters of cerebral thought to embrace the natural world—indeed the entire world; eventually, his oeuvre included botany, zoology, physics, astronomy, chemistry and meteorology. Lacking the basic tools for experimentation (which hadn't yet been invented), many of his principles were formulated from observation, reason and primitive experimentation. In addition to his better-known writings on *Poetics, Rhetoric* and *Ethics*, he also assembled over twenty works which explored the natural world. These included a ten-volume *History of Animals*, the five-volume *On the Generation of Animals* and the four-volume *On the Parts of Animals*. He not only developed an eleven-tier system for the classification of living creatures, he did a fair bit of detailed dissection too, mainly of sea-life but also including cows and chicken eggs. In many ways, he was the prototypical Renaissance Man two millennia before the Renaissance.

Four hundred years later came our second truly remarkable polymath: Pliny the Elder, whose 37-book *Natural History* is, in essence, the first ever encyclopaedia, complete with citations and a comprehensive index.[40] In the preface, Pliny claims he has recorded 20,000 facts that he has gathered from 2,000 books and 100 different authors. To read the contents page

40. Montaigne was a Pliny fan—though, somewhat perversely, not for his knowledge: 'Is there anything more delicate, more clear, more sprightly than Pliny's judgment when he is pleased to set it to work? Anything more remote from vanity? Setting aside his learning, of which I make less account, in which of these excellences do any of us excel him?'

alone is to be humbled: maths, geography, ethnography, anthropology, physiology, zoology, botany (including agriculture, horticulture and pharmacology), metallurgy, mineralogy, statuary, painting, modelling and sculpture. For much of the day he would sit reading, or being read to, taking notes and ordering his findings—a process remembered fondly by his nephew, Pliny the Younger:

After dinner a book would be read aloud, and he would take notes in a cursory way. I remember that one of his friends, when the reader pronounced a word wrongly, checked him and made him read it again, and my uncle said to him, 'Did you not catch the meaning?' When his friend said 'yes,' he remarked, 'Why then did you make him turn back? We have lost more than ten lines through your interruption.' So jealous was he of every moment lost.

Both Pliny and Aristotle were commonly referred to as 'natural philosophers', possessed of sensibilities that cross just about all the epistemological boundaries we now erect around individual areas of knowledge. The whole world was their classroom. Science started to outgrow its parent Philosophy in Western Europe around the mid-16th century, one of the milestones in this process being the appointment of the first ever Professor of Natural Philosophy, Jacopo Zabarella at the University of Padua.[41] Plato had differentiated between knowledge that is the product of either theory or practice, and Zabarella's *Opera Logica* expanded on that dualism, using the work of Aristotle as his template. In summary, Zabarella postulated that:

The Sciences deal with the eternal world of nature; they are the product of contemplation and deep thought, and move in the direction of certainty and reliable knowledge of what already exists. Their ultimate aim is arranging and comprehending.

41. Zabarella was an almost exact contemporary of Montaigne, being born in 1532.

The Arts have their roots in the day-to-day human world; they create things and have no need of 'perfect' knowledge or precision. Their ultimate goal is to initiate.[42]

And so the rift had been opened, although Science's practitioners were still for the great part thinkers rather than hands-on experimenters.

The term 'scientist' did not supplant that of 'natural philosopher' until as late as the mid-19th century. By that time, science had grown far more visible, having acted as midwife to the Industrial Revolution. Massive engineering projects were clearly not the products of philosophy, but of disciplines which had been extracted from the motherlode of original knowledge; new overarching theories and the practical means of testing them witnessed science moving yet further from its roots and beginning to approximate how we understand it today.

As the subject continued to fragment and grow ever more involved, the chance that a single person could embrace both arts and sciences was looking ever more improbable and separate cultures began to evolve. Which brief whistle-stop summary brings us back to the two tribes in St. Catherine's JCR.

It probably sounds smug to claim that I was never particularly convinced by the arts/sciences schism—but I wasn't then and I'm still not. Most of my friends found themselves on one side or the other because of logistical shortcomings at our schools—my chosen combination of Maths, English and French was refused on the grounds that it was impossible to accommodate within the timetable. And just because we may not have an aptitude for one or the other area of knowledge doesn't preclude our being interested in it. Disciplines like architecture and many

---

42. Interesting how these days, we might think the Arts were contemplative and the Sciences practical.

of the social sciences still demand expertise that overlaps both areas.

Yet I always felt that any intellectual myopia was usually the fault of those in the arts, probably because science is so damned *hard,* and we mocked what we couldn't understand, which is, of course, pathetic. By contrast, many of my contemporaries in science were brilliant musicians; one was a fine comic book artist and another, damn him, wrote excellent short stories. He could do what I could do—yet I had no corresponding talent in any of his areas of knowledge. Which I found embarrassing and do to this day. Like when people from Holland or Sweden talk to me in perfect colloquial English. It reveals my ignorance, and I hate them for it.

In its more mature moments, the *Brideshead* gang did manage to debate the issue of arts versus sciences; I recall our major beef being that scientific thought was essentially reductive and constricting, whereas the impulse towards art was characterized by expansive and expanding vistas—in pursuit of which we curtailed our discussions, passed round the gin and dope, and listened to Tom Waits.

I suppose we were thinking along the right lines, but a little less dope and a little more digging would have revealed this rather pertinent observation from science historian William Whewell, who noted in 1840 that scientific method cannot be based on experience alone. Any form of 'Inductive Science', as he termed it, required 'invention, sagacity [and] genius' at every stage of a theory's evolution—a kind of oscillation between imagination and experience. Vague terms to be connected with scientific inquiry admittedly, but what Whewell sought to highlight was the quality of imagination that must drive science forward and be an intrinsic component in its methodology.

Maybe he saw what was coming in the teaching of science subjects in my school: the suspicion of non-linear thought when formulating ideas, and the temptation to banish imprecision of any kind from experimental activity. In short, the systematic purging of imagination from science. Which represents a travesty of true scientific method, because there's *tons* of mind-blowing imagination in science—which, to me at any rate appears worryingly superior to that demonstrated in, say, my chosen field of literature. Let me try and explain.

The writer can basically think what he wants—there are no limits placed on his imagination. He may spend a few years knocking out his *magnum opus,* and he may have to do some research if the subject carries him outside his comfort zone of immediate experience. Or, like James Michener, he might get whole teams of interns helping him do the research for his great historical wedges. Whatever, he controls the world he's creating, which may or may not resemble the one he's actually living in. Verisimilitude doesn't necessarily matter—it's the story that counts, and the writer's ultimately in control.

Scientists, on the other hand, have to use buckets of imagination but in a much more rigorous way, relying on evidence and theory; logic and hunches; observation and extrapolation. They are not completely in control; to some extent they are steered by circumstances that force them to think round and through fundamental principles of nature that cannot be changed. Yet they grapple with GIANT subjects that are often way outside the purview of the writer—like what happened in the first half-trillionth of a second after the Big Bang. Besides which most fiction appears pretty inconsequential. I love it when novelists claim that what they do is difficult—oh, that blank screen that mocks me first thing in the morning as I sit down to create; oh, the terror if my muse does not visit me; oh the utter despair and desolation of writer's block. Well. For a start it's not coal mining; and second, try wrestling with some of the problems scientists have to solve. Try coping with the failure of a costly experiment. Try coping when an entire theoretical structure collapses after five years' brain-melting work. *That's* hard. And it'll take more than a Starbuck's Frappuccino and a long walk on Hampstead Heath to put right.

Now I've no means of knowing for certain, but I'm prepared to bet the propositions that gave rise to, say, particle physics involved massive leaps of imagination. One of the biggest must have been the very first, namely that atoms exist at all. The Indian and Greek philosophers who first made the proposition couldn't see atoms either with the naked eye or any experimental equipment yet available; yet they were convinced they *had* to exist. And they were, of course, right. This was such an incredible step forward, it couldn't be improved on for almost fifteen hundred years. Similarly, when one of the fathers of nuclear physics, John Dalton, postulated his 'rule of greatest simplicity' in the creation of compound molecules from the atoms of different elements, he couldn't prove it, but his assertion, being broadly correct, represented a giant leap forward in our understanding of what everything on the planet is made of. Beside that, Proust looks like a load of onanistic tosh.[43]

This imaginative combination of precedent and prediction leads to forward intellectual movement that the artists among us might describe as faith, the scientists probability. If that probability is high enough, the search for proof begins. And, let's face it, faith doesn't come much more expansive (or expensive) than the construction of the LHC (Large Hadron Collider) beneath the borders of France and Switzerland. Its circumference is 17 kilometres, it's buried between 50 and 175 metres down, and it cost in the region of $6.2 billion. 60 countries have a stake in it, indicating to me that faith is pretty strong the LHC will prove what it's intended to. And the stakes are very

43. Actually, beside *anything* Proust looks like a load of onanistic tosh.

high; we are told we may finally learn what holds the universe together. Amazing? You bet. And an unexpected by-product emerged when Tim Berners-Lee pioneered the World Wide Web in 1989 while working there.

And what has the arts contributed to this astounding journey? Dan Brown's *Angels and Demons*, that's what. Partly set at the LHC, it involves the theft of some anti-matter which a disgruntled Papal Chamberlain threatens to use to destroy the Vatican.

Flippancy aside, the most frustrating aspect of *Angels and Demons* is the fault it shares with too many fictional representations of science; it resolves into a tired old binary plot of good versus evil, goodies and baddies, blah blah blah, with the scientists (as usual) being the unwitting tools of evil by inventing things that can be dangerous if they fall into the wrong hands. Or, of course, being evil themselves. It really doesn't matter that when the time came to make the movie, director Ron Howard tried to make amends for some of Brown's scientific howlers: the problem with the book was the plot, which was incredibly banal and unambitious when set against the fantastic subject matter scientists have been creating for over two-and-a-half thousand years.

The story of particle physics to me is just as compelling as any novel: it has a story and a cast; it's set on several continents; it must have involved success and failure and their accompanying elation and despair; and its biggest theme, which *A & D* only touches on, is the enduring question of who has the right to explain how the world works to those not equipped with the necessary expertise: the Church or Science? This fascinating argument that has raged for over 500 years is killed off when the character that embodies the theme is murdered by the mad guy—which takes place before the book even starts. Oh well. Another in the long tradition of novels that use science as window dressing.

At present, the Great Divide between the Arts and Sciences seems just as wide as ever. I really do feel sorry for those gifted men and women engaged in studying the latter who are marginalized by just about everybody, and not just arty oiks in Oxford JCR's. And I know the blame isn't all one-sided; until recently, science hasn't exactly gone out of its way to explain what it gets up to, although it has now woken up to the usefulness of PR, particularly when fundraising and recruiting the next generation of boffins. Hopefully, science won't prove the great turn-off it was for my generation if scientists themselves can help to demonstrate its excitement and relevance—and not rely on penny-plain teachers whose idea of sex education was dissecting a dogfish's bollocks. Or whatever they have. You can tell I was paying close attention.

It's probably a Sisyphean task, though: at the time of writing, the LHC has just been fired up again after a few months' break because the politicians and their attendant armies of bean-counters couldn't decide who was going to pay its massive electricity bill. Their solution? You can run it in summer when power's cheaper.

That's what scientists are up against when they try and tell us about the mysteries of our planet. That and Dan Brown.

Chapter Eleven

Don't Know Much About History

'There is a just liberty allowed in the schools, of supposing sim-
ilitudes, when they have none at hand. I do not, however, make
any use of that privilege, and as to that matter, in superstitious
religion, surpass all historical authority. In the examples which
I here bring in, of what I have heard, read, done, or said, I have
forbidden myself to dare to alter even the most light and indiffer-
ent circumstances; my conscience does not falsify one tittle; what
my ignorance may do, I cannot say.' (Book 1, Chapter 20:
'Of The Force Of Imagination')

Even as a 9-year-old doing my History homework, I was
confused by the year 1485. For it was on the 22nd August of
that year that the Middle Ages came to an end. No, they did:
my course book told me so. King Richard III was defeated by
Henry Tudor at the battle of Bosworth Field and the medieval
period was toast. Just like that.[44]

Being a child, and rather daydreamy, I wondered what people

---

44. As at the end of *1066 & All That* in which, after the First World War,
'America was thus clearly top nation and History came to a [full stop]'.
In addition, the War 'was the cause of nowadays'.

felt when they woke up the following day. After all, one thousand years of history had ended overnight. Were they excited or apprehensive?

'*Well*', I reasoned, staring out of the window at the plume of pollution rising from the ICI petrochemical works into the night sky, '*another name for the Middle Ages was the 'Dark Ages', which was all about mud and plagues. They'd probably be happy to see the back of that. But did Henry Tudor know before the battle that the Middle Ages would end that night? If he'd been beaten by Richard would it still have been the Middle Ages? Are historical eras always tied to regime-change or big battles? Or do they have a fixed shelf life?*' By now, the questions were snowballing, not least of which was '*Who decides these things?*'

While studying for my GCSE exams five years later, I at least partially resolved the issue—I discovered that the Middle Ages only ended in 1485 *in England*. Although a Europe-wide phenomenon, the Middle Ages came to a close on several different dates, ranging from 1453 (the fall of Constantinople) to 1516 (the death of Spain's King Ferdinand II). Some books cited the invention of the moveable-type printing press by Johann Gutenberg in 1455; others, the voyage of Christopher Columbus, and the fall of Muslim Spain (both 1492). But far earlier (and utterly preposterous) than any of these was the claim made by Italian historians that the Middle Ages officially ended when a contract was signed to build the north doors of the Florence baptistery (1401). So somewhere in the 115 years spanned by those events was the right answer.

I gave up on history right there. Obviously, historians were all idiots; they couldn't agree when the Middle Ages *started* either. Was it 410 (the Fall of the Roman Empire) or 476 (also the Fall of the Roman Empire)?

But at least they had a name that just about everyone agreed on; no-one even knew what the era that succeeded them was *called*. Was it 'The Renaissance'? Or 'The Modern Age'? And anyway, I reasoned, how can it be Modern when it's 500 years old? Sheesh.

Twenty years later, I was commissioned to research a radio programme entitled, 'What Was The First Ever Rock'n'Roll Record?'—and the same thing happened. Only this time, I learned far more about how history works.

Of course, there *was* no first rock'n'roll record. Yet to read some histories of the subject, you'd have thought Bill Haley went into the studio on April 12th 1954 saying to himself, 'Today, me and the Comets are going to invent rock'n'roll.' Well he didn't. The song in question, 'Rock Around The Clock', was at least 12 months old by that point, and had already been recorded by Sonny Dae and His Knights some weeks earlier—in a version not entirely dissimilar. Parts of the verse melody were lifted from country superstar Hank Williams's 1947 hit 'Move It On Over', which had borrowed from bluesman Charley Patton's 'Going To Move To Alabama', which in turn tipped its hat to Jim Jackson's 1927 song, 'Kansas City Blues'. The style of Haley's recording owed a lot to the kind of small ensemble black Rhythm & Blues that had been popular for well over ten years; to which Haley added a bit of western swing (his previous group, the Saddlemen, wore Stetsons and played country songs). His producer, Milt Gabler, had overseen many recordings by multi-million selling R&B artist Louis Jordan— another man credited with inventing rock'n'roll. Credited by none other than Chuck Berry, who has also been credited with inventing rock'n'roll.

So rock'n'roll was a great big mess of at least four distinct musical styles in greater or lesser concentrations—and was certainly not invented overnight or embodied in any single recording. Given that there's no 'recipe' for rock'n'roll, it's not surprising that there are dozens of other records that historians claim got there first, one—'Crazy About My Baby' by Blind Roosevelt Gaines—recorded as early as 1929. And some, apparently, came later—a popular contender is 'Blue Suede Shoes' by Carl Perkins, which simultaneously topped the Country, R&B *and* Pop charts in early 1956—the first record ever to do so.

There's no single derivation of the words 'rock' and 'roll' to help historians either. The joint term, 'Rock'n'Roll' (or 'Rock and Roll') also has quite a history ('roll' is nowhere mentioned in the lyrics of 'Rock Around the Clock'), and has been used in three different musical contexts. The obvious one is the name of the musical genre itself.

The second, also well known, is as a synonym for sexual inter-course, as in 'Sixty Minute Man' by the Dominoes from 1951, in which lerve machine 'Lovin' Dan' 'rock[s] 'em, roll[s] 'em all night long'; this 'hokum' interpretation had first been noted in a blues recording, 'My Man Rocks Me With One Steady Roll' by Trixie Smith in 1922.

The third context, rather more obscurely, comes from black gospel music; when a congregation was moved by some of the more uptempo songs, its members collectively swayed from side to side. This motion was described in the lyrics of 'The Camp Meeting Jubilee', recorded by an unknown male vocal quartet back in 1916, in which the singer claims 'We've been rockin' an' rolling in your arms / Rockin' and rolling in your arms / In the arms of Moses.' Here the meaning is clearly re-ligious rather than secular, and was repeated in the lyrics to several subsequent songs, in which the movement was likened to the back and forth motions of waves in the sea; the Boswell Sisters' song 'Rock And Roll' from 1934 refers to 'the rolling rocking rhythm of the sea', and in 'Rockin' Rollin' Mama' by Buddy Jones (another western/swing blues hybrid), the fol-lowing lines appear: 'Waves on the ocean, waves in the sea/

But that gal of mine rolls just right for me / Rockin' rollin' mama, I love the way you rock and roll / You ease my troubled mind and pacify my weary soul'. Religious and secular were also blended by Sister Rosetta Tharpe's 'Rock Me', in which the legendary gospel diva doesn't make it *entirely* clear whether she's on the side of God or the Devil.

So, that's the words and music dealt with. Lastly, it depends what point the historian is trying to prove as to which record gets the prize. If you date rock'n'roll from the first time a white vocalist sang in a black blues style, Elvis's debut 'That's Alright' from 1954 might be your Rosetta Stone. Or not. And so on. And who cares, anyway? Because history demonstrates there's plenty of routes that'll take you to from A to B, and on each route are plenty of resting places you might care to stop at. There's good stories whichever road you choose.

It's here that I think Montaigne and I differ in the way we like our history. Montaigne, as the quotation at the head of this essay makes clear, is wedded to the truth, the whole truth and nothing but the truth, he elsewhere distinguishes between 'true' and 'false' history: the facts of history exist to be sympathetically interpreted but never deliberately monkeyed around with. They may be misremembered, he admits, but that's another issue entirely.

I prefer instead the distinction between the 'official' history—which usually coincides with what's written in school textbooks—and 'unofficial' history, which is all the bits they leave out, which are often an amalgam of truth and supposition, sometimes warped beyond recognition as the stories are repeated until they are finally recorded by an expert witness. Who may have been drunk or misinformed. History is not about the laying down of facts—it's the accretion of different grades of source material, from truth to downright filthy lies, the survival of which is at the constant mercy of happenstance.

Which is why it's more fun than the stuff they teach you at school. My godfather, Victor Neuburg, himself a teacher and historian, was the first person to tell me that. And how right he was, even though, being a seven-year-old at the time, I hadn't a bloody clue what he was talking about.

Montaigne would have never have described the dozens of personal anecdotes he includes in the *Essays* as history. But in my book, they have their place, just as much as the deeds of the great and the good.

And besides, the first rock'n'roll record was 'Maybellene' by Chuck Berry. And talking of the Middle Ages, when does middle age start? I hit 50 yesterday.

Chapter Twelve

Yes, We Are All Individuals

*'Plutarch says somewhere that he does not find so great a differ-
ence betwixt beast and beast as he does betwixt man and man.'*
(Book 1, Chapter 42: 'Of the Inequality Amongst Us')

Montaigne debated the issue of equality throughout the *Essays*:
indeed, 'Of the Inequalities Among Us' ranks as one of his
longest. The general thrust of his argument is that whatever
our social ranking, there are many aspects of our lives that
serve as great levellers. Not least of which is illness:

*At the first twitch of the gout it signifies much to be called Sir and Your
Majesty!*[45]

A sentiment he echoes in practically the final sentence he ever
published:

*'Tis to much purpose to go upon stilts, for, when upon stilts, we must
yet walk with our legs; and when seated upon the most elevated throne
in the world, we are but seated upon our breech.*

---

45. Gout is colloquially referred to as 'the disease of kings'. Which
doesn't really explain why I've developed it.

Another related theme he often revisits is that of clothes: underneath them, we're all the same. Yet the age in which Montaigne lived was rigidly stratified to the point where social mobility was practically impossible. Everyone may have been equal in the eyes of God, but that didn't often translate into social or political policy that benefited the have-nots. As such, the following remark might be interpreted as dangerously socialistic:

*Why...do we not value a man for what is properly his own? He has a great train, a beautiful palace, so much credit, so many thousand pounds a year: all these are about him, but not **in** him...if we consider a peasant and a king, a nobleman and a vassal, a magistrate and a private man, a rich man and a poor, there appears a vast disparity, though they differ no more, as a man may say, than in their breeches.*

Having been raised among the peasantry in his native Bordeaux, Montaigne had a keener awareness than many other nobs of what it was like to live in humble surroundings. On several occasions in the *Essays,* he extols the dignity of labour, but it's clear that in 16th-century France, everyone was aware of his station and behaved accordingly—Montaigne included. The social ladder had no rungs to climb up or down.

Fast forward to the present, and equality—what it is, whether it's desirable and if so how we achieve it—remains an illusory ideal that has fomented bloody revolution all over the world. But as with so many subjects these days, to meaningfully engage with it is an incredibly complex proposition. *Pace* Montaigne, it cannot simply be reduced to the provenance of a man's trousers. Something that was driven home to me in the most ridiculous circumstances last year.

I was in America, jetlagged, wide awake and channel-surfing in the small hours, when I happened upon a double bill of 'Barney'—who, for those of you lucky enough never to have seen him, is a goofy purple and green Tyrannosaurus Rex, and ranks, along with the Teletubbies, among the most annoying characters on children's TV. So annoying, in fact, that his theme song, 'I Love You' (sung to the tune of 'Yankee Doodle'), has been used to torture detainees at Guantanamo Bay.

Barney peddles saccharine messages about good citizenship to the under-8s, and has been taken to task by no less an authority than the miserable bastards at *Parents* magazine, who testily observe:

[H]is shows do not assist children in learning to deal with negative feelings and emotions. As one commentator puts it, the real danger from Barney is denial: the refusal to recognize the existence of unpleasant realities. For along with his steady diet of giggles and unconditional love, Barney offers our children a one-dimensional world where everyone must be happy and everything must be resolved right away.

Sounds good to me—I wish my life were like that. Yet it's not so much Barney's wilfully myopic world view that caught my attention, but rather the unfortunate scheduling of two back-to-back episodes, which had seemingly been chosen completely at random, or possibly with a touch of subversion, from the large stockpile available.

In the first, Barney was stating 'Hey, kids! We're really all *the same*, kyuk, kyuk, kyuk', while in the second, which followed immediately, he was claiming, 'Hey, kids! We're really all *different*, kyuk, kyuk, kyuk.'

These mixed messages must really mess with the minds of the under-8s, as indeed they do with mine. It's enough of a leap of faith to receive instruction on civics from a singing reptile without him lapsing into philosophical schizophrenia.

Of course, both Barney's messages are impeccably PC; the first emphasizes equality while the second stresses diversity. But the act of bringing these big themes together in enforced juxta-position served, in my addled brain at least, to point up the central contradiction facing anyone working in the education/ equal opportunities/race relations industries, namely: a) none of us are the same, yet b) we all share a lot in common. As King Lear realizes when he's exposing his privates on the blasted heath in a thunderstorm, we are all, beneath our robes, 'poor, bare, forked animals'; yet, on the other hand, according to Bob Dylan, the only thing that truly unites us is the certainty that we're going to die. Clearly, one of those Barney episodes needs to be binned or philosophical confusion will stalk our play-grounds. But which one?

Let's start with 'Hey, kids! We're really all the same!' Or in other words, can we, and should we, aspire to a world in which everyone is equal? It's all very well blithely noting, as the US Declaration of Independence does, that 'all men are created equal', and that this truth is 'self-evident.' No problem with that as an ideal. But try to legislate for it, and the solutions are not so bleedin' obvious.

Issues raised by equality have been at the heart of much of the legislation passed in England for the last 800 years—since 1215, in fact, when the Magna Carta sought to limit the powers of the monarchy. Clause 29 of the 1297 version states that '*No Freeman shall be taken or imprisoned, or be disseised of his Freehold, or Liberties, or free Customs, or be outlawed, or exiled, or any other wise destroyed; nor will We not pass upon him, nor condemn him, but by lawful judgment of his Peers, or by the Law of the land. We will sell to no man, we will not deny or defer to any man either Justice or Right.*' This establishment of *Habeas Corpus* has yet to be repealed, so, in theory at least, we should all be equal in the eyes of the law. Which is not a bad place to start if you want to build an egalitarian society.

But as we know, the law is an ass, as current anti-terrorist legislation lays siege to many of the inalienable rights and freedoms we thought formed the unshakeable cornerstone of our constitution. While it's true that *Habeas Corpus* has been suspended at various times in our history, usually during wartime, given that the current 'war on terror' doesn't have a neat beginning, middle and an end like good old-fashioned wars, it could be said that for the unfortunate few, this ultimate protection may prove to have been fatally compromised forever. And they'll end up having Barney's rendition of 'I Love You' piped into their cells for an indefinite period as they await a trial that may never happen.

But then, the law never was the most successful vehicle for effecting change. As we all know, you can't successfully legislate against prejudice, so equality is not only difficult to inculcate, it's practically impossible to enforce in anything other than a superficial way. You can arrest, fine and imprison white soccer fans for racially abusing black players, but you can't remove that prejudice from what passes for their brains.

Or take the Equal Pay act of 1970: forty years on, women in England are still paid on average 22% less than men for doing the equivalent jobs—and those are officially-compiled statistics revealing the abject failure of successive governments to get to grips with the problem. Then there's the Sex Discrimination Act (1975), the Race Relations Act (1976), the Disability Discrimination Act (1995), and the three main pieces of secondary legislation that protect against discrimination on the grounds of religion or belief, sexual orientation and age. All passed with worthy intentions—and all shot through with loopholes. As soon as one inequality is nailed down, another pops up, and the pieces of legislation listed above have grown so complex and unwieldy (and hence virtually unworkable), that as of last week (9th April 2010), a new overarching Equality Act has replaced them all. I wish it the best of luck.

But already there are exceptions to the new rules, with perhaps the non-ordination of gay, women and trans-sexual priests into the Catholic church being the most newsworthy, forcing the government to issue a so-called 'Myth Busting Document', stating that Rome can legally continue to discriminate against these groups just as it's always done—on the specious grounds that it always has.

So any Equality Act won't (and can't) create an egalitarian society overnight—if indeed at all, for any number of reasons—of which human perversity and political contingency are but two: it is perpetually, to borrow a phrase from one of those dreadful 1980s straplines, 'working *towards* equality'; it has to choose its targets carefully; and it has to tread warily or it will undo the very thing it sets out to achieve. It's all that legislation of any kind, no matter how cleverly drafted, can ever hope to do.

But then I guess we have to start *somewhere*, and passing a law is perhaps the least worst solution at our disposal. It may be generations before hearts and minds catch up, but at least a line has been drawn and the gesture has been made. Take the American Civil Rights Act of 1964. Not even fifty years later, to have racially segregated restaurants is unthinkable; but at the time, a sizeable number of Americans thought Congress had taken leave of its senses when it proposed their abolition. So, thanks to this pioneering piece of legislation (whose troubled passage into law witnessed the largest mass arrest of rabbis in US history), we can all eat our Happy Meals together under the same roof. And a good thing too.

Which brings us to our second Barney concept—that we're all different (kyuk, kyuk, kyuk).

I'm pretty sure I prefer the idea of a diverse society to an entirely homogeneous one, even though Trevor Phillips, the current head of the UK's Equality and Human Rights Commission tells me that it's discredited and old-fashioned to think that way, certainly within his sphere of operations. In his view, and he does have a point, multiculturalism legitimises separateness, an unwillingness to adopt the manners and practices (and even the language) of a host country. Which is equally true for wilfully clannish expat Brits on the Costa Del Sol drinking their Earl Grey and reading their two-day old *Daily Mails* as it is for the many distinct immigrant communities in East London. In the borough of Hackney, for example, almost 100 languages and dialects are spoken in an area of just 7.36 square miles—and in 12% of households, no English is spoken at all. Which makes life rather difficult, say, for a doctor and his patient: without a common language (or an interpreter), the patient can't explain his symptoms and, unless those symptoms are obvious, the doctor has no idea what treatment to administer. In situations like that, it's in everyone's interest, not least the patient's, to take some steps in the direction of integration; it's not being a traitor to your culture—it's simply practical to establish common links that benefit all concerned. And this necessarily happens slowly and incrementally from one generation to the next. Once again, the law doesn't get a look-in. It just happens because it has to.

Trevor Phillips has referred to such tiny steps as the necessary fostering of 'a core of Britishness'—for which he was pilloried by the then Mayor of London, Ken Livingstone, who somewhat emotionally accused him of cozying up to elements at the far right of British politics. Because in the UK at least, multicultural societies tend to be favoured by the left-leaning; integrated societies by the right, and by using the term 'Britishness', Phillips (himself of West African extraction) was seen to be allying himself with those who favour citizenship ceremonies and so-called 'cricket tests' over respect for cultural autonomy.[46] A respect which has seen certain local authorities re-branding the Christmas season as a 'Winterval' holiday to make it more inclusive and less alienating for those communities in the UK who don't celebrate it.

Now things are totally confused: the attempt to make Christmas 'relevant' to as many people as possible involves playing down the reason it exists for those who continue to mark it as a Christian festival. Yet this attempt at levelling the cultural playing field has been inspired by the need to recognize diversity. At this point, my brain started to hurt—and I began to think that Barney, by totally ignoring the distinction between equality and diversity, was not so dumb after all.

After a long period spent staring out of the window, I had an idea: why don't I take a sample citizenship exam to see how integrated I am? After all, I hold a UK passport, and have done my whole life, so, being 100% British, at least officially, let's see how I perform against my own government's criteria of Britishness.[47]

Well, I failed miserably, scoring a mere 58% from a standing start—and what's more, I even flunk the cricket test: I don't

---

46. The cricket test or 'Tebbit test' was a controversial phrase coined in 1990 by Conservative politician Norman Tebbit, commenting in the Los Angeles *Times* about the loyalty or otherwise of certain groups of British immigrants to the England cricket team. Tebbit posed the question, 'Are you still harking back to where you came from or where you are?' Perhaps he should have read the works of Alfred Polgar, in which the subject is addressed with greater subtlety and intelligence: 'It is the destiny of the emigrant that the foreign land does not become his homeland: his homeland becomes foreign'.

47. When in France, however, I'm often mistaken for a German, as I have blonde-ish hair. In Germany, they take me for Belgian. In America, I was once accused of being Irish. In my home city of London, some people reckon I'm Swedish.

support the England team because my life has enough frustration and disappointment in it already. Not to mention the national soccer team...

By this token, if you're an aspiring British citizen, and (a) can demonstrate a grasp of the British constitution, and (b) cry tears of rage when our middle order batsmen spectacularly collapse in the course of two overs, it's perfectly possible, in the eyes of government at least, to be more 'British' than people who've been living there for half a century (OK, me). Which could prove any one of a number of things, including that an essential aspect of *true* Britishness is knowing bugger all about the country you live in.

Incidentally, do you know what the reward is for passing the test (apart from becoming a citizen, that is)? A welcome pack ('Greetings, citizen of the UK!') and a commemorative lapel pin. And it doesn't end there. Soon, you'll be able to take the 'advanced citizenship test', which will involve a period as a 'probationary citizen' before being granted full status, which you can accomplish by working as a volunteer in a charity shop and not visiting your doctor. No really, I'm not making this up. This is what equality is all about in the fevered brains of the Whitehall mandarins.

Of course, these shenanigans are spectacularly patronizing to longstanding naturalized citizens like my friend Sue, who originally hails from Brooklyn: she still has to jump through these hoops even though she's lived here 40 years and drinks tea for pleasure. As does my Texan friend Bob, who, within weeks of arriving in the UK went totally native, developing a taste for warm pints of bitter, Friday night curries and steam engines. On that showing, he should have been awarded his pin immediately.

But I digress, so I once more turn to the internet to see if I can get any pointers that will help me effect a reconciliation between equality and diversity, which seem further apart than ever. In fact, they now appear mutually exclusive, or else hopelessly muddled—I'm not sure which...and then my partner walks in, having spent an exhausting day treating special needs patients in Britain's most ethnically diverse local borough—Hackney again. She asks what I'm doing. I explain. And then she tells me I needn't have bothered, as the answer to the equality/diversity dichotomy has already been solved courtesy of something called 'Maslow's Hierarchy of Need' which was first proposed in 1943 by the American psychologist, Abraham Maslow. Here it is in diagrammatic form:

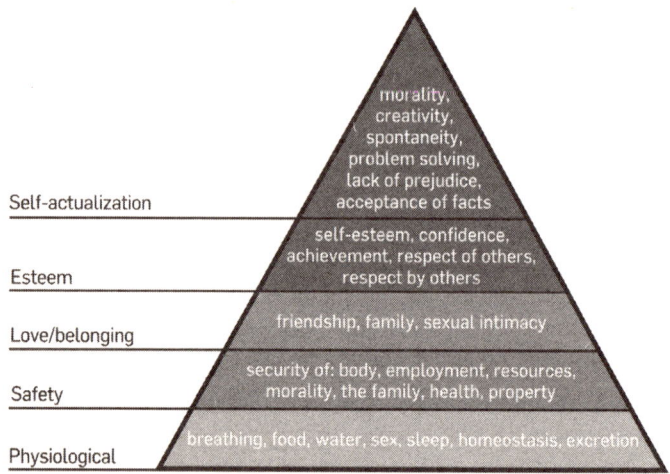

At the base of the triangle are attributes shared by all mankind—our lowest common denominators, or, if you like, things that make us equal—from breathing to excreting. Moving up towards the apex are those qualities that progressively emphasize our diversity, or 'self-actualization' as Maslow puts it.

The great thing about this model is that race, religion, nationality, and all the things we tend to get in a flap about when discussing equality and diversity are neatly short-circuited; what *actually* contributes most to our diversity, claims Maslow, is open-mindedness or, to borrow a phrase from the top section, 'lack of prejudice'. Montaigne would have loved it.

It's a wonderfully inclusive and *unified* model which cleverly accommodates both equality and diversity, combining anthropology, sociology and psychology, and moving in a logical sequence from man as King Lear's 'poor, bare, forked animal', through his preoccupations as a member of society and on to the ways his individuality asserts itself.

And yes, it's perfectly possible to pick holes in it, but it's the clearest methodology I've come across for resolving the issues first awoken by the wretched Barney on that sleepless night in America last year.

The galling thing is that the giggling purple bastard was right all along: we *are* the same and we *are* different. And there's your proof in that little triangle.

Of course, Montaigne got there before all of us, as the sentence which opens Book 2 of the *Essays* effortlessly demonstrates:

[T]here never were, in the world, two opinions alike, no more than two hairs, or two grains: **their most universal quality is diversity.** [emboldening mine]

Ex Uno Plures. Or *E Pluribus Unum.* Take your pick.

Chapter Thirteen

Infamy, Infamy, They've All Got It Infamy

'A man may play the fool in everything else, but not in poetry: Neither men, nor gods...permit mediocrity in poets.' (**Horace, from 'De Arte Poetica', quoted in Book 2, Chapter 17 'Of Presumption'**)

I'm in two minds about conspiracy theorists. Their limitless ingenuity, coupled with the total denial of any evidence, however compelling, that refuses to fit their paranoid schemata is both a source of rich amusement and profound irritation. As a firm believer in the cock-up theory of history, I've very little time for those who try to make things more complicated than they need to be; wading through primary evidence is often difficult and time-consuming enough without building delusional constructs on top of, around and behind it. You can fabricate too much structure, dig too deep or indulge your predilections too far. A cut-off point has to be reached before two and two makes five and you start thinking *The Da Vinci Code* is a credible repository of hidden truth.

Back in Montaigne's day, a conspiracy was a simple thing: you and your associates conspired to kill or discredit an individual, a family or an institution and you either succeeded or failed.

Our man was both fascinated and repelled by the perfidy that resulted in the assassination of his hero Julius Caesar, perhaps the most notorious conspiracy of the classical age. Now, though, that would be small beer, since there are conspiracies perpetrated by national governments whose target is THE WHOLE WORLD. I suppose it's in the nature of the beast that if you want your theory to be taken seriously, it's got to involve as many innocent dupes as possible.

Such is the heightened level of paranoia in the United States, Congress has gone on the offensive with its own theory-busting website 'Conspiracy Theories and Misinformation', the pre-amble to which is this:

Conspiracy theories exist in the realms of myth, where imaginations run wild, fear trumps facts, and evidence is ignored. As a superpower, the United States is often cast as the villain in these dramas...

To which one might respond 'WHY ARE YOU SO SURPRISED?' If you continually feed your citizens a steady diet of misinformation about real or perceived threats to their way of life, is it any wonder they'll embellish them or even make up a few of their own? Not to mention those of us in other nations who remember the Cold War. So various are these theories, the website arranges them under nine separate headings: 9/11, health, military, outer space, economic, U.S. domestic, U.S. and Islam, Latin America and 'others'. It's a great site—check it out.[48] Just about all human paranoia is represented here.

Yet no matter how ridiculous I find them, there is one particular pretty minor conspiracy theory which, in a shamefully Pavlovian way, pushes my buttons every time—the Shakespeare

---

48. http://www.america.gov/conspiracy_theories.html. If you can't access the site, it's because they're on to you.

Authorship Question. As P.G. Wodehouse once summed it up in an essay for *Vanity Fair:*

...there is a carping minority who hold that he did not write [the plays] at all, but simply lent his name to a limited company consisting of Sir Francis Bacon, Sir Walter Raleigh, the Earl of Oxford, the Earl of Essex, Queen Elizabeth, Mr Gordon Selfridge, and the second girl from the end in the front row of the chorus of the Merry Widow *Touring Company.*

Which good natured ribbing indicates old P.G. clearly viewed the theorists with the same amused disdain as me. There's also an apposite Monty Python sketch that focuses on a TV quiz programme called 'Stake Your Claim', in which Mr Norman Voles from Gravesend (played by Michael Palin) claims to have written all the plays normally attributed to Shakespeare, 'and my wife and I wrote his sonnets.' John Cleese as the quizmaster then asks Mr Voles his age. '43', comes the artless reply. Then how, Cleese continues, could you have written plays that we know to have been performed over 300 years before you were born? At which point, Voles replies, 'Well, that's where my claim falls to the ground.' He then congratulates Cleese on his shrewdness, noting that 'you're more than a match for me.'

However, unlike Norman Voles, the Shakespeare conspirators simply won't admit defeat and go away, no matter how conclusively their arguments are demolished. For example, we know that Shakespeare died in 1616, and that the currently fashionable pretender to the throne, the Earl of Oxford, shuffled off his mortal coil in 1604, at which point 'Shakespeare', whoever he was, had yet to write *Antony & Cleopatra, Coriolanus, The Winter's Tale, The Tempest* and, possibly, *King Lear* and *Macbeth.*

Get out of that, as Eric Morecambe used to say.

Easy, reply the conspirators. Oxford, knowing he was on the

way out, stockpiled manuscripts like crazy which his executors drip-fed for publication following his demise. The more objections are raised, the more elaborate the explanations need to be, the more desperately the facts have to be twisted to fit the premise. Yet the anti-Shakespeareans refuse to go away.

And these aren't necessarily stupid people. Famous sceptics include Mark Twain, Friedrich Nietzsche, Sigmund Freud, Charlie Chaplin, Malcolm X and Walt Whitman. Even Shakespearean worthies of the calibre of John Gielgud, Derek Jacobi, Jeremy Irons and Mark Rylance have all expressed their misgivings. It's an issue that's been addressed by the U.S. Supreme Court, and in September 2007, the *Shakespeare Authorship Coalition* sponsored a 'Declaration of Reasonable Doubt' to encourage new research into the question of Shakespeare's authorship, which has been signed by more than 1,700 people, including 295 academics. Which latter information indicates that 'Who *actually* wrote Shakespeare' is going to pass into academic curricula as a legitimate subject for research. Which to me at any rate is profoundly depressing. More wasted time and resources spent chasing chimaeras...

Now I'm not going to bore you (or myself) with rehearsing the same old tired theories which are rapidly accreting round this seemingly vexed question: instead, in the true spirit of Montaigne, I'm going to try and analyse the source of my irritation.

I think it has its roots in 'Bardolatry'—the belief that everything Shakespeare wrote is utterly fantastic. So great in fact, that a mere glover's son with little formal education couldn't possibly be its creator.

It's difficult to pin down the precise origins of this unthinking worship, but many lay the blame at the door of actor/impresario David Garrick. In 1769, 153 years after Shakespeare's death, Garrick thought it would be good for business to declare Shakespeare a God, and set himself up as his high priest by inaugurating a three-day festival in the sleepy market town of Stratford-on-Avon, at which he would unveil a new statue of the Mighty Bard to the accompaniment of processions, a horse race, fireworks and a whole Disneyesque panoply of gim-cracks and gewgaws. But the fickle English climate put paid to this monumental act of hubris, with torrential rain causing the river Avon to burst its banks and submerge the festivities. Supplies of food and drink ran out; the specially-constructed pavilion collapsed, the procession was ruined and the fireworks wouldn't light.[49] The narrow streets were gridlocked as the audience attempted to leave *en masse*.[50]

Garrick did manage to salvage something from the disaster, delivering, according to some, the performance of his career: having planted a fellow actor in the audience dressed as a French fop, whose role was to complain that Shakespeare was vulgar, provincial and overrated, Garrick mounted a spirited defence of the national playwright, the climax of which—''Tis he! 'Tis he! The God of our idolatry!'—was enthusiastically received by its waterlogged auditors. Garrick then returned to London with his tail between his legs, egg on his face, and the prospect of an awkward visit to the bank manager, having dropped a cool two grand.

But Garrick soon found himself in exalted company; even the normally sceptical Dr. Johnson grew uncharacteristically moist. Shakespeare, he wrote, 'opens a mine which contains gold and diamonds in unexhaustible plenty.' Then along came the Romantics, with their notions of god-given inspiration,

---

49. A visit to Stratford hasn't changed much in the interim. The theatre aside, it's still an ordeal—not a single decent pub in the whole town.

50. James Boswell, Doctor Johnson's fawning biographer was in at-tendance, and, true to form, wrote a hilarious account of the entire proceedings.

proclaiming Shakespeare not just a bloody good playwright, but a transcendent genius. Even if they stopped short of declaring him a god, he was the next best thing—a force of nature. John Keats, in his letters, wrote of 'Sun Moon & Stars and passages of Shakespeare', as if the plays were akin to celestial bodies, but it was perhaps the self-proclaimed opium addict Thomas de Quincey who went most absurdly overboard:

O, mighty poet! Thy works are not as those of other men, simply and merely great works of art; but are also like the phenomena of nature, like the sun and the sea, the stars and the flowers,—like frost and snow, rain and dew, hail-storm and thunder, which are to be studied with entire submission of our own faculties, and in the perfect faith that in them there can be no too much or too little, nothing useless or inert…

And it wasn't just the Romantics, with their pantheistic tributes: here's Thomas Carlyle, the grumpy old man of Victorian philosophy in the uncharacteristic act of practically wetting himself:

[Shakespeare]…I say, is an English King, whom no time or chance, Parliament or combination of Parliaments, can dethrone! This King Shakespeare, does not he shine, in crowned sovereignty, over us all, as the noblest, gentlest, yet strongest of rallying-signs; indestructible; really more valuable in that point of view than any other means or appliance whatsoever? We can fancy him as radiant aloft over all the Nations of Englishmen, a thousand years hence. From Paramatta, from New York, wheresoever, under what sort of Parish-Constable soever, English men and women are, they will say to one another: 'Yes, this Shakespeare is ours; we produced him, we speak and think by him; we are of one blood and kind with him'.

Given, as P.G. Wodehouse put it, that 'It is never difficult to distinguish between a Scotsman with a grievance and a ray of sunshine', this was praise indeed. And it's a view that has echoed through the ages down to the present day. It's a central plank of the intellectual legacy all students inherit: 'Shakespeare is the best. A genius. Period. Live with it.'

So is it any wonder the Bardolaters look at what we know of Shakespeare's biography and declare that a man of humble origins couldn't have written what he did? How could he know so much, how could he be that good, this refugee from the English *Midlands* (not renowned either then or now, as a hotbed of creativity).

No, 'Shakespeare' must be a front for an *educated* man, and to enjoy the benefits of an education in the 16th-century, you had to be an aristocrat. *Ergo*, Shakespeare was Edward de Vere, Earl of Oxford. Or Sir Francis Bacon. Or Sir Henry Neville. Or even Sir Walter Raleigh, who had plenty of time to write plays while he was banged up in the Tower of London on charges of high treason. By the by, the first proponent of 'Oxford was Shakespeare' was one J. Thomas Looney, whose surname really does nothing to lend his causes credibility.[51]

Anyhow, I digress. Notice the parade of knighthoods in the above list of contestants. The snobbery is breathtaking, and I think perhaps the main reason I regularly lose my rag with these conspirators. Why shouldn't an ordinary Joe rise to be Carlyle's 'English King'? The world is full of auto-didacts: my Dad for a start—an amazing man with an amazing intelligence whose depth and versatility he never fully appreciated. Yet he was a butcher's boy from West London who left school at 13 and never went to college. And my grandfather, a Blackpool

---

51. Although it is pronounced 'Loney', apparently. Oxford was an odd choice, being a consummate arsehole: in an eventful life, he committed acts of adultery, blasphemy, buggery and murdered an unarmed cook called Brincknell, who, Oxford claimed, committed suicide by deliberately running onto his sword. By comparison, Shakespeare's alleged deer-rustling is pretty small beer.

tram driver, possessed of a ravenous curiosity and passion for learning. And that's just in my family. I'm not saying either of them could have tossed off Shakespeare's plays, simply that they were far more gifted intellectually than their early biographies would lead one to expect.

So I have no problem with Shakespeare being exactly the man history tells us he was. Yet the conspirators can't because Bardolatry has cast him in the mould of a Romantic genius, his brow furrowed, anxiously waiting (probably alone in his garret) for his Muse to descend from the Gods. I recently bought a Victorian effigy of Shakespeare cast in Britannia metal which represents him, head bowed, hand on heart, eyes downcast, rounded shoulders clearly weighed down by the burden of his genius. Or else he's constipated, I can't decide which. Anyway, it cheers me up whenever I'm glum, because it's so diametrically opposed to my own mental picture of Shakespeare, who would be laughing and gesticulating, waving a dog-eared manuscript and sharing a joke with an actor who's fluffed his lines in rehearsal.

My Shakespeare was a theatre addict, a peerless entertainer. We don't truly know where the passion originated, but what we can fathom from fragments of his biography is that he lived, ate and drank theatre. He wasn't simply a playwright, but an actor, impresario and businessman too. He was completely immersed not just in writing plays, but the production, staging, casting, performing and financing of them. He thoroughly understood every aspect of his craft. And he learned his trade, it's thought from the bottom up, first as a script doctor, then as a trainee, and finally as a published playwright. He knew how to play his audiences like a pitch-perfect instrument because he too was a fan of the theatre, just like them. His plays acknowledged contemporary trends and also poked fun at them; he continually tested theatrical formulae to destruction, and created some new ones. He wrote to order, and to make money for himself and the company in which he was a major shareholder. So in other words, he wasn't a plaything of the Muses who died unacknowledged in noble poverty. By the time he retired, Shakespeare owned the second-grandest house in Stratford, and a property in London. He was the Andrew Lloyd Webber of his day. Only he was good.

OK, I hear you ask, where's your evidence? Well, lots of it, and too much to summarize here. But the key, I think, lies in a brilliant *apercu* by W.H. Auden, which states:

I find Shakespeare particularly appealing in his attitude towards his work. There's something a little irritating in the determination of the very greatest artists, like Dante, Joyce, Milton, to create masterpieces and to think themselves important. To be able to devote one's life to art without forgetting that art is frivolous is a tremendous achievement of personal character. Shakespeare never takes himself too seriously.

I wouldn't go so far as to claim that Shakespeare considered his art frivolous, but there is a strong case to be made that it's Shakespeare's absence of pretension that most completely identifies him as a true man of the theatre and not some dilettante aristocrat who wouldn't have needed the money.

For a start, Shakespeare clearly didn't regard himself as an 'Artist'; he never saw a complete edition of his plays published in his lifetime, and he doesn't seem to have been terribly interested in leaving a legacy, other than a financial one. In fact, his plays were not collected until 1623, seven years after his death. Shakespeare was, rather, a businessman who happened to write plays for a living, using the proceeds to support his abandoned wife and family back home in Warwickshire, and indulge in a little speculation on the property market.

And in any case, he was far too busy writing new material to bother about old stuff. The theatres of Elizabethan London devoured plays voraciously, and writers had to keep pace with their punishing schedules. That Shakespeare wrote around 38 plays of such high overall quality in the 20 or so years his talent flourished is a testament to his efficiency and professionalism as well as his undeniable literary gifts. He had to keep writing—his work was hugely popular from the outset of his career to the end, and his entire acting company (and its shareholders) relied on him to keep churning out the successes that kept paying the bills. The pace of his writing was not dictated by the intermittent visits of inspiration, but by the (very real) threat of insolvency. Particularly when outbreaks of the plague, Puritanism, bad weather and monarchy change constantly disrupted your performing schedule. Inevitably, not all his plays were of *Hamlet* standard—but give the guy a break—most of them were.

His capacity for play and mischievous experimentation also demonstrates a total immersion in his *métier*. Shakespeare based his early drama *The Comedy of Errors* on a Roman play by Plautus which cast identical twins in its lead roles. You can almost hear Shakespeare challenging himself to go one better and craft a plot that featured *two* sets of identical twins. Just because he could. Or he had a bet with a mate down the pub.

He was still playing almost two decades later in *The Winter's Tale* when he wrote the most notorious stage direction in theatre history, [*Exit, pursued by a bear*], no doubt to the great chagrin of the stage manager, who had to make it work. Perhaps he owed Shakespeare some money.

Then there's the torture porn that is *Titus Andronicus*, which, on balance, can only be considered a satirical *riposte* to the vogue for the so-called 'revenge tragedies' of the late 1580s and early 1590s—plays such as Thomas Kyd's *The Spanish Tragedy* that were the box-office smashes of their day. 'OK', Shakespeare says to the theatregoing public, 'you want blood, here we go.' And in the course of the play, there are no fewer than 13 deaths, including: Titus's daughter Lavinia, who has her hands removed and her tongue cut out, and the two sons of the Goth queen Tamora who are murdered and served to their mother in a pie. 'Top that!', Shakespeare seems to be saying to his fellow playwrights, in the spirit of a 16th-century Tarantino.

But perhaps the most audacious demonstration of Shakespeare's mastery of dramatic theory occurs in Act 4 of *King Lear* when Gloucester, having had his eyes gouged out, is being led to Dover by his disguised son Edgar, with the intention of committing suicide by throwing himself off the White Cliffs. Edgar, in character, guides his father to what the old man supposes is the edge, then leaves him to jump, having painted this breathtaking word picture of a scene that doesn't exist:

> *Come on, sir; here's the place: stand still. How fearful*
> *And dizzy 'tis, to cast one's eyes so low!*
> *The crows and choughs that wing the midway air*
> *Show scarce so gross as beetles: half way down*
> *Hangs one that gathers samphire, dreadful trade!*
> *Methinks he seems no bigger than his head:*
> *The fishermen, that walk upon the beach,*
> *Appear like mice; and yond tall anchoring bark,*
> *Diminish'd to her cock; her cock, a buoy*
> *Almost too small for sight: the murmuring surge,*
> *That on the unnumber'd idle pebbles chafes,*
> *Cannot be heard so high. I'll look no more;*
> *Lest my brain turn, and the deficient sight*
> *Topple down headlong.*

In reality, they're both on *terra firma*, and in launching himself into oblivion, Gloucester merely falls to the ground. Then Edgar adopts the guise of a second character, convincing his father that he has tumbled over the cliff, landed on the beach, and that he's had a miraculous escape at the hands of

Providence. He's *flown* down. Gloucester is completely taken in by Edgar's artful psychology, and vows in future to endure anything life can throw at him. If I've survived this, he reasons, I'm not meant to die yet.

It's a ritual which uses drama in a way that even four hundred years later feels incredibly daring. Essentially, it's an old blind bloke falling over. In Shakespeare's hands, it's powerful testimony to the redemptive powers of drama—and, of course, to the imagination and skill of the playwright who dreamed it up.

So sucks to you conspirators, I'm enjoying Shakespeare while you're chasing shadows. Shakespeare's genius was not born of education or privilege, but from ability and experience. He was my player, not your gentleman.

Chapter Fourteen

Feel The Need In Me

'Nature has mother-like observed this, that the actions she has enjoined us for our necessity should be also pleasurable to us; and she invites us to them, not only by reason, but also by appetite, and 'tis injustice to infringe her laws.' (Book 3, Essay 13: 'Of Experience')

Montaigne could have taught King Lear a thing or two. If he'd managed to nobble him prior to abdication, Shakespeare's play would never have been written:

Now the end, I take it, is all one, to live at more leisure and at one's ease: but men do not always take the right way. They often think they have totally taken leave of all business, when they have only exchanged one employment for another: there is little less trouble in governing a private family than a whole kingdom.

Never were truer words written, as Lear found to his cost. There's no such thing as retirement—only the substitution of one set of worries with another. So better the devil you know. And if you insist on stepping down and giving the governance of your kingdom to a pair of conniving harpies, you're *really* asking for trouble. But anyway, on to the essay—which is all about NEED.

If Lear's Britain was being given the once over by the Dark Ages equivalent of PriceWaterhouseCoopers, Accenture, KPMG, DeLoitte's or some such army of management consultants, they'd probably take a dim view of this rant from Act 2, Scene 4, as howled by the former Chief Executive at his elder daughters, Goneril and Regan, both recently admitted to the Board of Directors:

> *O, reason not the need!: our basest beggars*
> *Are in the poorest thing superfluous:*
> *Allow not nature more than nature needs,*
> *Man's life's as cheap as beast's: thou art a lady;*
> *If only to go warm were gorgeous,*
> *Why, nature needs not what thou gorgeous wear'st,*
> *Which scarcely keeps thee warm. But, for true need,—*
> *No, you unnatural hags,*
> *I will have such revenges on you both,*
> *That all the world shall—I will do such things,—*
> *What they are, yet I know not: but they shall be*
> *The terrors of the earth.*

'O reason not the need' is an exhortation that has haunted me since I first read *King Lear* for 'A'-Levels at the age of sixteen. It's the cry of a man at the end of his rope, who is both cornered and powerless—a situation which must have tapped into some kind of primal fear in my subconscious even at that tender age.

Lear enjoys regular father/daughter dust-ups with Goneril and Regan, and the above example is the last of a series of harangues occasioned by his regular monthly visits to their houses. But unlike the case with most lone parents coming to stay, there is the added complication that Lear is regularly accompanied by one hundred roistering knights who behave like a pack of unneutered polecats on a stag weekend. Goneril describes them as:

> *Men so disorder'd, so debosh'd and bold,*
> *That this our court, infected with their manners,*
> *Shows like a riotous inn: epicurism and lust*
> *Make it more like a tavern or a brothel*
> *Than a graced palace.*

Clearly, something must be done to curtail the fun and games—and this is where the play starts to resemble a meeting with McKinsey's. Goneril opens the negotiations by informing her father that accommodation scenario has become wasteful and unworkable, and he needs to downsize his retinue by 50% if the household is to remain well-run and efficient.

Lear refuses point blank. His staff, many of whom have been with him for years, are:

> *…men of choice and rarest parts,*
> *That all particulars of duty know,*
> *And in the most exact regard support*
> *The worships of their name.*

And so we must remain *in statu quo*. Regan now enters the negotiations with a counter-offer: Lear can come to hers with a net headcount reduction of 75, citing duplication and inefficiency within the management structure of the care delivery team:

> *How, in one house,*
> *Should many people, under two commands,*
> *Hold amity? 'Tis hard; almost impossible.*

Goneril then proposes that her own staff, and those of Regan, take on additional duties to offset the cuts in the royal retinue:

> *Why might not you, my lord, receive attendance*
> *From those that she calls servants or from mine?*

A more horizontal structure, Regan argues, would shorten lines of communication, lead to greater staff accountability, and promote an enhanced quality of care:

> *Why not, my lord? If then they chanced to slack you,*
> *We could control them.*

Lear refuses the revised offer. His daughters remain inflexible, citing the generous care provision in both their households:

> *What need you five and twenty, ten, or five,*
> *To follow in a house where twice so many*
> *Have a command to tend you?*

But Lear has clearly forgotten he's no longer the CEO of Ancient Britain—in fact, having abdicated in favour of his children, he doesn't even wield the clout of a non-executive director. He's utterly powerless. And so Regan removes the iron fist from out of her velvet glove and asks…

> *What need one?*

Lear's not even going to be allowed to keep his Fool. No great problem, you might think—he's not funny anyway—but it sets Lear off on his heartrending tirade. *It's not just about need. You're destroying me.*

This exchange later popped into my mind when a team of management consultants was brought in to give BBC Drama yet another going over. As they powerpointed their latest plan to emaciate the department, my sympathies went out to Lear—I could readily identify with someone whose world as he had known it was being systematically destroyed. Nothing, but nothing in human experience is reducible to a simple set of needs, so why do the most basic tenets of management theory insist that it is? Yet it is precisely the consultant's job *to* 'reason the need', and to 'allow not nature more than nature needs'. To do otherwise is to promote waste and inefficiency.

Of course, I was far from alone in feeling threatened: most public sector organizations in the UK have had corporate maggots crawling over them for more than two decades: in the ten years from 1997 to 2006, the British government lined the pockets of the major consulting firms to the tune of a staggering £20 billion. For that money, UK PLC should by now resemble a well-oiled machine firing on all cylinders: instead, what all that expenditure typically achieved was a marked reduction in service and staffing levels, accompanied by an explosion of admin. In other words, the complete reverse of what needed to happen.

I think what first established the link between *Lear* and consultancy in my mind was Goneril's choice of language—she suggests that her father should 'disquantity' his retinue. Can't you just see that ugly verb on a powerpoint presentation? Then there's Regan's beautifully spare 'What need one?'—a consultant's question if ever I heard one, it's also one of the most economical and cruellest put-downs in literature. Cold, calm and calculating, it pierces Lear to the soul, leaving him to utter the kind of vague, impotent threats that wouldn't sound out of place in a children's playground.

On the surface, the sisters' united front appears logical and reasonable: after all, would you want a hundred drunks up to their knees in hookers and gin carousing in *your* house? I know I wouldn't. But what the proposed downsizing *actually* presages is Lear's total isolation—and he knows it. From being King of his people, he is being condemned to a future where he will be entirely dependent on the whims of others—and, most significantly of all—he will face his declining years utterly alone, stripped of all vestiges, human and material, of who and what he once was. Yes, he's angry, but he's also utterly terrified. Please, he's saying, don't rob me of everything I need, or you've reduced me to the level of an animal. Let me hang on to something to prove, if only to myself, that I matter.

At a lower social level, Lear's impassioned speech might be that of any eighty-plus senior who, having bequeathed his hard-earned goods and chattels to his kids, finds himself instantly booted out of his house and frog-marched to a care home that stinks of stale wee and steamed fish. Lear pleads to the gods for 'patience', for he rightly fears the intensity of his anger (his '*hysterica passio*'), fuelled by the injustices he is suffering, will drive him mad. Which of course it does. Because need doesn't answer to reason.

The denial of all but basic needs in a business setting is what used to be called 'trough planning'—you do just enough to achieve your goals and not one thing more. And trough theory usually works pretty well, except, of course, when your wonderfully emaciated super-efficient horizontal structure encounters an element of randomness over which it can exercise no control—and which the consultants didn't foresee or else strategically ignored. Then, having no built-in contingency or resilience, it crumbles immediately. It's the same principle that governs the finances of commercial radio in the UK and in America; if a single penny doesn't absolutely have to be spent, it won't be—usually, as they say, with hilarious consequences. The radio station at which I was Programme Director strictly adhered to that policy, so we pre-recorded the entire output and played it out in sequence using an automated computer system. That way, we didn't have to hire costly live presenters. Which was fine, until the computer crashed at the weekend. No one in the office to fix it, because that would involve paying someone double time. So, in the middle of a birthday piss-up,

I receive a 'dead air' alert on my mobile phone.

The computer maintenance company also had a trough staffing policy, and I found myself late one Saturday night trying to reboot our server under instructions from their on-call engineer on *his* mobile phone, who was up to that point enjoying his weekend skulking in a deer hide in rural Vermont, some 4,000 miles away from our London studios on an entirely separate continent. He had to talk to me in whispers, because his fellow hunters had spotted something in the woods that looked shootable, and he didn't want to risk their opprobrium by scaring it away. After all, these guys were *armed*. And probably drunk.

All the while, the radio station was, of course, silent, the ads weren't being played out, and there was hell to pay on Monday morning. But did the broadcast consultants who dreamed up this crazy system get it in the neck? No. I did. The Chairman, who wanted to know why it had taken so long to get the station back on air, was surprised by the vehemence of my reply when he questioned the truth of my story.

You can see why I'm not the greatest supporter of reasoning the need—and when the history of commercial radio in the UK comes to be written, I've got about 500 more stories along those lines, equally if not more ludicrous. Like when we couldn't afford a desk for the studio, so a national radio station ended up broadcasting from a microphone gaffer taped to my IKEA picnic table...

No, a bit of fat in the system is never a bad thing to a Virgo like myself, who expects everything to go wrong and is quietly elated, surprised and relieved when it doesn't. And us humans need that bit of fat to get us through the lean times. It's our insurance policy, lifebelt, comfort zone, call it what you will.

Anyway—back to Lear, who was absolutely correct when he

implied that need and reason are to some degree mutually hostile. Reason is primarily a tool for justification, and certain needs are so fundamental that they cannot yield to justification by employing *any* rational mechanism. Those needs just 'are'. We can all point to the obvious things no human can do without—an air supply and sustenance to name but two—but beyond these absolutely basic essentials, what do we actually *need*?

Conceivably, a management consultant in trough mode might reply that we need 'nothing'. If you're alive, and able to remain alive under your own steam, then you've got everything you need. Anything else is just desirable, or a 'want'. Wants become more difficult to justify, the further behind you leave the level of basic existence. Until you reach the ultimate frippery represented by, say, an Armani handbag. Yet some people will claim they 'need' one of those to make their life complete, before moving on to the next sparkly thing that catches their eye in Harrod's. That kind of ridiculous craving can't be explained using any analytical tool I've ever come across; but for those afflicted, it can prove a powerful compulsion. And don't get me started on Apple geeks, 600 of whom queued overnight outside the London store this week to get their iPhone 4, some of whom emerged clutching their prize and punching the air, as if they'd just discovered penicillin.

But what of spiritual things? We don't *really* need beauty or music, yet they're highly desirable, in that their very existence helps man to rise above his animal origins. These are qualities that give our lives meaning, in that we can clutch them to our souls, call them our own, while sharing them with everyone else.

And one of the abiding qualities of beauty, particularly when expressed in art, is that it resists reason—or, perhaps more accurately, challenges reason to interpret its message and even its very existence. Very often, reason isn't up to the task because it cannot justify or even explain the impulse that gave rise to art, or the quality of the reaction it elicits from its audience. Take Keats's 'Grecian Urn', for example.

> *Thou, silent form, dost tease us out of thought*
> *As doth eternity: Cold pastoral!*
> *When old age shall this generation waste,*
> *Thou shalt remain, in midst of other woe*
> *Than ours, a friend to man, to whom thou sayst,*
> *'Beauty is truth, truth beauty,'—that is all*
> *Ye know on earth, and all ye need to know.*

It wouldn't do for a management consultant to be teased out of thought. In fact, the Urn is the ultimate negator of that kind of reductive analysis.

There it stands, inscrutable and enigmatic, challenging anyone, even its creator, to define it. All Keats can really tell us about this alien creation is that it's 'a friend to man'; in other words, we must not feel threatened by the fact that it's challenging us—it's not a hostile challenge. Rather it's inviting us to suspend our need to understand. And that's no bad thing. Under these conditions, a statement such as 'Beauty is truth, truth beauty' can make perfect sense and even possess considerable power, which paradoxically is increased by its vagueness.[52] In fact, it's 'all (we) need to know'. Of course, we don't actually 'know' this to be the case—we have to take it on trust. Because the beauty we're perceiving when looking at the vase carries its own truth with it.

Now, of course, this opens up a whole can of worms for the

---

52. There's the typographical problems with those inverted commas which have been omitted or altered in different editions over the years. For the purposes of this essay, their appearance and positioning doesn't materially alter the argument.

empiricists among us; taking things on trust easily allows us to be hoodwinked by the unscrupulous. But we have to learn to trust our instincts if we wish to fully appreciate what is beautiful. That instinct to dissect negates and destroys beauty. Just as explaining a joke renders it totally unfunny. So just put down your clipboard and stop it.

Now I'm aware Montaigne's been taking a bit of a back seat for the last few pages, but here's a good place to drag him back from his extended tea break. There's no doubting that Montaigne the philosopher was a creature of reason, which he sometimes contrasts with 'fortune'. Fortune is capricious and ungovernable, and the philosopher should use reason to buttress himself from the uncertainty and indiscipline it represents. But there are occasions when Montaigne slips the lead—for instance, while he's reading poetry or engrossed in a play:

And here is a wonder... the true, supreme, and divine poesy is above all rules and reason. And whoever discerns the beauty of it with the most assured and most steady sight, sees no more than the quick reflection of a flash of lightning: it does not exercise, but ravishes and overwhelms our judgment. The fury that possesses him who is able to penetrate into it wounds yet a third man by hearing him repeat it; like a loadstone that not only attracts the needle, but also infuses into it the virtue to attract others. And it is more evidently manifest in our theatres, that the sacred inspiration of the Muses, having first stirred up the poet to anger, sorrow, hatred, and out of himself, to whatever they will, does moreover by the poet possess the actor, and by the actor consecutively all the spectators. So much do our passions hang and depend upon one another. Poetry has ever had that power over me from a child to transpierce and transport me...

This is positively Keatsean. It's Montaigne with his guard down, actually finding something good to say about *un*-reason and the way it can hypnotize us. For poetry and drama— and by extension, art in general—moves too quickly; it's like a nimble cat burglar being chased by a copper with big heavy boots—it makes off with our reason before we realize a crime's been committed. Yet it's a joyous theft, liberating and *beyond need.*

In the same way, I often wonder what early man's reaction was when he first saw the sun: I dare say some of the tribe thought it so wonderful they prostrated themselves and worshipped it; some wanted to find out what it was and how it worked; some freaked out and the Yorkshireman said 'it's nowt'. But Keats would have accepted it on its own terms; his experience over the course of a few days would inform him that it was a source of light and heat, and his aesthetic sensibility would have confirmed its beauty. But here he would stop. Of course, he'd say, it's interesting to know the sun is 93 million miles away, the Earth orbits round it and it's 865,000 miles across. But like the Urn, it is what it is. Utterly incredible. And no amount of knowledge or analysis can hope to encapsulate that splendour. One hopes that Montaigne would have reacted similarly and that he gave his reason regular vacations. After all, an exclusive diet of reason is rather dull and constricting, like eating porridge for breakfast every morning...

One last example: wandering round the new galleries in the Museum of London the other day, I was intrigued by a feature on the Festival of Britain, which took place in 1951. Life was still hard after the end of World War Two, and the London site of the Festival was surrounded by bomb craters and burned-out wharves and houses. In the midst of this devastation, a collection of modernistic buildings started to take shape, containing exhibitions that looked to the nation's future, hoping to promote a feeling of recovery and progress. Its chief booster, Herbert Morrison, dubbed it 'a tonic for the nation'. Its aims and objectives were vague, some of them unquantifiable; and for the time, it was hugely expensive, costing £8 million the country couldn't really afford. I imagine even the most cursory cost/benefit analysis by the most junior consultant would have damned it to oblivion. Yet it went ahead, and proved an enormous popular success. 10 million people paid to see it in the five months it was open, and the Festival actually returned a profit. My parents were somewhere in the crowd, having just started courting.

One of its centrepieces was the Skylon, a 300-foot tall aluminium-clad steel frame, in the shape of a cigar but pointed at both ends, and supported forty feet above the ground on slender, tensioned cables slung between three asymmetrical beams. Illuminated at night, it served no other purpose than to elicit wonder as it appeared to float above the festival site. It was a beacon, and a potent symbol of a new age.

Clearly those who commissioned the Skylon were not reasoning the need; or perhaps they had a rather more sophisticated understanding of human need than those who rely on figures, charts, projections and systems for their evidence. The trouble is, that kind of understanding will only ever give the appearance of a hunch which, should it succeed (as with the Festival of Britain), will be put down to luck. How else to explain an act of faith?

So perhaps this essay is less about need than intellectual generosity. By all means reason the need—but remember that there are more things in heaven and earth than are dreamed of in that philosophy. And, evidently in Winston Churchill's, one of whose first acts in regaining power in the General Election of 1951 was to have the Skylon torn down. After all, what useful function did it serve?

As the world embarks on another period of fiscal austerity in 2010, there will be a lot of reasoning the need as governments wrestle with their enormous deficits. Let's hope, for the quality of all our lives, that some of them have read *King Lear*.

P.S. How Consultancy Works: here's how teachers have to approach the teaching of Shakespeare in British schools, according to the Department for Education's website. Clearly, this 10-stage programme has been drawn up at vast expense by a consultant. How can I tell? a) if you can penetrate the jargon, it's all screamingly obvious, and b) Shakespeare, the object of the exercise, isn't even mentioned until Clause 6, and doesn't re-appear. In fact, substitute any word for 'Shakespeare' in the text below, and you have a consultant passing off a slightly modified boilerplate document as a piece of original, commissioned work.

'Improved learning' can be achieved by:

- *reviewing the current provision*

- *seeking to develop the department leader's vision for improving performance*

- *departmental discussions to secure understanding of expectations and criteria for success*

- *developing departmental vision for improvement*

- *department training and workshop sessions to share and develop active engagement strategies*

- *departmental meetings to adapt/rewrite plans for teaching Shakespeare*

- *joint observation, classroom support and co-teaching with SL and/or consultant*

- *peer coaching and/or team teaching*

- *interim review and further planning*

- *a final review that leaves a clear vision of continuing improvement.*

Or you can just hire a good teacher. And that advice comes free.

Chapter Fifteen

Physical Jerks

'Mothers are mightily pleased to see a child writhe off the neck of a chicken, or to please itself with hurting a dog or a cat; and such wise fathers there are in the world, who look upon it as a notable mark of a martial spirit, when they hear a son miscall, or see him domineer over a poor peasant, or a lackey, that dares not reply, nor turn again; and a great sign of wit, when they see him cheat and overreach his playfellow by some malicious treachery and deceit. Yet these are the true seeds and roots of cruelty, tyranny, and treason; they bud and put out there, and afterwards shoot up vigorously, and grow to prodigious bulk, cultivated by custom.'
(Book 1, Chapter 22: 'Of Custom, And That We Should Not Easily Change A Law Received')

The World Cup 2010's on at the moment—and, of course, it's ubiquitous, not just on TV, radio and the internet, but out in the street. England flags are everywhere, fluttering from the roofs and windows of countless cars, vans and trucks. No problem. I have no desire to spoil anyone's fun—unlike one pundit I heard on the radio this morning, who reckoned that the flags' drag factor reduces a car's average fuel consumption by 3%. In the U.K. alone, this will account for an extra 1.22 million litres of extra fuel being burned, resulting in 2.8 million kilograms of CO2 being pumped into the atmosphere. The inescapable conclusion is, of course, that flags should be banned if we want to save the planet. Another tosser reasoning the need…

Montaigne doesn't have a great deal to say about sport: being an avowed bookworm, he usually employs the term to describe some frivolous pastime or other. He pays lip service to the classical ideal that the training of the mind should proceed hand-in-hand with physical activity, but otherwise he is largely silent on the subject. However, he clearly draws the line at cheating:

…there is no game so small wherein from my own bosom naturally, and without study or endeavour, I have not an extreme aversion from deceit. I shuffle and cut and make as much clatter with the cards, and keep as strict account for farthings, as it were for double pistoles; when winning or losing against my wife and daughter, 'tis indifferent to me, as when I play in good earnest with others, for round sums. At all times, and in all places, my own eyes are sufficient to look to my fingers; I am not so narrowly watched by any other, neither is there any I have more respect to.

This conjures up a lovely image of a long winter evening *chez* Montaigne, when, after dinner, Dad gets the cards out for a few hands and some quality time with the family, before scuttling back upstairs to scratch at his manuscript. And even if we hadn't been treated to this little anecdote, you just *know* that Montaigne would be a true Corinthian if he'd taken part in *any* sporting activity: it's not the winning, or even the taking part—it's the way you conduct yourself when you're playing that he would find important. I also get the feeling that were he to witness anyone cheating at cards, he would probably never trust them to have honest dealings in any other aspect of their lives.

I can only agree. There is a master cheat of my acquaintance who not only palms Scrabble tiles, but will even 'accidentally' upset the entire board if they're losing. That same person has also twice been known to 'accidentally' slip and fall on a recently-mopped floor in the local supermarket, in the hope that a large wedge of compo will be forthcoming. *In ludo veritas.*

So if Montaigne had watched the match between Brazil and Ivory Coast last night, I think he might have been inspired to write the essay I'm going to start in a moment. Even though I know very little about 'the beautiful game', sport, we're told, is the world in microcosm. Great international events like the World Cup and the Olympics shine a light on our collective humanity, as much as they showcase skill, dexterity and stamina. And of course, shameless cheating.

So we're in the final minutes of the game, and Ivory Coast sub Kader Keita charges towards Brazilian star Ricardo Kaka, who nonchalantly puts out his elbow. The replay clearly shows that contact is made in the chest area. Keita then suffers a loss of verticality, writhing around and clutching his face. Kaka, with one yellow card to his name already, is then sent off by a referee who didn't witness the incident since it took place way off the ball. None of the other officials saw it either, but the incident was of course captured on camera—inadmissible as evidence apparently, for reasons best known to FIFA.

Now Kaka is no saint, and his protruding elbow could either be interpreted as an act of aggression or self-protection. However motivated, it clearly makes contact with Keita's sternum and not his face. Keita's subsequent play-acting was of such intensity that when he's done with soccer, there's a career waiting for him on the stage. One newspaper correspondent noted that Keita was 'making a meal of it'—which is something of an understatement. It was more like a Chinese banquet. His pained expression led you to believe there was a procession of chilli-covered fire ants marching up his urethra.

But what started me thinking was my own reaction to the foul, and my subsequent opinion of Keita, of whom I'd absolutely no prior knowledge. Do I condemn his behaviour as cynically calculating, or applaud his opportunism and *chutzpah*? Of course it's all rather pathetic—yet not without its serious consequences[53]—but does any of it matter if the net result is the same? In short, what is THE PERFECT FOUL?

This dilemma brought to mind George Orwell's 1946 essay 'The Decline of the English Murder', in which he compares a good old home-grown British slaying with a more Al Capone-type professional slaughter. Setting the scene in an English parlour some time prior to the outbreak of the Second World War, he pictures a typical Sunday afternoon at the home of the man who's going to serve as his judge:

The wife is already asleep in the armchair, and the children have been sent out for a nice long walk. You put your feet up on the sofa, settle your spectacles on your nose, and open the News of the World. Roast beef and Yorkshire, or roast pork and apple sauce, followed up by suet pudding and driven home, as it were, by a cup of mahogany-brown tea, have put you in just the right mood. Your pipe is drawing sweetly, the sofa cushions are soft underneath you, the fire is well alight, the air is warm and stagnant. In these blissful circumstances, what is it that you want to read about? Naturally, about a murder. But what kind of murder?

Ah, the perfect evocation of those interminably dull Sunday afternoons of my youth, when absolutely nothing happened—endlessly. An era when the shops and pubs didn't open, and all we had to look forward to was pork pie with piccalilli for tea.

But it's all different for our modern-day umpire: substitute a

---

53. Kaka was banned from playing in the next round—but Brazil won anyway.

40-inch plasma TV for the newspaper, pizza for roast beef, 24-packs of lager for mahogany-brown tea and the wife driven out shopping by your drunken mates, and you have the 2010 World Cup version of Orwell's scenario. So what kind of soccer match do we wish to see as we settle down into our leather-effect armchair? Let the parlour game begin…

OK. First things first. Who should the perpetrator be? Over to Orwell—his ideal murderer is:

…a little man of the professional class—a dentist or a solicitor, say— living an intensely respectable life somewhere in the suburbs, and prefer-ably in a semi-detached house, which will allow the neighbours to hear suspicious sounds through the wall. He should be either chairman of the local Conservative Party branch, or a leading Nonconformist and strong Temperance advocate. He should go astray through cherishing a guilty passion for his secretary or the wife of a rival professional man, and should only bring himself to the point of murder after long and terrible wrestles with his conscience.

In other words, someone you would never suspect would be capable of murder in a million years.

My footballing equivalent would be the wonderfully-named Harry Haddock, who played for the Scottish team Clyde from 1949 to 1961 and was never sent off, booked or even shouted at by a referee in all that time. Voted player of the year in 1959, he could throw the ball 'remarkable distances' despite being 'not particularly tall'. Clearly a great man, and someone who never committed a cynical foul. A more recent candidate is former England captain Gary Lineker, who was never shown the yellow card, although he did come close on one occasion by committing the unpardonable sin of 'grinning at a referee in Spain'. Only these men could formulate the perfect foul.

So we've got our murderer/fouler. What about the ethos in

which the crimes take place? Orwell now tells us what kind of slaughter he *doesn't* like—an example of which was the so-called 'Cleft Chin Murder', in which the perpetrators were unduly influenced by 'the anonymous life of the dance-halls and the false values of the American film'. They were young, urban, and guilty of the 'utmost callousness', clearly not the products of a 'stable society'. The whole affair was, Orwell concludes, 'meaningless'. Murders just ain't what they used to be.

Back to football, and my corresponding bad ethos, as symbolized by the 'professional foul'—which in the eyes of some British commentators is a nasty foreign importation. The concept was first mooted in the UK after a notorious incident in the 1980 FA Cup Final when Arsenal's Willie Young deliberately fouled West Ham's Paul Allen who was in the middle of a clear scoring run. A free kick was awarded, which was deemed insufficient compensation for the loss of a certain goal. After much head-scratching by the authorities, fouls were now to be divided into either 'professional'—an automatic red card offence; and whatever the opposite of professional is—presumably 'amateur'. Official recognition that, seemingly overnight, fouls had just got nasty and premeditated. This symbolic loss of innocence was further compounded when TV rights auctions suddenly made some clubs very rich very quickly, and football was elevated to the echelons of big business. Suddenly there was a lot more to lose than just pride—and there was a lot more to win. A loss was not to be accepted with a *que sera* shrug of the shoulders; it was a catastrophe. Ejection from a major cup competition could mean the loss of millions in revenue. Pressure mounted on the teams. Managers played musical chairs every few weeks. More money rolled in. Star players bought Lamborghinis with a single week's wage packet and still had change to binge drink their way into an entrapment *exposé* in the *News of the World*. Hey, why not commit a professional foul? Your manager might publicly deny you, but if the foul won the game he'd be patting you on the back once the cameras were turned off. A stiff fine? A short suspension? So what? The club will pay, you'll have a rest, and the finance director will jump for joy.

Is it any wonder the team's regular fouler metamorphosed from a loveable rogue into a sneaky conniving git? Like Orwell's murderers, the net result was the same, but it was all so much more...dishonest and, well, *squalid*. Kaka's behaviour would have appalled Ron 'Chopper' Harris, master of the late tackle, who debuted for Chelsea in 1961, and whose playing style has been euphemistically described as 'uncompromising'. Or how about Norman 'Bites Yer Legs' Hunter, whose similarly physical games for Leeds United became legendary: on one occasion, an assistant rushed into the changing room to inform the team's trainer, Les Cocker, that Hunter had broken a leg. His response was 'Whose is it?'[54] Oh *où sont les fauteurs d'antan?* The REAL MEN? Never mind holding your poncy little face with your threaded eyebrows and sports moisturiser and squealing like a girl—if someone's fouled you that badly GET UP AND LAMP HIM!

So much for the ethos... Let's now merge our two lines of inquiry and imagine Orwell was alive in 2010 and working as a sports journalist covering the Brazil/Ivory Coast match. Unlikely, I know, but...anyway.

He'd probably be tapping out a piece bewailing football's loss of innocence, and tracing the origins of this fall from grace back to the early 1960s. As, I think, would Montaigne, were he to be writing a column for a rival newspaper. Both would have been attracted to the story, because it marked the death of amateurism, the nostalgically cheat-free environment beloved of both. Cue harp glissando as we reminisce, our misty eyes

---

54. On that occasion, for once, it was Hunter's own.

blinking through rose-tinted spectacles, back to that pre-lapsarian world where piles of jumpers served for goalposts, stumps were chalked on the wall...

In British cricket, the status of 'Amateur' (or 'Gentleman') was officially abolished in 1962; thereafter, everyone became a 'Professional' (or 'Player'). From that point, the 'Gentlemen versus Players' match, a fixture in the English social calendar which had been held most years from 1806, ceased to have meaning and was ended by the cricketing authorities. At around the same time, the English Football Association finally caved in to players' demands and abolished the 'maximum wage' clubs could pay their team members, paving the way for the ludicrously high salaries they enjoy now.[55]

Within a few weeks, England's entire Corinthian heritage as enshrined in its two great national team games had been sold down the river. All those stories of ex-public schoolboys who eschewed training, relying instead on instinct and camaraderie; the working-class heroes who enjoyed a meat pie, a beer and a fag before taking part in the Cup Final; Bert Trautmann, Manchester City's goalie playing on, not realizing his neck was broken...and so on. And look at the modern Olympics—another British invention. Oh yes, never mind Baron de Coubertin and Athens in 1894—what about Much Wenlock in the sleepy county of Shropshire in 1850 and the Games's true inspiration, Doctor W.P. Brookes?

Brookes believed that physical exercise was better for the locals than boozing so, like a true Victorian English Gentleman who played a straight bat and believed in *mens sana in corpore sano*, he

---

55. In 1960, the maximum wage was £20 per week, the average wage in England then being around £15. Kaka, who currently plays for Real Madrid, is estimated to earn £154,000 per week as of March 2010. Manchester City offered him £500,000 per week in 2009, which for reasons best known to himself, he rejected.

founded the Much Wenlock Society for the Promulgation of Physical Culture in 1841, and the Olympics were reborn with just four events (football, cricket, quoits and the long jump). Miniscule cash prizes awaited the victors. By 1850, the list of sports had grown to incorporate a blindfold wheelbarrow race, a pig race, and jousting.[56] Then, in 1890, who should rock up, plant a tree in the village and walk away with the idea—Baron Coubertin. And while his version of the Olympics has degenerated into a rolling transcontinental caravan of bungs, bribes and performance enhancement, the Much Wenlock Games continue to this day, as their website proclaims, 'Preserving The Ideals Of Doctor William Penney Brookes.' Hoorah!

But amateurism is now a distant memory: some footballerss (the English most definitely among them), still pay lip-service to the old ideals, while shamelessly ignoring them on the pitch. Diving, for example, was exclusively confined to overseas players like Jurgen 'The German' Klinsmann[57], if you believe these testimonies from two current England players:

'I have never intentionally tried to dive…It isn't fair for players to dive and try to cheat the other team. And it is not just cheating your opponents, you are cheating the fans as well'—Wayne Rooney.

'If I ever saw one of my team-mates diving, I'd definitely have a word'—Steven Gerrard.

And this from players who have both been shown the yellow card for precisely this offence. I'd love to be a fly on the wall

---

56. Now wouldn't you love to see *that* in the London games of 2012? Even a sportophobe like me might be tempted to go and watch. One of the hideous mascots at the event is to be called 'Wenlock' as a belated tribute to Dr. Brookes. I doubt he would be flattered.

57. Interestingly, in Germany, diving is something that only Spaniards do, apparently.

when Gerrard has a word with himself.

And then there's the former England captain, John Terry:

'*I can speak about the England lads and I think it is something we don't do. We're too honest*'.

Ah, the England lads are too *honest*—and this from a man sent off once and booked seven times in the 2009/10 domestic season alone, and more notoriously who cheated on his wife *with the girlfriend of a team-mate who was his best friend!!!*

Clearly, John Terry can neatly compartmentalize his life on and off the pitch whereas, of course, a true Corinthian wouldn't have to, because the pitch was simply an extension of his life. *In ludo veritas,* remember?

If you're an avid reader of Edwardian school stories, as I am, Terry's offence is the lowest of the low. There are, it's true, few wives and girlfriends involved in most school stories, but to cheat at sport *and* betray your best friend is the hallmark of a total rotter, a cad, a scoundrel and a bounder. I mean, I'd be more than happy to lend Harry Haddock a tenner and be confident of its prompt and safe return; but in the unlikely circumstance of one of today's footballing plutocrats being temporarily embarrassed, I'd definitely ask for a receipt. And even worse than that, Terry has shown himself to be a world class fibber—something Montaigne would have *utterly* condemned.

But perhaps it's unfair to compare modern world cup football with Roy of the Rovers or Montaigne's evening games of cards. It's apples and oranges, surely? Just like Orwell's vision of the English murder being coarsened by the war and the intrusion of American culture, so football has evolved over the last twenty years courtesy of money, and lots of it. The stakes are higher, and he who dares, wins. By any means necessary.

We can't go back to the Edwardian glory days of the Casuals, or even to the heyday of soccer's hard men in the 60s and 70s, so we should not be surprised that a concept such as the 'professional foul' is alive and well. We've got to live with it because it's a situation that's not going away any time soon. It's a good job Orwell died when he did.

But hold on a minute: on second thoughts, maybe that's too glib. After all, my Mum taught me that a cheat is a cheat is a cheat, no matter what the circumstances. Yes, a sporting infrastructure wallowing in a jacuzzi of cash creates an awkward tension between the ideals of sportsmanship, and the economics of winning at all costs. Which is a pretty fertile breeding ground for hypocrisy and humbug. But footballers could try and resist the temptation to be hypocrites, couldn't they?

Cue a little research…[58]

Looking at football fan sites on the internet, or listening to sports phone-ins on the radio in the UK, I was surprised to find hypocrisy is such a hot topic—and not simply because we're in the middle of the World Cup. I just Googled the single word 'hypocrite', and on page one of the results, three concerned politics, two marital infidelity and no fewer than *five* football. Clearly there's a lot of it about—and it doesn't seem to be popular.

As to the question I posed ages ago about what kind of game we want, having now spent a few enjoyable weeks immersed in the *minutiae* of football, I'd conclude the following: fans would like players to develop a closer understanding of what 'sport' actually is and the values that underpin it, and behave accordingly; their hero status should be completely separate from the size of their wage packet and potential transfer value; and they

---

58. Actually, it took me a month, as I know nothing about football.

should behave like heroes, not heroes compromised by extra-curricular shenanigans, or, indeed, cissies who writhe on the ground after being elbowed in the sternum.[59]

Put simply, heroes shouldn't cheat. With the ultimate sanction that if they do, chilli-covered fire ants *should* be introduced into their urethras. I'll bet FIFA could make a fortune selling Sky or ESPN the TV rights to *that*.

So if I were Keita (or indeed whoever), knowing the eyes of the world were on me, would I have wanted to brand myself a lousy stinking cheat in front of all those TV witnesses? Or, indeed if I were Montaigne, and my wife caught me palming cards? The principle's the same even if the audience is far smaller. In either circumstance, could I ever consider myself honest again, without being guilty of the rankest hypocrisy? What it boils down to, is whether Keita said to himself, as he looked in his bathroom mirror that night after the match, 'Well, that worked OK, tee-hee-hee' or 'I'm thoroughly ashamed. I have betrayed myself, my team and my country.' We can only guess the outcome, but as far as I'm aware he didn't play the Roman and fall on his sword. Which *would* have hurt.

It's an easy dilemma for the morally scrupulous and the sancti-monious to answer. For the rest of us, maybe it's a bit less clear cut. For example:

In the same match, Brazil's Luis Fabiano was guilty of a double handball which resulted in him scoring his team's second goal. Once again, the hapless ref's gaze was elsewhere. Now if I'd been in his position, would I have fessed up? And even if I had, would the officials have taken any notice, since their

---

59. Several bloggers chose to question Kaka's much-publicized religious affiliations—his favourite book is the Bible, and he has the words 'God Is Faithful' stitched on to the tongues of his match boots.

judgement is the ultimate arbiter of what happens? Would my honesty have done me any good?

On a personal level, yes it would—I could look in the bathroom mirror with no pangs of guilt or remorse. But if, as the result of my honesty, the goal was subsequently disallowed and it cost my team its place in the next round, there'd be hell to pay: the manager, the press, the fans, the accountants, the shareholders would all be after me, some of them with pitchforks and flaming torches. What price honesty if you're living in fear of your life?

One thing's for sure though, now the world knows Keita's a dastardly cheat, he'd better not try falling over in the supermarket because it *simply won't work*.

Chapter Sixteen

Same As It Ever Was

'*...obstinacy is the sister of constancy*' (Book 2, Chapter 32: 'Defence of Seneca and Plutarch')

When I was at secondary school, I spent what must have totalled many hundreds of hours in our small library. Most of my fellow pupils never darkened its doors, so I usually had the place to myself. It felt (to me at any rate) more of a sanctuary than a learning resource, having once been the school chapel, until its function was usurped by a far larger Victorian excrescence in the 1860s, situated a long salt-flecked walk out towards the sea.

A copy of the London *Times* was displayed on a large lectern in the reading room, and a bell rope hung from the ceiling, which was rhythmically tugged to mark the start of each period by a man of military bearing who sported a tweed jacket and a waxed moustache known as 'The Marshal'. His visits were the only interruption in this otherwise peaceful harbour, where one could enjoy a can of beer and a cigarette without fear of being caught.

The half-height shelves contained the most utterly eccentric assortment of books, including no fewer than ten copies of the *Collected Poems of Owen Seaman*, and all 39 four-inch thick volumes of the *Library Edition* of the works of John Ruskin. I don't recall ever dipping into either at the time; I could only wonder at the Ruskin's incredible productivity—and why any librarian, however drunk, would buy ten copies of a poet I'd never heard of.

Once at college, and studying Ruskin, I began to feel sorry for him; 39 volumes of erratic, often brilliant scholarship, and the only thing anyone remembers about him is his wife's pubes, some aspect of which rendered him impotent for the entire period of the marriage. Which is an entertaining, but utterly implausible story, and a vile calumny on his wife who successfully remarried and bore her husband, the artist John Everett Millais, no fewer than eight children, one of whom became a celebrated dog-breeder.

No, the *useful* thing I remember about Ruskin are these few words spoken by my tutor: 'For every statement made by Ruskin in his writings, there is elsewhere in his work a refutation of it.' Which, on further investigation, proved a fairly accurate assertion. I was reminded of that particular tutorial the other day when leafing through an anthology called 'The Genius of John Ruskin' in a second-hand bookshop, the foreword of which asserts;

His works are as burdened with contradiction as experience itself... Ruskin was always changing and always himself. Even his contradictions have a certain consistency. At different stages of life he reacted differently to the same things, yet each response was absolute in its integrity, reflecting a unity of sensibility rather than a system. Throughout his career, his mind was capable of change, and hence of growth ; but the change, as he once remarked, was that of a tree, not of a cloud -

Which is, in my opinion, a healthy way of appreciating the

world, and one not unadjacent to Montaigne's outlook.

A rigid adherence to being consistent doesn't just stifle desirable qualities such as imagination, creativity and experimentation; it can ultimately compromise essential attributes like independent thought and discretion. That's not to say the lifetime of one's thoughts and opinions should mimic the attention span of a 6-year old with ADD and a Coke addiction; more that the mind should permit itself (and be permitted by others) a certain flexibility which acknowledges that our opinions, and, just as importantly, the context in which we have them, necessarily evolve over time. And if that generates contradictions, well, that's to be celebrated rather than condemned. Don't be a cloud, Ruskin argues, changing shape every time you look at it; make like a tree, slowly and organically growing and evolving.

What's not to like in that? Yet the world appears, in my view at least, to be moving in the opposite direction—towards a fetishization of consistency with its attendant emphasis on precision, clarity and rigidity. Which is not only boring, but plain lazy and sometimes even cowardly. Admitting that you've changed your mind sometimes takes guts—not necessarily about your hairstyle, lippy or hemline, but where you stand on, say, a knotty political issue.

Certainly around where I live in West London, a regular example of this is the spectacle of nice, left-leaning middle-class parents who, when childless, swore they would never send any of their offspring to private school as it contravened their political principles; then, of course, when junior comes along, those ideals are consigned to the wayside. Next thing, the elderly Citroen 2CV with the agitprop stickers in the window is up for sale and the kids are being ferried to school in a black BMW SUV with tinted windows. If you're a fan of consistency (or lucky enough to be childless), you'll point out the hypocrisy of this behaviour, to which I would reply, let he who is without sin cast the first stone. We all do it. We get older. Our circumstances change. Our opinions change. It doesn't make us evil—it's when we attempt to *justify* our lack of consistency that we stoop to folly; imposing, like the politician, a spurious continuity on our opinions. I know I've done it. On many occasions.

The main thrust of Ruskin's evolution was his gradual politicization: when he began writing his seminal work of art criticism *Modern Painters* in the early 1840's, it was conceived as a piece of aesthetic criticism. Gradually, as he wrote more of those 39 volumes, he discovered that the principles governing the art he was so adept at elucidating could also be extended outwards into life. Which precisely what he started to do—and by the time *Unto This Last* appeared almost twenty years later, he had morphed from an art critic into a Christian socialist, whose thinking radicalized many younger disciples, among them William Morris.

Yet even though Ruskin's artistic and philosophical principles cannot, with any honesty, be assembled to form a coherent system, they remain powerfully relevant despite their inconsistency. And it's *that* conundrum I want to examine in these scribblings. Apologies for taking even longer than usual in getting to the point—I must really be channelling Montaigne now, as I've finally discovered my argument now the essay's halfway finished...

Perhaps we should look firstly at the upside of consistency: if something's consistent, you know where you stand in relation to it. It offers no shocks, no surprises. Which is why it's a quality beloved of the law and moralists.

Montaigne himself bewailed the tendency of humans to act inconsistently in the opening sally of his second book of essays,

'Of The Inconstancy Of Our Actions':

We fluctuate betwixt various inclinations; we will nothing freely, nothing absolutely, nothing constantly. In any one who had prescribed and established determinate laws and rules in his head for his own conduct, we should perceive an equality of manners, an order and an infallible relation of one thing or action to another, shine through his whole life.

Which is the equivalent of saying, 'So-and-so never changes, does he?'—which may sound like a compliment, but to my ears always carries with it an undertone of regret, i.e. 'So-and-so's really dull, don't let him corner you in the pub.' Montaigne examines the pattern of thought that equates inconsistency with immorality—if you don't behave consistently, you clearly don't know *how* to behave, and therefore your moral compass points to 'lost'. It's a problem he's constantly wrestling with and doesn't appear able to overcome:

For my part, the puff of every accident not only carries me along with it according to its own proclivity, but moreover I discompose and trouble myself by the instability of my own posture; and whoever will look narrowly into his own bosom, will hardly find himself twice in the same condition. I give to my soul sometimes one face and sometimes another, according to the side I turn her to. If I speak variously of myself, it is because I consider myself variously; all the contrarieties are there to be found in one corner or another; after one fashion or another: bashful, insolent; chaste, lustful; prating, silent; laborious, delicate; ingenious, heavy; melancholic, pleasant; lying, true; knowing, ignorant; liberal, covetous, and prodigal: I find all this in myself, more or less, according as I turn myself about; and whoever will sift himself to the bottom, will find in himself, and even in his own judgment, this volubility and discordance. I have nothing to say of myself entirely, simply, and solidly without mixture and confusion. 'Distinguo' is the most universal member of my logic.

'I differentiate', he says. Which is not at all consistent with the kinds of high office Montaigne held in Bordeaux, which would have required anything but this habitual 'volubility'. One might hope that when the time came to make formal judgements, the above quotation represented a private acknowledgement that different circumstances *can* affect different decisions on different days, and that he needed to be careful. A legal system that operates on precedent isn't going to survive long if its representatives start behaving capriciously, moodily, or whimsically. So, for example, you wouldn't want to be up before Mayor Montaigne on a charge of petty theft if he had a thundering hangover, or you might end up being hanged. But Montaigne was by and large thought to be an excellent public servant, so it looks like he did actually take notice of his own *caveat,* and his honest self-appraisal proved useful.

Yet although binding tariffs are established to prevent judges letting their emotions get in the way when banging people up, they can often prove too rigid, not just for tabloid editors, but occasionally for the judges themselves: when a particularly horrific murder has been committed, magistrates have been heard to lament their powerlessness, as neither precedent nor human longevity will permit those found guilty to be sentenced to a million years behind bars. The same with sentencing minors; when the crimes committed are identical to grown-up crimes and the perpetrators show no remorse, why does the law exercise clemency on the grounds of youth? Only last night on the news, a London judge complained he wasn't able to incarcerate a couple of particularly vicious, murdering happy slappers for the rest of their miserable lives on account of their being juveniles. And he was sore about it because his hands were tied.

Or how about the example of the guy caught speeding for the third time receiving an identical custodial sentence to another guy found guilty of malicious wounding? The first has been given the maximum penalty for his offence because there are no mitigating circumstances, the second the most lenient because there are—the law's working perfectly yet the net result seems unfair.

Back in the 16th-century, Mayor Montaigne—this time with his *distinguo* hat on—had the answer—which involved abandoning precedent almost entirely:

'[E]very particular action,' he writes, 'requires a particular judgement. The surest way to steer, in my opinion, would be to take our measures from the nearest allied circumstances, without engaging in a longer inquisition, or without concluding any other consequence.

Which simply means that every case should be judged on its own merits with reference not to formulated rules, but to an occurrence as closely allied to the offence as possible. Which is, of course, a nice distinction worthy of a lawyer. He cites a case of attempted rape in which a woman unsuccessfully tries to commit suicide rather than have her virtue compromised by a soldier, 'that she appeared another Lucretia'.[60] Yet, he wryly adds, 'I have since been very well assured that both before and after she was not so difficult a piece.'

So, Montaigne's saying, don't judge the past by the present. Nor should one project forwards beyond the immediate circumstances. A case should be looked at in isolation. If the woman was known to be indiscriminate with her sexual favours either before or after the alleged offence, the attempted rapist might escape justice. But on this occasion, it appears she wasn't—and that's what counts. So this time the charge *did* stand up in court.

---

60. Lucretia was a legendary figure whose rape and subsequent suicide ultimately brought down the line of Roman kings. By Montaigne's time, her name had become synonymous with constancy and honour.

A modern equivalent of that principle is, I suppose, the with-holding of evidence from juries: if there's a rapist in the dock charged on a single count, any similar crimes he's committed are often kept quiet until after the verdict lest they prove preju-dicial. So there's a case where the law fails to use precedent in reaching judgment, but will aim for consistency when passing sentence. Which strikes me as reasonable. At least I think it does. My head's starting to swim.

With the arts, problems of inconsistency are all so much easier, since nobody dies: Ruskin, being a Victorian Englishman and therefore immune from doubt, brooks no opposition. In a prose style quivering with authority, he comes out squarely on the side of what he alternately calls 'changefulness' and 'variety', probably because he'd enjoyed the luxury of never having had to preside over messy legal deliberations of life and death. Here's his definitive statement from *The Stones of Venice:*

...great art, whether expressing itself in words, colours, or stones, does not say the same thing over and over again; that the merit of archi-tectural, as of every other art, consists in its saying new and different things; that to repeat itself is no more a characteristic of genius in marble than it is of genius in print; and that we may without offending any laws of good taste, require of an architect, as we do of a novelist, that he should be not only correct, but entertaining.

Odd that Ruskin, who throughout his writings, shows himself addicted to formulating rules and codifying experience should be, at times, such a denier of precedent; but, as my tutor said, we can't expect consistency in a genius. I can't resist quoting Ruskin's summation of this particular strand of his argument, because it's not a bad principle to live by:

If we pretend to have reached either perfection or satisfaction, we have degraded ourselves and our work... The vital principle is not the love of Knowledge, but the love of Change. It is that strange disquietude of the Gothic Spirit that is its greatness; that restlessness of the dreaming mind, that wanders hither and thither among the niches…and yet is not satisfied, nor shall be satisfied…and it can neither rest in, nor from, its labour, but must pass on sleeplessly, until its love of change shall be pacified forever in the change that must come alike on them that wake and them that sleep.

Montaigne, however, can produce no such manifesto, and voices no such unequivocal pronouncement. In short, he's all over the place. Unlike Ruskin, who views consistency as bad yet sees it everywhere in bad art, Montaigne views it as good but can't find it when he's most in need. He sort of concludes that inconsistency in outward actions isn't really the point when exercising our judgement, which, rather, must penetrate to the very soul and seek out *motivation*. Then he helpfully adds, in what is almost a throwaway parting shot, *that* particular process is fraught with difficulty to the point where he wishes fewer people would attempt this 'high and hazardous' undertaking. And then, in another essay, 'Of Custom, And That We Should Not Change A Law Received', he seems to perform a 180-degree U-turn:

There is a vast difference betwixt the case of one who follows the forms and laws of his country, and of another who will undertake to regulate and change them; of whom the first pleads simplicity, obedience, and example for his excuse…the other is a much more ruffling gamester; for whosoever shall take upon him to choose and alter, usurps the authority of judging, and should look well about him, and make it his business to discern clearly the defect of what he would abolish, and the virtue of what he is about to introduce.

On balance, laws have been formulated for a reason, are sanctioned by precedent, and so you'd better have a bloody good reason for mucking about with them. It's certainly not a job for a 'ruffling gamester'.

It's Montaigne at his most infuriatingly indecisive—or honestly realistic, depending where you stand on the issue. Me? I don't stand anywhere. I have the first stone ready in my hand, but don't feel sufficiently confident to cast it. All in all, to be perfectly honest, this essay's turned into something of a mess. Which is ironic given its subject matter. Not being a Victorian gentleman, or a public official dealing with matters of great pith and moment, I'm both taxed by consistency yet often reassured by it. On the other hand, I can find inconsistency maddening, yet I'm often in the mood to be surprised. From that, I doubt it'll come as a shock that I still haven't worked out if it's OK to send my kids to private school. Perhaps I'd better get some first and see what happens.

P.S. Two not entirely unrelated stories re: consistency. Head honcho of Creedence Clearwater Revival, John Fogerty, was sued by his record company for 'self-plagiarizing'. And Neil Young was sued by *his* record company for making music that was 'unrepresentative of himself'. You just can't win in that crazy world of rock'n'roll. I guess we're all consistent in our inconsistency. Or inconsistent in our consistency. Or something.

Chapter Seventeen

Biggie Smalls

'So many words for words only.' (Book 3, Chapter 9: 'Of Vanity')

When I first went to the U.S.A. twenty-odd years ago, store assistants would routinely complete a transaction by saying, 'Have a nice day.' At the time, I remember some of my fellow Brits getting very aerated about this uncalled-for and hence redundant intimacy between themselves and a member of the lower orders. 'And it's not as if they mean it,' huffed one BBC colleague on her return from holiday in Florida, revealing how little she'd learned of Americans in their native habitat.

As time passed, we started doing it over here. And I didn't mind one bit, particularly if the send-off contained even the slightest scintilla of sincerity, and/or was accompanied by a smile, however perfunctory: after all, it's better than 'Fuck off and die' which, implied rather than spoken, remains the norm in Paris.[61]

---

61. You've got to love 'em. Earlier this year, I went to a friend's wedding at a hotel/chateau near Paris and was shown to a room in which the air conditioning had packed up. It was perhaps 110 degrees in there. When I pointed out that this was not acceptable, the manager refused to help, simply noting, 'I do not make the weather'.

Then, on a trip across the pond about ten years ago, I noticed things had moved on: 'Have a *great* day' was now in regular use. A tad exaggerated, I felt—a nice day was probably achievable, but a great day could prove a trickier proposition. It certainly upped the pressure.

And now I've just returned from New Orleans with a bartender's 'Have a *perfect* day!' ringing in my ears. So where do we go from there? I know we haven't *quite* reached the linguistic summit of how good a day can be—I suppose that would be something like 'have the quintessential day' or the clumsier, 'have the acme of days'—but we're rapidly running out of superlatives as we aspire towards the best 24 hours it's humanly possible to have.

We're not talking about a new phenomenon here; Montaigne's essay 'Of the Vanity of Words' notes that much the same linguistic inflation was happening 2,500 years ago: he reports that in Sparta, 'rhetoricians', who 'make little things appear great' were regularly whipped. And a good thing too, he implies. He goes on to note, and here Charles Cotton's 1877 translation becomes confusing, that linguistic inflation usually occurs 'when the public affairs were in the worst condition and most disquieted with intestine commotions.' I don't think he means to imply any link between rhetoric and trapped wind, but you get the gist: when things are going badly, we big things up. And various political and religious groupings throughout history realized the deleterious effects of this tendency—Montaigne (in Grumpy mode) cites the Cretans, the Persians, the Macedonians, the Athenians and the Mohammedans as having no truck with exaggerated language, as its use was considered not just deceitful, but likely to incite the plebs to revolution should a troublemaker with the gift of the gab come along:

...for the stupidity and facility natural to the common people, and that render them subject to be turned and twined and, led by the ears by this

*charming harmony of words, without weighing or considering the truth
and reality of things by the force of reason.*

Which, as a definition of advertising, takes quite some beating.
More of which in a moment. I doubt that Montaigne could
have added the modern Western World to his kingdom of
Enlightenment, since inflated language is such an integral part
of the way we express ourselves. We're all familiar with the
way journalists routinely pump up language to the point where
mild irritation becomes 'fury'; a supermodel's broken heel a
'crisis'; a two-hour flight delay a 'living hell'; a mild surprise a
'shock'; a minor cock-up 'turmoil'; worry 'anguish'; three cars
at a stop sign 'gridlock'. And it's not just confined to the fourth
estate—although they own the copyright on all this.

Perhaps the best example of this tendency in general use is
the ubiquitous 'awesome'; everything even mildly interesting or praiseworthy is 'awesome'—or, as the wonderful *Urban
Dictionary* defines the term: 'something Americans use to
describe everything', or alternatively:

*a 'sticking plaster' word used by Americans to cover over the huge
gaps in their vocabulary. It is one the three words which make up most
American sentances* [sic]*: Omigod, awesome and shit.*

To which, of course, should be added 'like', and 'I dunno'.
And it's not confined to America: if you dare, travel on the top
deck of a London bus at school chucking out time to test the
accuracy or otherwise of this statement.

Now Moses parting the Red Sea was probably awesome, in that
it struck fear and wonder into anyone who saw it. Similarly,
should the Four Horsemen of the Apocalypse grace us with
their presence, that too would be awesome; unless, of course,
you're not one of God's Elect, in which case their appearance
would be shit. But the wanking kangaroo on YouTube isn't

quite in the same league. Funny—hilarious even, but not as remotely awesome as some reviewers have described it.

Or take the noun 'genius', which is used so frequently to describe subjects who clearly aren't, that it has become almost meaningless. These days, if you want to alert your audience to the fact that someone actually *is* a genius, it's almost compulsory to include a preamble along the lines of 'I know the word 'genius' is chronically overused, but on this occasion, we are gathered here to celebrate someone who is possessed of the real thing.' And only then could you welcome a genius of the calibre of Frank Sinatra on stage, and not, say, Michael 'Bloody' Bublé.

Notice I've just used the past tense—because even this disclaimer has now become a cliché, and probably *has* been used to welcome Michael Bublé on stage.[62] Yet the word 'genius', and the concept behind it, has a venerable history. In Montaigne's time, the idea of the 'genius' of the artist grew out of neo-Platonic philosophy, and the conviction that creativity comes to the poet in a 'fury' (as opposed to a mild irritation). From the start it identified true art as being created while the artist was figuratively (and in some cases literally) 'out of his mind' while communing with his Muse. It was most definitely a term to be applied sparingly to those who had quite clearly been 'touched' in this extraordinary way. So by that token Picasso is a genius and Damien Hurst isn't. Ditto Shakespeare and Harold Pinter. Mozart and Salieri. Aretha Franklin and Lady Ga Ga. The point is, we have to keep a word in reserve for those who genuinely are geniuses—and the term's overuse by journalists lionizing this week's new thing is robbing us of an essential constituent of our vocabulary. 'Genius', and other words signifying quality

---

62. There is, incidentally, a page on Facebook called 'Michael Bublé is awesome', but fortunately at the time of writing, it only has 17 members. There is yet hope.

and excellence, need to be somehow ring-fenced to prevent their true meaning being diluted and ultimately lost. Which isn't going to happen in a month of Sundays.

But that doesn't stop the notorious *Académie Francaise* having a pop at keeping the French language pure and unsullied—and you have to admire their quixotic and slightly loopy mission which, having no legal authority, is a complete waste of time. What I didn't know was that the Spanish have a similar organization, which publishes the wonderfully-named *Pan-Hispanic Dictionary of Doubts.* Not to be left out, the Swedes established the *Svenska Akademien* (mission statement: to protect 'the purity, strength and sublimity of the Swedish language'); and then there's Brazil, whose august linguists are known as 'the immortals'. Not to be outdone, the UK has Stephen Fry and his wretched iPad.

But I digress. Another word that's regularly abused is 'passion'. Particularly, I've noticed, in connection with food. At London's Victoria Station, there's a branch of a franchised sandwich outlet that claims to be 'passionate' about its products. Well, that passion was not manifest in the quality of its BLT; I suspect it never existed outside the marketing exec's imagination (the passion, not the BLT). And even if the company was responsible for the finest sandwiches ever created, would they elicit 'passion', either in their manufacture or consumption? I'd prefer to reserve my passion for, say, a gorgeous woman—who I'm sure would be mortally insulted if I equated the way I felt about her with my love for a stale, tasteless, underfilled, overpriced baguette. No, passion existed between Romeo and Juliet, Paris and Helen, Tristan and Isolde, Dante and Beatrice—not commuter and sandwich. Even if the sarnies were any good, I'd restrict the description of their makers' motivating energy to 'enthusiastic' or, at the outside 'dedicated', if we want to keep things in proportion. But clearly we don't, as two other sandwich chains up the concourse are declaring their 'passion' too.

During my radio days, I presented a short-lived weekly discussion on food and drink (more often the latter) called 'Foodstuff'. For the pilot show, we had three Italian chefs come in to puff a local trade fair. Well, the amount of passion flying around that tiny studio was obscene. Everyone was so 'passionate' about food you thought they were fucking it, not cooking it. Half way through the recording, I called a halt, suggested we start again, this time minus the 'p' word, the use of which was becoming tediously repetitive and hence meaningless. They collectively shot me a hostile look, quickly replaced by one of panic as the realization dawned they'd have to go off script. Which, given that two of them turned out to be actors employed by the PR agency proved rather tricky. I should have spotted their ludicrous off-the-shelf Italian accents from the outset.

And it was by no means the last time guests on the show declared their passion without any means of explaining *why* they were passionate. On one occasion, we had a journalist in who, the briefing document explained, was 'passionately knowledgeable' about Southern Italian cuisine. Turned out her knowledge was based on an all-expenses-paid weekend junket to Naples, during which she'd consumed vast amounts of pizza and ice-cream.

Coincidentally, Montaigne's essay on this very subject was prompted by a foodie issue—and he too had dealings with an Italian chef, who discussed 'palate-science' with a 'magisterial gravity' that went beyond pretension, much to the great man's annoyance.

Now I'm not just in from Texas, and I know the worlds of PR, marketing and advertising are venal and enjoy, shall we say, a casual relationship with the truth. Fine. Most of the time, it's all good fun and nobody loses an eye. I'll even confess to having been on a junket or two. On one level, I think it's all rather jolly, and it's not going to hasten the end of civilization as we know it.

But the thing that concerns me is this: if we carry on as we are, within a generation we'll have lost the knack of describing things—*anything*—accurately. Because even the lowliest or least-deserving subject will have a wildly inappropriate superlative attached to it. We'll have entered a phase in which everyone is their own ad executive, as we routinely transform everyday reality into a hyperbolized version of that reality in which everything will be either awesome or shit, with nothing in between. Omigod.

What we will be doing is *dramatizing* reality, creating an unearned significance for subjects that don't merit or demand it. And we also need to address the issue: why would we do this? Is it because we're dissatisfied with reality the way it is? Is life so dull? Why would an ad agency think we'd be more attracted to a sandwich made with passion rather than, say, skill, expertise or care? Why, in the teeth of the evidence, would fans and reviewers almost *will* Michael Bublé to be better than he is or can ever be? Why do we need to have a perfect day every day? Perhaps, as Montaigne hints, we *are* in trouble. I worry when I get to the front of a tailback on the motorway to see that it's been caused by my fellow motorists gawping at an accident, however small, presumably to see if anyone's lying on the carriageway covered in blood. Do they experience relief or disappointment when they discover there's no casualties? Do they need a fix of drama that badly? And yes of course I look too—although I try not to slow down *too* much, as that would be hypocritical.

The problem is that we have been weaned onto the idea that everything we see and do carries with it the potential for drama, some of it real, some of it manufactured. And we'll look for it in the most unlikely places—even a car crash. In this respect, we're not so much ad executives as tabloid journalists waiting for our adrenalin shot from the next big scoop. So we pay ludicrous amounts of money to watch sport, where there's plenty of drama—and don't the TV trailers let you know it. I can't recall a recent promo, be it for rugby, darts or synchronized swimming, that doesn't feature the word somewhere ('passion' creeps in occasionally too). Which is fine, even though it's becoming rather tedious; sport is genuinely adversarial, unpredictable, involves combinations of skill, strength, ability, experience, endurance—all the ingredients of a first-rate drama. Unless, of course, you're stood in the rain back in 1969 watching a goalless draw between Blackpool and QPR, during which, shall we say, drama was at a premium.

But there are many areas in life where an overemphasis on drama would be inappropriate. Take the law.

The other day on the Tube, I saw an advert for a law school featuring a recent inductee who claimed he was attracted by 'the drama of the courtroom.' Which is a pretty superficial way of choosing a career—and an odd claim for the college to want to advertise. How about upholding the law as a worthwhile ambition? Defending the weak? Making sure the guilty get their just deserts? Or even being paid a fortune? Do they actually teach law at this seat of learning, or do they major in acting skills?

I suspect said student watched *A Few Good Men* and was inspired by the duelling between Tom Cruise and Jack Nicholson. Or even, if I'm being more charitable, *The Merchant of Venice*. Having graduated, he might want to revisit his motivations after fifteen straight days in the small claims court, and reflect that he's been sold a pup. A career in the law, except on the rarest of occasions, isn't *A Few Good Men* or even *Judge Judy,* nor should it be. It's about the administering of justice, not queening about in front of the jury. Most of the time, it's a relentless, ultimately dispiriting parade of offenders and their crimes, misdemeanours, motivations, life stories and excuses played out against the rigid formalities of the justice system. At least that's what my friend the Queen's Counsel tells me. He's over the moon on those rare occasions when there's a good old barney in his courtroom. It relieves the monotony and lets him bang his gavel.

But it's the reporting of the news on TV where drama really doesn't belong—and is now endemic. And it wasn't always like that. Ironically, back in the 1950s, the BBC's news bulletins were all-scripted and read not by journalists, but trained 'announcers', some of whom were former actors, employed because they knew how to speak clearly with the correct intonation. And they needed to—primitive technology meant that sound quality was extremely variable. Being able to *hear* what was being said took priority. And back then news *was* news—it was a calm *resumée* of what had actually happened that day, delivered in an efficient, authoritative if sometimes over-formal way. It was not drowned in tidal waves of speculation, analysis and 'on-the-spot' interviews and actuality. News anchors were not 'personalities'—in fact, they weren't even on screen during the early years of TV, for fear they would distract viewers from what was being said—there was usually a still of the Big Ben clock tower for the duration of the broadcast, or relevant still photographs.

We all know what the news has become—all over the world—and how an emphasis on drama has long since eroded editorial standards. I remember being shocked back in 1987 watching news reporters being winched onto the semi-submerged hulk of the capsized car ferry 'Herald of Free Enterprise' by helicopter, poking their cameras through portholes, presumably to see if they could spot any of the 193 men, women and children drowned inside. And all this while salvage operations were still going on. Now, in these days of febrile sensationalism, I'd *expect* this kind of behaviour. Sad, isn't it?

What possible value can an emphasis on drama bring to our appreciation of the day's events? The drama is already right there in the story if the duty editor's doing his job properly—it needs no further amplification. We, as viewers, should be left to decide its significance for ourselves and how we're going to react—if, that is, the news media credited us with any intelligence. What we're fed isn't 'news' at all; it's entertainment masquerading as news. Or the other way round—I can't make up my mind which. Yet it's a burlesque the entire media seems to be lost in, which does few favours for those of us who actually want an unvarnished, matter-of-fact account of what's going on around us.[63]

The question that we need to keep asking, and one for which I demonstrably have few answers, is whether all this rannygazoo is the news simply reflecting society's values—or, put another way, do we really need a fatal car crash to make our day complete? And would that be a nice/great/perfect or awesome day?

Perhaps the solution to all the hype is to take a leaf from the bankers and engineer some worldwide linguistic and histrionic crash to return the world to some kind of normality, at least in our use of language. Just as share prices can't keep rising exponentially, or a nation's economy continue to grow indefinitely, so this level of what Montaigne might term 'vanity' surely can't last forever. It's high time the bubble popped and we had what the financial commentators call a 'necessary period of readjustment'. Or we could borrow Montaigne's Spartan solution and just beat the perpetrators senseless. Strictly *pour encourager les autres*, of course.

---

63. I know—I've just contradicted myself. Maybe I'm in a worse mood than when I wrote what I did on page 14.

Chapter Eighteen

The Future Ain't What It Was

'Whoever saw old age that did not applaud the past and condemn the present time, laying the fault of his misery and discontent upon the world and the manners of men?' (Book 2, Chapter 13: 'Of Judging Of The Death Of Another')

(N.B. all ages quoted in this essay are correct-ish as of May 2010)

When Montaigne started writing his Essays, he was 38. By the time the first batch was published, he'd reached 47. He died aged 59 after a long illness, which for Renaissance France was a pretty good though not exceptional innings. And so it's only slightly presumptious of him to devote an essay to old age and death (Book 1, Chapter 57), although I have to say, it's one of the rare ones where I totally disagree with him.

One of Montaigne's heroes was the younger Cato, who crops up a fair few times in the *Essays* as the benchmark for honour, nobility and integrity. And nothing became his life so much as the leaving of it. During the Roman Civil War (the one between Julius Caesar and Pompey the Great), Caesar finally came out on top following the battle of Thapsus in 46BC. Cato was loath to live in a country with Caesar in control, and so committed suicide, according to the good old Roman tradition, by stabbing himself with his sword. However, because of an injury to his hand, he botched the job, and merely managed to open his stomach. And there he lay helpless, his bowels spilled out all over the floor, until assistance arrived in the form of a surgeon, who, given that Cato's giblets were intact, offered to stuff them back in, sew him up, good as new, bish bash bosh, right as rain. Cato was having none of this, and tore at his innards, ripping them out and expiring instantaneously. A noble, if messy, death. (I always feel sorry for the poor buggers who have to clean up after these grand gestures—you never read about the person who had to scrape Anna Karenina's mortal remains off the railway line, do you?)

Clearly, Cato wasn't afraid of shuffling off his mortal coil. In fact, he embraced death as a lover. And, says Montaigne, at 48 years old that's fair enough. After all, you've achieved everything you're likely to by that age. So let's give people responsibility when they're young, as they're likely to be sharper, braver and more savvy than a doddery geriatric. Take Hannibal, for instance: brought the mighty Roman Empire to its knees before he was 32, which, coincidentally, was the age at which Alexander the Great died, having achieved equally magnificent feats of arms:

For my part, writes Montaigne, *I believe our souls are adult at twenty as much as they are ever like to be, and as capable then as ever. A soul that has not by that time given evident earnest of its force and virtue will never after come to proof... Of all the great human actions I ever heard or read of, of what sort soever, I have observed, both in former ages and our own, more were performed before the age of thirty than after... For this reason it is that I complain of our laws, not that they keep us too long to our work, but that they set us to work too late. For the frailty of life considered, and to how many ordinary and natural rocks it is exposed, one ought not to give up so large a portion of it to childhood, idleness, and apprenticeship.*

Of course, it was only the better off who could fritter away their youth in idleness; the poor kids would be rammed head first up the nearest chimney, or whatever the Renaissance equivalent was. But this denigration of age is shared by Montaigne's disciple T. S. Eliot who, in his poem *East Coker*, ruminates:

> *There is, it seems to us,*
> *At best, only a limited value*
> *In the knowledge derived from experience.*
> *The knowledge imposes a pattern, and falsifies,*
> *For the pattern is new in every moment*
> *And every moment is a new and shocking*
> *Valuation of all we have been.*

And then he concludes:

> *Do not let me hear*
> *Of the wisdom of old men, but rather of their folly...*

Which actually scares the hell out of me as I enter my 50s. No, Tom, I *want* to hear about the wisdom of old men, be-cause—and maybe I'm witnessing the beginning of denial here—with middle age comes greater understanding and appreciation of life. Doesn't it? Or rather, shouldn't it?[64] I'm already painfully aware of my fading ability to recall the year Lulu won Eurovision, or even why it was I just climbed the stairs, and all I have available to shore up the fragments of my intellectual ruin is that I'm rich in experience. It's the only thing I've got that trumps the young. And now you'd rob me even of that. So what if every moment is 'new and shocking'?

---

64. Eliot once denied that Montaigne had 'any philosophy whatever.' Which makes me wonder how a man who usually got things right on this occasion managed to be so spectacularly wrong.

That's not scary—it's *energizing*. But then you retreated into the sanctuary of Anglo-Catholic bells and smells when you were a mere 39. Ya quitter.

From that little rant you'll have gathered that for once I'm also disagreeing with the Master, who was writing his Essay 'On Age' from the perspective of a 45 year-old who had similarly retired into the contemplative life. In mitigation, however, he does remark that to die of old age is rare in the late 16th-century, what with the regular outbreaks of plagues, wars and malnutrition—not to mention all the normal shocks that flesh is heir to.

Now, however, with average life expectancy nearly double that in Montaigne's time (UK figures), it's rather more difficult to justify disembowelling yourself at 48 on the grounds that you probably haven't got long to go, and besides, any talent you may have had is well past its sell-by date. But staying employed and useful from 48 to normal retirement age isn't always easy if you choose to hang on to your innards: these days, old age isn't automatically associated with wisdom and ability; rather it equates with 'expensive' and therefore 'expendable'. And no amount of anti-ageist legislation is going to stop companies haemorrhaging hard-won experience if they can reduce the wage bill.

So, to put it bluntly, I'd like to know whether I'm all washed up or not. Can I still make some sort of positive contribution to society? Or has the NHS created a generation of latter-day Tithonuses who achieve immortality having omitted to ask for a halt to the ageing process and regular paid employment? Thanks to the miracles of modern science, I may be possessed of a *mens* reasonably *sana in corpore* reasonably *sano* at 50, but that's no damn use if *I'm* no damn use. It's what they call 'the curse of fulfilment', apparently. All revved up with experience and no outlet for it.

Of course, back in the day, old age was a simple affair: as Groucho Marx noted, all you had to do was live long enough. But at what point do you *become* old? Chronologically, the threshold has kept moving upwards, largely thanks to the stardust and golden 60s generation. Being the greatest bunch of self-obsessed revisionists that ever strode the earth, they took it on themselves to continuously re-define 'middle-' and then 'old-' age to suit their need to keep feeling young. And so 40 became the new 30. Then they collectively reached 50—which had to become the new 40. And so on, just to prove they weren't all washed up. And now they're marching towards 70 and shouting from their wheelchairs how relevant they still are. Which is, I suppose, healthy, if faintly ridiculous. So maybe all that self-regarding 'tree-hugging hippie crap' (as Cartman so rightly calls it) did have one useful outcome.

And nowhere is this better exemplified than in the field of pop music, where, it seems, you're never too old to rock'n'roll.

F. Scott Fitzgerald once told a reporter that no-one in showbiz should have the decency to live beyond thirty, and several rock stars duly obliged by dying tragically young. But many more endured to sail the uncharted waters of middle and even old age. In the past year, I've attended performances by three musicians who couldn't even stand up—Solomon Burke (because each of his legs is the size of a morbidly obese five year-old); Etta James (worn out by a life of heartbreak, hardship and heroin but who still hopefully rubs her groin suggestively on stage) and, the Methuselah of music, B.B. King, because he's 84. Eighty-four!! Now there are limits to what old Blues Boy can perform on stage these days, but when he plays the occasional stinging riff or fill, the heart still leaps. Over 65 years in showbiz, sharp as a tack, and keeping up a punishing schedule of live appearances, 'It's all I know to do' [sic], he says, mercifully free from the pernicious influence of T.S. Eliot.

And the white *arrivistes* are following suit: Johnny Winter (sedentary at age 66 due to chronic illness, but always magnificent); John Mayall, who still bounds on stage and sings, plays harp and keyboards at 77 as if it's his first time in front of an audience. His latest (57th) album is described as 'a new start with fresh new blood'. I'm not sure if it's the band line-up he's talking about or 8 pints of type O—either is plausible—but you've got to hand it to him, he's always searching, and still knocks out 'Hideaway' like a bitch 45 years on. And, lest we forget, there's the wonderful Ian Hunter, who played a storming set at Hammersmith the other week aged 70 with a re-formed Mott the Hoople.

And then, in a field of one, there's Keith (he doesn't need a surname any more)—a man whose face makes WH Auden's look like a Nivea model's[65]—sort of alive and sort of well at 67, and still welded to his guitar, his kidneys and liver down to their last few functioning cells. A quarter of a century ago, in their 40s, he and Mick were nicknamed 'the Zimmer twins'—and yet the Stones' last world tour between 2005-7 grossed 558 MILLION DOLLARS, indicating that their earning potential is still cashing cheques even if their bodies aren't.

Now you may think it's somehow undignified for the hellraisers of yore to die with a whimper rather than a bang, to fade away rather than burn out (the writer of that second epithet, Neil Young, is 64): after all, if your teenage idols are old, that's pretty conclusive evidence that you are too—a fact that most of us would rather ignore. And 558 million bucks does argue that there's way too much wistful nostalgia in the world.

But I still think all those artists are inspirational. For all their

---

65. I've been unable to establish corroborative evidence for the notorious comment about W.H. Auden, 'if that's what his face looks like, imagine his scrotum'—but the finger points in some quarters at Dylan Thomas.

frailties, for every strained top note, for every fumbled solo, they're refusing to go gentle into that good night and sit in old folks' homes with salmon-coloured upholstery, watery vegetables and a Yamaha keyboard playing hits from the war years (the Vietnam war, not World War 2). They don't have to be creative powerhouses any more, they just need to be *there*. Symbols. Icons. Call them what you will, dammit they're *necessary*. One of my favourite poems from my teenage years remains Roger McGough's 'Let Me Die a Young Man's Death'—but not until he's a) 73—mown down by a red sports car on his way home from an all-night party; b) at 91 in a mafia-style execution in a barber's chair or c) at 104, cut into pieces by his mistress when she discovers him in bed with her daughter ('and fearing for her son'). The poem struck a chord when I first read it 35 years ago and it resonates ever more loudly as I nurse my gout. And I'm also reminded of the sainted John Betjeman who, when asked if he had any regrets, answered almost without hesitation, 'I haven't had enough sex.'

But this is just my opinion, of course, and to offer it gratuitously or without qualification would run counter to the principles of this book. So how to settle the issue of young versus old...

...Cut to three weeks later...and I think I may have a solution... There's a brilliant essay by Greil Marcus, collected in his 1993 volume *In the Fascist Bathroom,* entitled 'Rock Deaths in the 1970s—A Sweepstakes' [sic], which is not only a great read, but proposes a perfect pub game to play in the snug after a few pints and there's a lull in the conversation. When carefully adapted, it fits the bill admirably, in that it ignores age entirely and focuses on achievement instead.

It goes like this: when the first pop stars died (cf. Buddy Holly at 22, Eddie Cochran at 21) these were thought to be exceptional events and just sheer bad luck (or the devil giving these ungodly varmints what they justly deserved). But as the 60s progressed, more pop stars succumbed to the attentions of the Grim Reaper, culminating in the famous quadruple deaths of the so-called 'Forever 27 Club'—Brian Jones, Jimi Hendrix, Janis Joplin and Jim Morrison (they all stiffed aged 27 in 1969, 1970, 1970 and 1971 respectively). Now it started to look like death was a hazard of the profession, to the point where many convinced themselves Paul McCartney was dead even though he clearly wasn't. And indeed still isn't, aged 67. Although the current 'Paul', it's suggested, could be a ringer, on the grounds that he hasn't written any songs of 'Hey Jude' calibre just lately.

By the 70s, as the cumulative effects of life in the fast lane continued to push up the mortality rate, and record sales of the dead artists actually rose with every re-issue, some were starting to view death as not so much a tragedy, more a shrewd career move. And then came The Big One—Elvis dead at 42 on August 16th, 1977. I was attending the RSC Summer School in Stratford-upon-Avon at the time, first hearing the news on the radio as I entered the breakfast room of Mrs Barnacle's B&B on the Alcester Road. Too upset to go to lectures that day, me and a fellow Shakespearean called Judy sagged off and got drunk. Actually, I wasn't upset at all, but Judy was, and she was rather attractive so I naturally sympathized and plied her with alcohol. I also recall that a Dutchman, Danny Mirror, rush-released a tribute single entitled 'I Remember Elvis Presley'—not exactly a remarkable feat of recollection, as The King had only been dead less than a week.

At this point, value judgments were becoming hopelessly confused, particularly when rock journalists were trying to evaluate how 'great' musicians both dead and alive actually were now their acknowledged ruler had pegged it: Greil Marcus was disturbed by two things: first, he felt dead musicians, however good or bad, were being given an unfair advantage simply because they had died; and second, the ones who had enjoyed a lengthy career were being similarly favoured just for having survived in an industry not (then) renowned for longevity. Waters were being muddied and, given that the dead ones had no voices, Marcus decided to help them level the playing field by formulating three questions, each carrying a possible 10 points:

a) for the contribution the artist had made to music up to his or her death;
b) the contribution they would have made had they lived;
c) the originality of the manner of their death.

And there are some surprising results, with Question 3 often being the clincher. And this is where my modification comes in, to cope with those artists who are still alive: first, go through the stiffs, using all three questions; then the survivors, using Q1 and Q2 only. Pick the winner in each category. Then subtract the live winner's score from the dead winner's, and see what the survivor has got to die from to be equally successful. So, in answering Q3, you'll have to decide how many points you're going to award:

- a plane crash (The Big Bopper, Stevie Ray Vaughan, half of Lynyrd Skynyrd), when set against, say;

- a motorcycle crash (Duane Allman). Or;

- an argument with a concrete lamp post on the A4 outside Chippenham (Eddie Cochran).

This calls for some fine distinctions and difficult choices:

- a brain haemorrhage (Sandy Denny), versus;

- a heart attack aggravated by rheumatic fever (Billy Fury);

- bleeding ulcers (Gene Vincent).

If you get stuck, my advice is to have another drink.

Anyway, let's have a dry run: (by the way, these are my own scores, not Greil's.)

Take Jimi Hendrix. No question, 10/10 for Q1. Q2 is more doubtful—his muse was clearly waning by the time of his death, so let's say 7/10. And then 1/10 for Q3: drugs are the rock star's common cold: choking on vomit equally so (although, as Spinal Tap pointed out, choking on someone else's vomit does demonstrate considerable originality. Not to mention 'a bizarre gardening accident' or even spontaneous combustion, all three of which carried off Tap members). However, in the case of Gram Parsons' death from drugs, you may like to add extra points to his notional low score because his body was stolen and burned in the desert by two fans according to the singer's wishes. The pair was the subject of a high-speed car chase by local policemen, who lost the fugitives, because, quote, they were 'encumbered by sobriety'.

Then there's the problem of hip-hop acts: would shooting (which did for Tupac Shakur, the Notorious B.I.G. and Jam Master Jay among others) be the rap equivalent of drugs, i.e. somewhat inevitable and low-scoring? Or perhaps not. It's entirely up to you.

So Jimi, after all that, scores 18/30.

Now take Rory Storm. You know. The lead singer of Rory Storm and the Hurricanes, one of whose early drummers was Ringo. Until the Beatles came along, they were arguably the best band in Liverpool, regularly winning or coming close to the top of popularity polls. So we should give them 7/10 for Q1 and a charitable 2/10 for Q2, as they disbanded having only released two (admittedly good) singles. But then, coming up on the rails, Rory gets 10/10 for Q3—tragically found dead in

1972 alongside his mother in what some have interpreted as a pill-fuelled suicide pact.

Which late rally gives Rory a total of 19/30. Who would have thought?

So, say, Rory wins for the stiffs.[66]

Now we'll take our living act, and who better than the world-wide best-selling artist of 2009, Susan Boyle, whose debut album shifted an incredible 8.3 million copies in its first six weeks. Contribution to music = 0. Future contribution to music = 0. Total = 0. Now take away Susan's score from Rory's (19—0 = 19). Susan can't win, having to score an impossible 20 from Q3. Or she *could* win, if her death was *so* bizarre you decided to bend the rules. If you can't decide, my advice is to have another drink.

And you don't have to stick to rock stars—why not try poets or novelists? Painters? Or footballers? Or Stoics? (ripping out your own entrails must surely score high in Q3).

It's not hugely scientific, but callously brooding on other peoples' mortality can prove a wonderful distraction from fretting about one's own. And before you accuse me of taste-lessness, don't forget that Montaigne wrote something similar in his essay 'Of Judging of the Death of Another' (once again, Cato gets a namecheck and wins the competition hands down, with Socrates and his self-administered hemlock a close second).

I still haven't categorically decided if I'd have stuffed my bowels

---

66. Unlikely, if you include the mighty Sam Cooke (10, 10 and 9, shot to death practically naked in a tussle with a motel receptionist); or even Marvin Gaye (10, 8 and 10, shot by his father who was a church minister)—but remember this is just a working example.

back in had I been Cato. On balance, I think I would, a) being a devout coward and b) on the grounds that you never know what's coming round the next corner. It might even be good, *pace* Montaigne and Thomas Stearns Eliot. So let's banish the faint heart: after all, to quote Bette Davis: 'Old age is no place for sissies'.

P.S. I've just discovered that Tony Bennett is 84 and still standing at his gigs. Does that top B.B?

Chapter Nineteen

The Ultimate Sophistication

'...the very names of goodness and innocence are... in some sort grown into contempt. **(Book 2, Chapter 11: 'Of Cruelty')**

I'll be perfectly frank—I've been dreading this essay, partly because it's going to be quite a wrestle and secondly, I'll probably end up looking like a complete twit. But Montaigne is a stern and uncompromising taskmaster, so I suppose I'd better get on with it. Because somewhere within this subject, I think, lies the key to Montaigne's habits of thought, and why his writings remain as profound as ever over 400 years on from their composition.

It's at moments like these I feel his honesty to be somehow oppressive—I'd love to misrepresent my true self in what follows, because honesty can make you vulnerable and I don't like feeling vulnerable. Certainly not in front of an audience.[67] But the bastard won't let me tell porky pies. That's not what he's about, so, therefore, nor am I. But after all, where's the harm in a few white lies? Who would know? We all like wearing

---

67. One can hope. I can only guarantee two people will read this book; me and the editor.

our best bib and tucker in public, and I'm no exception. Or as Randy Newman so sagely puts it, 'I want everyone to like me/ 'Cause I'm a little bit insecure.'

I suspect Montaigne is more at ease with this self-imposed vulnerability than I am because, underneath it all, he has that unshakeable core of aristocratic self-confidence that I simply don't possess. And I certainly don't have the advantage of a thick skin, so the temptation to perjure myself is that much greater.

And besides, I've no way of knowing if old Michel *is* being 100% honest; sometimes, his candour looks a bit too routine and studied to be true. After all, here is a man who received the finest classical education, sailing through the curriculum by the prodigious age of 13; he was a counsellor of the Court des Aides of Périgueux and, in 1557, was appointed to a similar role in the Bordeaux Parlement. From 1561 to 1563 he was courtier to King Charles IX, and was awarded the highest honour of the French nobility—the collar of the order of St. Michael. Yet, for all his sophistication, here he is affecting a philosophical simplicity.

His stated aim in writing the *Essays* is one of honesty and guilelessness—what's the point, he implies, of embarking on a voyage of self-discovery if I'm going to falsify the log? It'll be of no use to anyone, least of all me. And while Montaigne gives me few reasons to doubt his sincerity, there's always that nagging suspicion that what we've got here is a beautifully contrived pose. Too good to be true, as the saying goes. Or too true to be good. My distrust probably says more about me than him. But then I come across a passage like this, from Book 1 Chapter 20, in which he starts discussing the vagaries of his penis:

The indocile liberty of this member is very remarkable, so importunately unruly in its tumidity and impatience, when we do not require it, and so unseasonably disobedient, when we stand most in need of it: so imperiously contesting in authority with the will, and with so much haughty obstinacy denying all solicitation, both of hand and mind.

This may be carrying openness and honesty a stage too far. I mean, you wouldn't get a serious philosopher like Bertrand Russell waving his old chap about in front of his readers, would you? And then it gets worse. In defence of his member's seemingly random malfunctions, our man reels off a few fart gags: the anal sphincter, he says, is similarly unruly—ask Saint Augustine, who claimed to have…

…seen a man who could command his rear to discharge as often together as he pleased; Vives, his commentator, yet further fortifies with another example in his time,—of one that could break wind in tune; but these cases do not suppose any more pure obedience in that part; for is anything commonly more tumultuary or indiscreet? To which let me add, that I myself knew one so rude and ungoverned, as for forty years together made his master vent with one continued and unintermitted outbursting, and 'tis like will do so till he die of it. And I could heartily wish, that I only knew by reading, how often a man's belly, by the denial of one single puff, brings him to the very door of an exceeding painful death; and that the emperor [Claudius] who gave liberty to let fly in all places, had, at the same time, given us power to do it.

He must have read and enjoyed Rabelais to come out with the conceit of putting his cock in the dock and defending it from a charge of affray brought by his other organs. It's masterly stuff, but perhaps reveals a little too much of what goes on within the confines of his doublet.

Of course, I'm not using those passages to get cheap laughs; I'm merely demonstrating that nothing seems off limits to our lad. And so it shall be with me. I may well end up looking an arse, but if I'm going to investigate simplicity, I'm going to have to be, well, Simple. Unsophisticated. Unvarnished. Direct. Plain. Straightforward. Innocent. Honest. And look stupid.

The trouble is that simplicity is complicated. Just defining it will give you a migraine, because all its meanings bleed into one another.

I like simplicity. It makes life easier. Operating on a policy that something's not necessarily obvious until you know it, I always made a point of always stating the bleeding obvious when communicating things to my staff—taking an issue back down to its foundations and building up from there. That way, there was less chance of them misunderstanding me—and thus saving me time. It worked pretty well, barring a few complaints that I came over as patronizing. Overall, though, I felt this was worth the risk: often, I'd get back to basics just to get things straight in my *own* mind, let alone anyone else's.

Keep it simple. And don't tell lies—that's another route to complication, because as Mama used to say, lies beget lies and it all just gets too darn difficult to keep track of which lie you told to whom and why and in what order and for what reason. So my default settings of simplicity and honesty were motivated by the desire for an easy life, not because I wanted to resemble a beacon of virtue smugly shining above the cesspit of internecine BBC squabbling. I think the large Dilbert poster I attached to my office door subtly implied as much: it read 'Always Postpone Meetings With Time Wasting Morons.' And, being intelligent people, my staff took the hint. For those that didn't, I helpfully added, 'This Means You'. Unfortunately, the latter group included my boss, who made me take the poster down on the grounds that it was 'offensive'.[68] 'Yes, but only if

---

68. One of the most disarmingly honest performers I worked with during that BBC period is Miriam Margolyes, who went on to star in the *Harry Potter* movies. Whereas most actors would sidle into the office and request you not to 'forget' them in your next production, Miriam

you're a time wasting moron,' I wanted to say, but of course didn't.

Which was all fine and dandy when addressing those less senior; when I was in a room with the other bosses (there are enough bosses in BBC Radio to fill a large suburb), keeping it straightforward just didn't work. I don't recall anyone actually saying we should lie to our staff, or that we should try to blind them with science—but having volunteered my sixpen'orth in the Tuesday morning management meeting I'd regularly get *that look* which expressed something like 'Who do you think you are? Fucking Candide?' (these were drama producers, after all). Which relegated my contribution to the level of 'Oh, why can't we all just be nice to each other?', or something equally nauseous and footling. Because simplicity is regularly confused with being simple-minded or credulous; as is innocence itself—which is what I'm going to try and put right in this essay. Oh yes. We're going to try and demolish Alfred North Whitehead's dictum that instructs us to 'Seek simplicity and distrust it."

But I found myself in excellent company. I remember when the UK's most popular TV cook Delia Smith received a critical mauling from certain harridans in the Fourth Estate for daring to instruct her audience how to boil an egg. 'Patronizing cow! Everyone knows that!', they collectively screeched.

But the harpies had to eat their words when sackfuls of appreciative letters arrived thanking Delia for having the balls to start with the simple things. Turns out that boiling an egg is one of those things your parents ought to tell you how to do but often don't. Because they probably didn't want to reveal that *they* didn't know something that should have been passed on to

---

would stand (all 4 feet 9 of her) in the middle of the main corridor and bellow, 'Have any of you arseholes got some work for a fat old dyke?'

them with their mother's milk. I mean, how many grannies do you know that can *actually* suck an egg? The public's response was doubly satisfying to me because most of the journalists I know couldn't find their own arse without a map—let alone prepare the perfect soft-boiled egg. Or, in some cases, breathe unaided.

And this is not an isolated example: I don't know what it's like in other countries, but here in the UK there seems to be a whole range of basic stuff we need to know in order to lead our lives as citizens that we're never taught. And I don't just mean sex. It's like this information is supposed to ooze into us by some mystical form of osmosis. And if it hasn't, too bad.

Back in 1987, it took my brother-in-law Pete to explain in words of one syllable the implications of the mortgage I'd just taken out. He managed that in the time it took to collect a Chinese takeaway, and suddenly he made it all seem so simple. Which all the literature I had read and the mortgage broker who sold it to me had singularly failed to do, no doubt deliberately. During that period in the mid-1980s, it's been estimated that 60% of endowment mortgages in the UK were mis-sold to people who had no idea about the nature of the agreements they were entering into—me being one of them. It's all a bit like the Emperor's New Clothes; 'surely', we must reason with ourselves in a particularly dysfunctional area of our brains, 'it's better to be thousands out of pocket than look stupid for a few minutes in front of an oily git in a cheap suit by asking him bovine questions about projected redemption values in 25 years' time.'

I mean, what was I afraid of? Probably *that look*. No, my opening question should have been: 'What's a mortgage?', and worked from there. So cheers, Pete. Not only did you save me a ton of money, you taught me that if in doubt, it's always worth playing the stupid card. As my friends and colleagues will testify, I now do it all the time. Very convincingly.

But since when did simplicity start getting a bad press? At what point was simplicity identified with being credulous? That's the next thing I needed to research. After all, Jesus was pretty much into it. Here's the relevant bit from Matthew 18:

> *At the same time came the disciples unto Jesus, saying, Who*
> *is the greatest in the kingdom of heaven?*
> *And Jesus called a little child unto him, and set him in the midst*
> *of them,*
> *And said, Verily I say unto you, Except ye be converted, and*
> *become as little children, ye shall not enter into the kingdom*
> *of heaven.*
> *Whosoever therefore shall humble himself as this little child,*
> *the same is greatest in the kingdom of heaven.*
> *And whoso shall receive one such little child in my name*
> *receiveth me.*

So you've got to be simple and accepting as a child when you have faith, and God'll see you right. Montaigne himself refers to this passage in his letter to Monsieur de Mesmes, Councillor to the King of France, in a prefatory note to the *Essays,* wholeheartedly concurring with its sentiments.

But then the Skeptic in him might say, not so in real life: if you behave with the simplicity and innocence of a child when you're in the bank, the oily guy in the cheap suit will win, and sell you an inappropriate product which will not suit your needs, leaving you in the gutter with the neighbourhood dogs licking at your sores. In this life you've *got* to be distrustful, or you might as well have RUBE tattooed on your forehead in mile-high day-glo letters. In fact it is the mark of an educated man that he resembles Thomas the Doubter and not Thomas the Sucker.

This doesn't imply that God's stock was necessarily falling during the Renaissance, but it's fair to say that man's was rising, bringing a greater emphasis on the life we all live rather than the ideal existence that awaits us after death. Which in turn brought with it a greater appreciation of how men are rather than the way they should be. And how children are too. Montaigne was under no illusions about the little ones' potential for duplicity: in *Of Liars* (Book 1, Chapter 9) he recommends that if children are caught fibbing, they should have it 'severely whipped out of them' before they find themselves managing hedge funds.

But how do you equate this fallen world where children tell fibs with the existence of God? Well, you could subscribe to the ideas most famously expressed in Gottfried Leibniz's theory of optimism which states that if God is perfect (which is a given), he would be incapable of creating anything but a perfect world. So the world we live in is as perfect a world as it is possible to create. With all its imperfections. At the root of Leibniz's philosophy is the belief that man is ultimately perfectible, so he can cultivate that pre-lapsarian state of childhood innocence and acceptance through the good offices of his reason—and through education. Which makes him a philosopher firmly rooted in ideas that were common currency throughout the Age of Enlightenment. Nobody's managed to give convincing dates that bookend this period of intellectual thought, but it roughly stretches from the mid 17th-century to the 1790s, when the lofty ideals of the French Revolution almost instantly degenerated into the bloodbath of *La Terreur.*

However, not everyone was sold on this kind of enlightened thinking, and the satirists' knives were soon unsheathed. In 1669, the wonderfully-named Hans Jakob Christoffel von Grimmelshausen published *Simplicius Simplicissimus*, a picaresque novel whose protagonist is characterized by his credulity and simplicity. In 1726 came *Gulliver's Travels*, in which

Swift's hero is a gullible (see what he did there?)[69] individual who learns about the harshness of life and ends up a recluse who prefers the company of horses to humans. And then of course there's the best of them all, *Candide*, in which Voltaire shows himself far from gruntled with the idealism of Candide's tutor Pangloss, whose Liebnizian optimism is so ingrained, he can justify the existence of syphilis by claiming that it indirectly led to the discovery of chocolate and cochineal.

And so we see a cluster of associated ideas forming around simplicity—it's good, because it connects us with the concept of man living up to his billing as a divine creation; and bad, because man just isn't like that. So to believe in simplicity or innocence would be great if only we could—hence to do so is to be credulous and sentimental.[70] And then there's the children thing—those convenient metaphors for what we could be if only we could divest ourselves of our worldliness and venal instincts.

It's no coincidence that the Age of Enlightenment witnessed an explosion in pedagogy, with loads of heavy-hitters weighing into the discussion about the relationship between children and the adults they grow into. John Locke published *Some Thoughts Concerning Education* in 1693, in which he implied that children are not of themselves innocent or simple; but they are *tabulae rasae* on which we must ensure the correct things are written. So as adults, instead of trying to connect with our inner child to regain our goodness, we must make sure that goodness is taught from an early age so we won't have to wistfully look back to a time before the world corrupted us. Because by then it will be too late to do anything about it.

---

69. The brilliant American short story writer Ring Lardner published a volume entitled *Gullible's Travels* in 1917.

70. It's probably coincidental, but the maiden name of Liebniz's mother was Schmuck—which lent added credibility to his opponents' argument that he came from a long line of schmucks.

But not all the Enlightened hankered after a world governed purely by reason: and here we come to that wonderful bridge between the Enlightenment and Romantic eras, Jean-Jacques Rousseau. His utopian novel *Émile où de l'Éducation* which appeared in 1762 really set the cat among the pigeons: it was ridiculous, he thought, to try and work up a program to educate children—no National Curriculum for young Émile. Instead, Rousseau creates a Panglossian tutor named Jean-Jacques (!) who illustrates the argument that a child is not necessarily good because it has been brought up by lovely, sympathetic parents who wrote all the right things on his *tabula rasa*: no, Émile (who is an orphan anyway), is good because he is *part of nature.* So education and the acquisition of culture can only spoil this natural spirit. Jean-Jacques bans all books (with the telling exception of *Robinson Crusoe*), because children should learn from real-life encounters, also insisting that Émile is reared in the country, where he can be free from the taint of urban sophistication and not be led into temptation.

So simplicity was back—big time. It's OK to be natural—you're not a Rube, you're a child of nature. Your simplicity is an asset, not a handicap.

But then certain parents started putting Rousseau's theories into practice.

Perhaps the best known of these experiments was conducted by Richard Lovell Edgeworth, who certainly had plenty of children to choose from, having fathered 22 little Edgeworths, including the future Gothic novelist Maria. And he invented the caterpillar track—so he was no slouch.

Anyway, Edgeworth decided to conduct 'a fair trial of Rousseau's system' on his son Dick, with, shall we say, mixed results. Dick showed promise early on, and his proud father even took him to visit Rousseau who he thought might be interested in the child's progress. Basically the great man thought the kid to be a cocky little bastard, who quickly alienated almost everyone he met. Edgeworth then sent Dick to join the Navy where, he hoped, some sense would be hammered into him. But then Dick deserted, and ended up in America, which at least had the benefit of being 3,000 miles away. So not a resounding success, then. Nonetheless, there are some fairly obvious parallels between Émile and certain modern 'progressive' systems of education—so if you're like many of the parents here in West London who long to send junior to a Montessori academy, you might want to give Rousseau a read first.

To be fair to Rousseau, he claimed that *Émile* was never intended to be a 'How To' book; rather, it was a set of general principles for reforming education so that it stood a better chance of moulding useful citizens, not precocious irritating brats with a marked absence of social graces.[71] But the Romantics took what they wanted from Rousseau and discarded the rest, leaving the poor guy to be credited with inventing the Noble Savage (which he didn't), and being a cheerleader for Primitivism (which he wasn't).

Until the 17th-century, all things primitive were, in the main, more to be scorned than embraced; after all, according to Thomas Hobbes, life in a state of nature could only be 'solitary, poor, nasty, brutish, and short', as indeed it is today in the eastern suburbs of Glasgow (average male life expectancy 53.9 years). Dickens held similar views about so-called 'natural philosophy':

To come to the point at once, I beg to say that I have not the least belief in the Noble Savage. I consider him a prodigious nuisance and an enormous superstition...I don't care what he calls me. I call him a savage, and I call a savage a something highly desirable to be civilized

---

71. Hello—we're back in West London again.

off the face of the earth...

But in the poetry of Wordsworth, for instance, 'primitives' such as the Leech Gatherer, The Old Cumberland Beggar and The Idiot Boy are promoted to the status of philosophers. In his Preface to the *Lyrical Ballads* (1798), Wordsworth sums up his fascination with this seemingly unpromising subject matter:

Humble and rustic life was generally chosen, because, in that condition, the essential passions of the heart find a better soil in which they can attain their maturity, are less under restraint, and speak a plainer and more emphatic language; because in that condition of life our elementary feelings coexist in a state of greater simplicity, and, consequently, may be more accurately contemplated, and more forcibly communicated; because the manners of rural life germinate from those elementary feelings, and, from the necessary character of rural occupations, are more easily comprehended, and are more durable; and, lastly, because in that condition the passions of men are incorporated with the beautiful and permanent forms of nature.

'Essential', 'plainer', 'elementary', 'simplicity'—all speak of Wordsworth's belief that pure unadorned nature could teach mankind more about who he is—and should be—than any formal program of learning. Meeting one of these 'natural men' is like having an instant brain detox, purging all the pollution civilization has put in there.

The poet's encounter with the Leech Gatherer (from the poem *Resolution and Independence*) beautifully, and to a large extent unintentionally, illustrates the difference between the worlds of innocence and sophistication. Wordsworth, the Cambridge-educated mathematician-turned poet, finally plucks up the courage to speak to this adamantine figure wandering among the hills: in an approach worthy of British Royalty, he asks: 'How is it that you live, and what is it you do?' The Leech Gatherer burbles on for a couple of lines or so about how leech gathering's not what it was—but Wordsworth's already in a reverie and has stopped listening. Then it hits him—there's a moral to be drawn from this encounter: when he's out of sorts, he'll think about this poor old bugger and he won't feel so bad: fine, but he manages to express this resolution in one of the most bathetic couplets in the whole of poetry:

> *'God,' said I, 'be my help and stay secure;*
> *I'll think of the Leech-gatherer on the lonely moor!'*[72]

And of course, being intellectually attracted to the primitive, it wasn't going to be long before children intruded. 'The child is father of the man', Wordsworth announced in 1802[73] after he had written the first draft of his finest poem *The Prelude*, which, at considerable length, chronicled his own early years. Focussing on a writer's formative period would have been almost unthinkable for a poet even a few decades previously: childhood was to be glossed over in a few sentences as a period of abject ignorance and pant-wetting. Who'd want to draw attention to that? Way too embarrassing. Rather begin the autobiography at a more seemly age, when manhood and majority had been attained and all that mewling and puking was for the most part over.

And there's so much more we could look at, but regretfully haven't the space, so I suppose it's time for some conclusions after all these ramblings.

I remain very ambivalent about where I stand between simplicity

---

72. One of my favourite bathetic Wordsworth couplets occurs in *The Thorn,* in which Wordsworth the poet gives way to Wordsworth the statistician. He sees a small pool amid the hills, noting: 'I've measured it from side to side/'Tis three feet long, and two feet wide.'

73. As did Blood, Sweat and Tears in 1968 with the title of their dreadful debut album

and sophistication. I think Wordsworth is an amazing, ground-breaking poet, but for me at least, he demonstrates that the chasm between these two ways of appreciating the world is almost unbridgeable. Once you've lived with the curse of sophistication, can you ever regain your childhood simplicity, even assuming it ever existed? It reminds me of some lovely friends of mine who bought a holiday home in the countryside, so they could reconnect with 'the simple things in life' and get closer to nature. As we sat on their veranda, gazing at the sunset, they realized we'd run out of champagne—then cursed that they weren't in London where the champagne shop doesn't shut at 5pm, and there's fresh antipasti available 24/7.

But I still have this gut feeling that simplicity and all its synonyms we've flitted between need not argue a lack of sophistication, an incomplete understanding of the world, sentimentalism, ignorance, naivety or any of the reactions that provoke *that look*. After all, what are the alternatives? A society that grows ever more hard, mistrustful, superficial and needlessly complex because it can't (or won't) address the fundamental principles on which it is constructed because it has a deep-seated fear that it's over-simplifying things.

So I'll come clean. I'd rather:

- approach the world with the freshness and energy of a child, and not the weary familiarity of a *fin de siècle* sophisticate;

- accept more than reject;

- learn to be more trusting and less suspicious;

- admit ignorance and not feign knowledge;

- be more a *tabula rasa* than a smartarse;

- believe there's much to be gained from a stiff dose

of wide-eyed innocence;

- be just as happy with a Delia boiled egg as lobster.

All of which, you might say, leaves me looking like a twit—or, even worse, a HIPPY.

But I'm really not—and by way of proof, I genuinely don't think that *Woodstock* was the pinnacle of Western civilization. I just happen to think sophistication, call it what you will, is limiting. That's all.

But then again, so did Montaigne's dad, who sent his son, at a very early age, to be raised in his local village among the peasantry, probably for the very same reasons we encounter in Wordsworth and Rousseau.[74] But unlike the Edgeworth experiment, here's your proof that it actually worked, taken from Montaigne's late essay, 'On Experience':

As if it were more to the purpose to borrow our proofs from the shops of Vascosan or Plantin, than from what is to be seen in our own village; or else, indeed, that we have not the wit to cull out and make useful what we see before us, and to judge of it clearly enough to draw it into example: for if we say that we want authority to give faith to our testimony, we speak from the purpose; forasmuch as, in my opinion, of the most ordinary, common, and known things, could we but find out their light, the greatest miracles of nature might be formed, and the most wonderful examples, especially upon the subject of human actions.

So, says Montaigne, philosophy can (and he implies, should) arise from the 'most ordinary, common and known things'. But the great thing about this essay is that it doesn't make fatuous recommendations about getting down and dirty with the peasantry: Montaigne is all too aware of the yawning social divide separating himself, his servants and the locals. But its

---

74. And, of course, predating both of them by a couple of centuries.

existence is not the occasion for snobbery, cruelty or, indeed, some well-meaning yet misguided Romantic attempt to establish a level playing field between them. Instead, he riffs on ideas of change, variation and flexibility, concluding that it is our duty to accustom ourselves and our minds to 'every variety and inequality of life,' while never losing sight of what unites us. Remember, he says, everybody defecates (or 'goes to stool' as Cotton translates it). Even kings, philosophers and ladies.[75]

So really, although this essay began by examining questions of simplicity, it will end with ideas of comprehensiveness. Of not letting prior considerations, or things that have been bred into us get in the way of how we look at things. Which, I think, is what my own list is mainly about.

And of course, as my friends continually remind me, I dismally fail to incorporate these considerations into my daily life, and I have to admit they're right. In those situations, I try to reconnect with my inner Candide by recalling a passage from William Faulkner's 1958 novel, *The Town*. It's a bit on the Delphic side, so I'm still not 100% sure what it means, but I think it fits what I've been saying. It describes a young woman who seems utterly immune to anything the world can throw at her. The trap would be to think that she's hard, cynical and loveless. Yet the reverse is the case. Her friend and mentor Gavin Stevens attempts to analyse the quality she radiates, which, for want of any better word, he terms 'innocence':

Innocence is innocent not because it rejects but because it accepts; is innocent not because it is impervious and invulnerable to everything, but because it is capable of accepting anything and still remaining innocent; innocent because it foreknows all and therefore doesn't have to fear and be afraid...

---

75. A rare example of Montaigne being ungallant, proving that a Yorkshireman, who will spare no-one's blushes, lurks in all of us.

To me, this sounds mighty like a passage from Montaigne's essay 'On the Art of Conference', in which he professes to:

...enter into discussion and argument with great freedom and ease. No propositions astonish me, no belief offends me, whatever contrast it offers to my own. There is no fancy so frivolous and so extravagant that it does not seem to me quite suitable to the production of the human mind... The contradictions of judgments, then, neither offend nor alter, they only rouse and exercise me.

True simplicity is hard won. To arrive at the state of mind described by Montaigne is bloody difficult, and all kinds of trivial occurrences can throw it off-kilter, as he readily admits. It's a constant struggle not to fall prey to baser considerations that threaten the mind's equanimity, 'liberty' and 'independence'. So to this reader, Montaigne's habitual acceptance seems less instinctive, and more philosophical in origin; I'd be prepared to bet that such a simple conclusion was hard-fought and taxed his powers of reason to their limit. Which leaves me with the intriguing yet ironic proposition that his simplicity may not have been possible without his philosophical sophistication. The frustrating thing is that I'll never know for certain—but I think of all Montaigne's pronouncements, it's certainly the one which offers the key to practically everything he wrote.

And for the rest of us? Well, the path of acceptance isn't a bad one to tread. And if people look at you funny, so what?

Chapter Twenty

The Great Fatsby

'I love to have all meats, that will endure it, very little boiled or roasted, and prefer them very high, and even, as to several, quite gone. Nothing but hardness generally offends me... not for want of teeth, which I ever had good, even to excellence, and which age does not now begin to threaten; I have always been used every morning to rub them with a napkin, and before and after dinner.' (**Book 3, Chapter 13: 'Of Experience'**)

Montaigne was quite the trencherman. So it's just as well he was blessed with a good set of teeth to help him get outside a whole range of dishes and ingredients he mentions throughout the *Essays*. Although in later life his gastric problems limited his intake of food and drink, he could nevertheless still appreciate a chef's talent. During his travels in France, Switzerland and Germany, as chronicled in his travel journal, there are plentiful descriptions of the local provender. In fact, at one stage (at Lindau in Bavaria), he regrets his omission to bring his own chef along, as he could then reproduce his favourite dishes on his return home.

At his hotel, 'The Crown', he found 'a vast abundance of provisions...in the matter of soups, sauces and salads, that nothing in our own way of living can be found to equal it.' He dined off quince, apple and cabbage soup, followed by trout livers and a variety of excellent game, which was among the tenderest he had ever eaten, and accompanied with bread containing both fennel and cumin. The wine was good too, although they refused to serve it with water, as was his taste. Dinner was a long drawn-out affair, eaten in a leisurely and convivial atmosphere. And it wasn't too expensive either. Result.

In Augsberg, he was served crayfish 'of a wonderful size', pasties 'large and small' accompanied by 'sweetmeats and boxes of confectionery'. At Kolmann, in the Austrian Tyrol, he consumed eggs poached in butter. But on reaching Italy, his appetite seems to fail him, on account of his stomach problems (which are described in some detail and not for the squeamish).

In gastronomy, as in all things, Montaigne is a creature not just of moderation, but of plainness and honesty, which is perhaps why he's such a fan of German cuisine. He appreciates quality ingredients served with the minimum of fuss. As a child, he tells us, he was never in thrall to a sweet tooth, and he does not approve of 'pampering [the] palate':

There are some who affect temperance and plainness by wishing for beef and ham amongst the partridges; 'tis all very fine; this is the delicacy of the delicate; 'tis the taste of an effeminate fortune that disrelishes ordinary and accustomed things.

'Per qux luxuria divitiarum taedio ludit.' [*'By which the luxury of wealth causes tedium.'—Seneca, Epistulae., 18.*]

Not to make good cheer with what another is enjoying, and to be curious in what a man eats, is the essence of this vice:

'Si modica coenare times olus omne patella.' [*'If you can't be content with herbs in a small dish for supper.'—Horace, Epistulae., i. 5, 2.*]

So—not too much in the way of fancy food, and don't be picky. In fact, anyone who professes to being indifferent to food is just plain weird.

There are some nations that will not be seen to eat. I know a lady, and of the best quality, who has the same opinion, that chewing disfigures the face, and takes away much from the ladies' grace and beauty; and therefore unwillingly appears at a public table with an appetite; and I know a man also, who cannot endure to see another eat, nor himself to be seen eating, and who is more shy of company when putting in than when putting out...

I doubt Montaigne ever deliberately tried to lose weight by dieting or exercise, and quite what he would make of the religion that is modern gastronautical eating I can only shudder to think. Being a philosopher, he might have been amused about what happened to me the other night...

So there I was, unaccustomedly dining in one of London's posher eateries when the waiter comes up and demands, 'Are you familiar with the *philosophy* of our restaurant?' To be fair, I had primed myself by looking at the eatery's website, and I was fully expecting them to pull something like this. For a start, it was so flash their web page took ages to load; its design was so minimal I couldn't find the information I wanted; and when I finally arrived at the 'ambience' page, it described itself as a 'high energy' venue, set in a 'spectacularly colonnaded space', featuring a 'fusion menu' run by a 'world-renowned' chef who would not so much deliver a meal as an 'experience'. And as I wasn't paying, and therefore happily ignorant of the potentially high price tag that would inevitably accompany such flummery, I invited our waiter to continue. He explained that all dishes were served in 'sharing' portions, so that diners could, well, share them and promote harmony and togetherness around the table. Reading between the lines, my companion and I speculated this meant we should expect something a) big and b) expensive. Well, we got it half right.

Given that he was probably an unemployed actor living off tips, we were gentle with our waiter and said no more, all the while pondering how such a simple process as going to a restaurant, ordering food, eating it, paying and then leaving had managed to crawl so far up its own arse. Earlier that same evening while getting ready, I had witnessed a TV chef describe cooking a meal as a 'journey' like it was some kind of shining path to enlightenment. And what lay at the end of this Ninja-esque quest for the truth? Meatballs.

When I was presenting my weekly foodie programme on the radio, I decided to drop the series after the first season because it turned out that my guests, who included chefs, journalists, restauranteurs, food critics, farmers and retailers were all saying, at base, the same thing. Their 'philosophy' of food could distilled as follows: get the freshest, best quality ingredients you can afford; cook them; don't get too fancy; if you're worried about sustainability, buy local stuff. Errrr...that's it. So simple, in fact, it got rather repetitive. As did the message to those running a catering business: serve good food; at reasonable prices; in a pleasant atmosphere. The End.

Occasionally we'd discuss what Montaigne was hinting at by the inclusion of those earlier classical quotes—the artificial 'hierarchy' of flavours which has developed over the years, mostly influenced by fashion and the laws of supply and demand. Is lobster any tastier because you've paid a hell of a lot for it or because film stars eat it? Course not. Is it more delicious than cod? Not unless you don't like the taste of cod in the first place. So what *does* make food taste bad? Poor quality ingredients; too much buggering about, either by the supplier or the chef; you're in a bad mood; or, like poor old

Montaigne scattering kidney stones round every spa town in central Europe, you have a debilitating illness.

And that was kind of it. No more to say. End of series. And the end of this essay.

Chapter Twenty One

Acts of Sordid Frightfulness

'Non pudeat dicere, quod non pudet sentire.'

'Let us not be ashamed to speak what we are not ashamed to think.' **(Plato, quoted in Book 3, Essay 5: 'Upon Some Verses of Vergil')**

Montaigne is the poet *par excellence* of the ageing process: get a load of this extract from the late essay 'Upon Some Verses of Vergil':

I was formerly wont to mark cloudy and gloomy days as extraordinary; these are now my ordinary days; the extraordinary are the clear and bright; I am ready to leap for joy, as for an unwonted favour, when nothing happens to me. Let me tickle myself, I cannot force a poor smile from this wretched body of mine; I am only merry in conceit and in dreaming, by artifice to divert the melancholy of age; but, in faith, it requires another remedy than a dream. A weak contest of art against nature. 'Tis great folly to lengthen and anticipate human incommodities, as every one does; I had rather be a less while old than be old before I am really so.' I seize on even the least occasions of pleasure I can meet.

And one of those pleasures was reminiscing about sex. 'Verses of Vergil' be damned, this essay's focus is men and women, seasoned by a fair amount of late flowering lust. And it's a whopper—25,000 words give or take a few. That's about one third of the projected length of the book you're now reading—and a mighty big twinkle he's got in his rheumy old eye.

I'm going to treat you to some plain talking on a subject, he writes, that's often clouded by euphemism, allusion, circumlocution—all the rhetorical tricks that help us avoid saying what we mean. But I'm going to give it to you straight. If you're guilty of a vice, why not fess up, so you don't make a prostitute of your honesty? And ladies can read this too, at the risk of courting their blushes:

I am vexed that my Essays only serve the ladies for a common piece of furniture, and a piece for the hall; this chapter will make me part of the water-closet.

So if you're easily embarrassed, girls, keep a copy in the toilet. We're delving beneath the table here, he writes, because someone's got to say what we're all thinking. And who better than I, a man who is about to renounce sex forever? This is my last waltz with Venus, so what have I got to lose? No one could take offence at the ramblings of a wizened old geezer who writes cheques in his mind that his body can't cash.

Montaigne was (worryingly) about my age when he wrote this, and sex wasn't the distant memory he makes it out to be. So his technique wouldn't be as rusty as he implies, and in all fairness, despite frequent assertions that he's an unreconstructed MCP, he doesn't make a bad job of being an agony uncle. Many, but by no means all, of his views are bang up-to-date, particularly those on sexual hypocrisy, indicating that he was either ahead of his time, or the *ars amatoria* hasn't changed that much in 500 years.

What I'm going to offer here is a rapid précis of Montaigne's essay which I've taken the liberty of radically re-organizing, as it rambles all over the place—at one point, he even includes a lengthy excursion slagging off modern poets. By its close, we can compare whether we are truly living in a liberated era… or just think we are; and whether we're any more obsessed with sex than our Renaissance forebears. Ladies and gentlemen, place your bets please…

Montaigne begins, conventionally enough, by contrasting sex and marriage, and it's here that Cotton's English translation, first published in 1685-86, unwittingly amuses the modern reader in its adherence to the strict rules of propriety.[76]

A man, says Aristotle, must approach his wife with prudence and temperance, lest in dealing too lasciviously with her, the extreme pleasure make her exceed the bounds of reason.

Is Aristotle concerned for the wife's psychological well-being, or is he worried on her behalf that the neighbours might hear? Difficult to tell, although it's probably the former: since classical times, it had been a recurring theme in philosophy that compared to men, women were utterly unreasonable. They couldn't think straight, couldn't apply themselves, and lacked the necessary calm and patience to consider any question dispassionately. Elsewhere in the *Essays,* Montaigne shares the opinion that being the playthings of emotion, it doesn't do to excite women too much, or there's no knowing what they'll do. In examining his relations with Étienne de la Boetie[77] in the earlier essay 'On Friendship' (Book 1, Chapter 27), he once again apes his classical forbears when he notes that a perfect friendship is only possible between men:

---

76. There will be many more examples dotted about the essay.

77. A man.

We are not here to bring the love we bear to women, though it be an act of our own choice, into comparison, nor rank it with the others. The fire of this, I confess, is more active, more eager, and more sharp: but withal, 'tis more precipitant, fickle, moving, and inconstant; a fever subject to intermissions and paroxysms, that has seized but on one part of us. Whereas in friendship, 'tis a general and universal fire, but temperate and equal, a constant established heat, all gentle and smooth, without poignancy or roughness. Moreover, in love, 'tis no other than frantic desire for that which flies from us: so soon as it enters unto the terms of friendship, that is to say, into a concurrence of desires, it vanishes and is gone, fruition destroys it, as having only a fleshly end, and such a one as is subject to satiety.

So women make you love them, but then your libido gets in the way and you end up losing *your* reason too, which is a high price to pay for a bit of slap and tickle. Or indeed a lot of same, because women can be sex mad. Take that 'Queen of Arragon' who claimed that a modest strike rate was six times a night, and compare her figure with the Greek statesman and poet Solon, for whom three times a *month* was sufficient. If a month has 30 days, the Queen would have sex 177 more times than the philosopher. Another philosopher, Polemon, was sued by his own wife for 'sowing barren seed in a fertile land'. So watch out for them womens—they're somewhat incompatible with philosophy.

However, before we return to the Vergil essay, it's important to note that nowhere in the above quote does Montaigne exclusively blame women for inciting this rather sweaty and unpleasant kind of love, as a medieval misogynist might have done. Rather, it may be 'an act of our own choice'. Men are not exclusively the innocent dupes of women's raving fleshly lusts; chances are they are led to bed by that 'one part' that robs the philosopher of his reasoned *sangfroid*. There's a lot of philosophers who've written about sex, and not just hypothetically, so they must have got their experience *somewhere*. They're not all cerebral eggheads who enjoy a distant, suspicious and ultimately scornful relationship with their genitals (or as Horace puts it in his *Epodes,* 'There are writings of the Stoics we find lying on silken cushions').

Montaigne takes great delight in listing them: Zeno, Strato (who wrote a book entitled 'Of Carnal Conjunction'), Theophrastus, Aristippus, Plato, Heraclides, Antisthenes, Aristo, Cleanthes, Sphaereus (whoever he is) and Chrysippus. And I haven't even *started* on the Epicureans yet, he says. All of which indicates that Montaigne was familiar with what passed for pornography in the classical era, and was aware of the deep hypocrisy which often lay at the heart of its dealings with sex. Then he cites a further reason why passionate sex isn't a great idea: apparently 'the seed' gets too hot, and it lowers the chances of conception. Montaigne helpfully passes on the latest medical opinion on sex and fertility which goes as follows: 'Take your time and leave good long gaps between sessions.'

But if you want to have kids, you should really be married, which is only possible once you've got over the concupiscent bit. For marriage consists of 'solid services' and 'mutual obligations', not mind-blowing sex. But although marriage can be 'the best of all human societies', it doesn't always get a good press; in fact, it resembles a cage—if you're outside you want to get in, if you're inside you want to get out. Or it's like Paris— great to visit but you wouldn't want to live there. It's OK for thick 'plebeian' people, Montaigne notes, but for those of us with restless minds it's a bit, well, *constraining. I* didn't want to marry, he says, I was persuaded into it by what Cotton translates as 'extrinsic occasions'—or what we might call his father twisting his arm. And 'as great a libertine as I am taken to be,' he confesses, he's been a faithful-ish husband.

And it's true; up to the age of 33, when he married Françoise de la Cassaigne, Montaigne had been a bit of a Jack the Lad.

After his best mate Étienne de la Boetie had died two years previously from dysentery, he screwed around a fair bit, some say to fill the hole left by his friend. This is perhaps why his father chose to intervene. By this point Montaigne *fils* had been a Bordeaux councillor for almost eight years, and his sexual licence may well have been remarked on by those to whom he owed his advancement. So Dad proposed he form an alliance with the daughter of one of his older colleagues.

So what sort of relationship did Monsieur et Madame Montaigne enjoy?

A glimpse is afforded us by a letter Montaigne addressed to his wife in the summer of 1570, following the death of the couple's first child, a two year-old daughter, who was apparently 'long looked for'. We'll examine it in greater depth in the following essay, but for my immediate purposes I need only quote the first few lines:

You understand well that it is not proper for a man of the world, according to the rules of this our time, to continue to court and caress you; for they say that a sensible person may take a wife indeed, but that to espouse her is to act like a fool. Let them talk; I adhere for my part the custom of the good old days… Let us live, my wife, you and I, in the old French method.

Two things here: he now realizes that if he's going to play by the rules, he needs to moderate his behaviour; and that his fellow 'men of the world' claim that you're an idiot if you love your wife. To hell with the rules, he says, I'll court and caress you as much as I please. And this he calls, 'the old French method'. What can he mean? A slap on the behind or a furtive snog while she's kneading the dough? Or making like Sacha Distel or Charles Aznavour? The frilly shirt, the single rose, the bargain weekend in a mid-range Bordeaux hotel, the steak frites, a bottle of cheeky red and an early night in satin sheets?

Who knows? I hope he treated his wife well…although sometimes I have my doubts…

Particularly when he says things like, 'Don't marry your mistress. Why shit in a basket and put it on your head?' No, really, he does.

But he immediately redeems himself, at least partially, by noting that marriage is bound to have its difficulties. There will be rows and disagreements which need to be worked through. But this will increase respect for one's partner—and besides, marriage without 'darts and fire' is no marriage at all. Incidentally, he got all this from Socrates, whose wife Xanthippe was an intolerable scold and a lousy cook (at least according to Xenophon). Rumour has it she poisoned him—and not with her food. But then Socrates, ever hungry for experience, noted of the 'blonde horse' (for so Xanthippe's name translates);

It is the example of the rider who wishes to become an expert horseman: 'None of your soft-mouthed, docile animals for me,' he says; 'the horse for me to own must show some spirit' in the belief, no doubt, if he can manage such an animal, it will be easy enough to deal with every other horse besides. And that is just my case. I wish to deal with human beings, to associate with man in general; hence my choice of wife. I know full well, if I can tolerate her spirit, I can with ease attach myself to every human being else.

Yikes. Well, if being a philosopher means your life is lived in some kind of social laboratory, then I suppose he had to do it in the interests of science. In accounts other than Xenophon's, however, Xanthippe is portrayed as a devoted wife and mother. So let's re-introduce some balance here. And to be fair to Montaigne, from this point in the essay he is almost scrupulously fair in doling out the sauce for both the gander *and* the goose.

For wives, says Montaigne, are marvellous creatures who often far exceed men in all points of behaviour and understanding. Much later in the essay, he notes that the calumnies heaped upon wives are usually born out of their husbands' inner demons and insecurities.

Take chastity, for example. Most men are happy to screw around, but would rather their wife was a murderer than an adultress. Ridiculous, he says, utter prejudice. It takes two to tango after all. Women lose their maidenheads not simply because they're randy—it's because they're assailed on all sides by horny men. Indeed:

I hold it more easy to carry a suit of armour[78] all the days of one's life than a maidenhead; and the vow of virginity of all others is the most noble, as being the hardest to keep. We have, doubtless, resigned to the ladies the most difficult and most vigorous of all human endeavours, and let us resign to them the glory too. This ought to encourage them to be obstinate in it; 'tis a brave thing for them to defy us, and to spurn under foot that vain pre-eminence of valour and virtue that we pretend to have over them; they will find if they do but observe it, that they will not only be much more esteemed for it, but also much more beloved.

And then, with a nod and wink to the lads, he remarks: 'Such an one may grant more, who does not grant so much.' Know what I mean, squire? Eh? But then taking the women's side once more, he notes that they often pay a high price for what men account so little.

And anyway, why *shouldn't* women enjoy sex and feel free to be honest about it? Men are always boasting of their conquests, so why not women too? In fact, says Montaigne, custom and

---

78. Back in translator Cotton's day, a 'suit of armour' was slang for a condom. Boswell uses the term frequently in his *London Journal* when discussing his bunk-ups with serving girls.

morality have decreed that women should be *over*-modest—that is if they feel they can discuss their sex lives at all. Which is nonsense; given that heterosexual coupling involves both a man and a woman, clearly women are having just as much sex as men. Montaigne distrusts women who are always claiming how chaste they are—unless, he says, they're 'an old toothless trot, or a young dry consumptive thing.'

He then begins to discuss (at great length) sexual jealousy—another vice to which men are highly susceptible. But not Montaigne. Because, he says, 'beasts feel it'. Especially goats. And Italians:

...their custom commonly imposes so rude and so slavish a law upon the women, that the most distant acquaintance with a stranger is as capital an offence as the most intimate; so that all approaches being rendered necessarily substantial.

Nothing's easier to instil than jealousy, nothing more difficult to cure, he rightly says, anticipating *Othello,* which Shakespeare wouldn't write for another twenty years. You can lock up your wife and surround her with guards, but who will guard the guards? And the more you guard against being a cuckold, the more your wife—and those men who are aware of your jealousy—will *want* to cuckold you. So the more you're jealous, the bigger the cuckold you'll probably turn out to be.

Valeria Messalina, the wife of the Roman emperor Claudius and perhaps (thanks to Suetonius and Robert Graves[79]), the

---

79. In their books *The Twelve Caesars* and *I, Claudius*—the latter a re-casting of the former. Juvenal also had a great deal to say about her in his *Satires:*

Then exhausted by men but unsatisfied, with soilèd cheeks, and begrimed with the smoke of lamps, she took back to the imperial pillow all the odours of the stews.

most notorious female serial adulterer in history, drove herself to insane acts of sexual athleticism to try and make her husband jealous. On one occasion, she even had a reluctant lover whipped into her bed. Still Claudius took no notice. Good move, says Montaigne; once she'd exhausted every possible means of rousing her husband's attention, she'd be chaste again. Only it didn't quite work out that way; Claudius suddenly snapped and had Messalina and many of her lovers put to death (including the reluctant one who had to be whipped. Which seems a trifle unfair). To which Montaigne adds that it's the quiet ones who have these explosive fits of temper, and to watch out for them.

On the whole though, men and women seem equally susceptible to jealousy. Bearing this in mind, and the tendency of both sexes to stray, he concludes:

He was, methinks, an understanding fellow who said, 'twas a happy marriage betwixt a blind wife and a deaf husband.

At one stage in the essay, we get one of those rare and delightful peeks into life *chez* Montaigne. His only daughter, he writes, is now of a marriageable age, (but only just), and has entered that transitional phase where the young woman is beginning to emerge. While reading aloud to her father, Montaigne *fille* encounters the word for 'beech tree' (*fouteau*), which sounds a lot like a widely-used expletive. Her governess stops her short before she can say it. Montaigne himself would have let it pass because, as he rightly says, twenty dockers couldn't better have impressed upon her how much of a social *faux pas* it would be to say the word in public. Which, of course, will make her want to say it all the more. But then, he says, you can't teach women much about swearing: why, only the other day in the village a group of young ladies was turning the air blue—so blue in fact, I can't repeat what they said for fear of offending my readers. To which one of Montaigne's editors has added a remark to the effect of 'Christ, it *must* have been bad.'

Even if you bring up your daughter in a strict regime, he says, it won't do any good; the world offers too many temptations. So he'll err on the side of lenience and generosity—and hope for the best.

But what sort of society will my daughter grow up in?, he asks next. Hopefully, not as sex-crazed as some of the places we now consider to be the cradles of Western civilization.

In Egypt and Rome, he notes, they worshipped the penis in elaborate public rituals—and what is it with the ridiculous codpieces we used to wear in France—and they *still* insist on wearing in Switzerland? Do they reflect the *actual* size of their contents, Montaigne ponders, his ever-alert lie detector twitching furiously. He hopes so. It's a big mistake to hide things like that. The Pope who ordered the genitals on all the statues in Rome to be gelded[80] was doing everyone a gross disfavour, because the imagination then steps in and distorts the often less-than-remarkable truth. Or the opposite—statues with small cocks 'give the ladies a cruel contempt of our natural furniture' (another magnificent euphemism from Mr Cotton). No, let's go around nude—at least it's honest, and there can be no misunderstandings. Nothing will then be thought un-remarkable, or considered a suitable subject for speculation.[81] Or arouse unnecessary lascivious thoughts. Which is not likely if anyone catches sight of the Montaigne jewels; by his own admission, his are 'shameful and pitiful'. And just to make sure we know he's telling the truth, he provides his readers with a little bit *too* much information (which of course I'm going to pass on):

---

80. A practice which continued into the 20th-century: on the front of the BBC's London HQ is a fantastic Eric Gill carving of Ariel, who had his bits sanded down for fear they would offend passers-by.

81. A theme Montaigne had already explored in an earlier essay, 'Of the Custom of Wearing Clothes' (Book 1, Chapter 35).

Nature should satisfy herself in having rendered this age miserable, without rendering it ridiculous too. I hate to see it, for one poor inch of pitiful vigour which comes upon it but thrice a week, to strut and set itself out with as much eagerness as if it could do mighty feats; a true flame of flax; and laugh to see it so boil and bubble and then in a moment so congealed and extinguished.

Oh dear. One thing Montaigne might have valued in our time is that small diamond-shaped blue tablet that raises the groinal Lazarus from the dead. At his advanced age (oh holy hell, yes it *is* the same as mine), he says that he tries the best he can with the vigour available to him, and tries never to feign more interest than he's capable of delivering. Although women often feign headaches and other reasons to excuse the failure of their libido, Montaigne gives of his best whenever he can. After all, he's a *gentleman.*

It's all a game, because when you look at it dispassionately, sex is simply an animalistic coupling that's highly overrated; the Gods must laugh when they see how much fuss we humans make about it. Particularly, he says, the French. No, let's be more modest, more discreet, like the Spanish and especially the Italians, those 'regents of lovemaking' (!). Let there be more teasing, more pleasure taken in the chase and not the conquest, or we shall remove all the mystery from sex and it won't be fun any more. If it's too available, we shall cease to value it. There's no need to brag about the number of notches on your bedpost, and as for rape… well, if you have sex with someone without their consent, you might as well be committing an act of necrophilia. For sex is about equal passion being given and received by both parties.

And now, in the latter stages of the essay, Montaigne begins to focus his full attention on equality and, yes, *real* love.

What *is* love after all? It's not just sex, and it's not just one person chasing another or being infatuated with them. You need two consenting independent adults who are also equal partners in the endeavour. Yes, Bono, two hearts may beat as one, and a good thing it is, but those two hearts belong to two distinct individuals, neither of whom is in thrall to the other. And there's no need of great sweaty deeds of sexual prowess to demonstrate that love either. Even Socrates, the philosopher's philosopher, could experience oceans of pleasure from a single tiny, seemingly insignificant, conjunction of flesh:

'Leaning,' said he, 'my shoulder to her shoulder, and my head to hers, as we were reading together in a book, I felt, without dissembling, a sudden sting in my shoulder like the biting of an insect, which I still felt above five days after, and a continual itching crept into my heart.' So that merely the accidental touch, and of a shoulder, heated and altered a soul cooled and ennerved by age, and the strictest liver[82] of all mankind.

So there's hope for us all. Montaigne accounts it an error on philosophy's part to make such a rigid distinction between the mind and the body.[83] For if, in old age, you wish to feel truly fulfilled, you need to call every one of your remaining resources into battle. But don't, whatever you do, have surgical procedures to try and make yourself look younger than you are. That is the saddest thing of all. Follow instead the advice of Marguerite Queen of Navarre: at the age of thirty, you should 'convert the title of fair into that of good' and stop being worried by that kind of thing.

And then, as the essay nears its end, our lad makes a brief and uncharacteristic excursion into self pity. Love, real love, would brighten up my old age no end, he says, but that can never

---

82. i.e. one who lives, *not* the organ.

83. My other favourite Morrissey lyric: 'Does the body rule the mind/ Or the mind rule the body??… I dunno.'

be, for 'we ask most when we bring least'. Young women (and men) may sport like hares on the mountain, but he can never join them again. Lookee no touchee, old feller. 'The old hook will not stick in such soft cheese'.[84] And in any case, no little stunner would ever have me. Not now. It's funny: men will excuse a woman being stupid if she looks beautiful; but a woman won't go near a man with the brain the size of a planet if he isn't totally buff.

Which is of course nonsense: anticipating those Victorian gentlemen who, in old age, ran into the arms of unsuitably young women (OK, Ruskin and Dickens), Montaigne formed a *very* close relationship with a certain Marie de Gournay, a writer 32 years his junior, who became his *fille d'alliance*.[85] He heavily influenced her first novel, written after he'd spent two months at her family home in Picardy. When Montaigne died, Madame Montaigne handed over her late husband's books and papers to Marie, who published a further edition of the *Essays*, including Montaigne's own final emendations (mostly in the form of fresh illustrative quotes) and an introduction of her own. She also named her cat after Montaigne's daughter Léonore.[86]

And that's it. I've cut away 7/8 of Montaigne's original essay, hoping I've left the vital organs and some of the meat which I've inelegantly paraphrased. The writer himself finishes by apologizing for his 'torrent of babble', which must have been to some readers 'impetuous and hurtful' by admitting that underneath it all, men and women are pretty much identical. When either gender finds fault with the other, it's usually a case of

---

84. An angling metaphor beautifully translated by Cotton, a close friend and collaborator of the most famous English fisherman ever, Isaak Walton.

85. Adoptive daughter.

86. She later published at least seven more revised editions of the *Essays,* and several tracts, the two best-known of which are *The Equality of Men and Women* (1622) and *The Ladies' Grievance* (1626).

the pot and kettle.

But what of his own marriage? Well, in this essay, his honesty once again overrides many of the doubts we may have entertained of him. And though he may not have been the perfect or even the most enlightened husband, his more liberal views were, shall we say, somewhat unorthodox for their time.

And he does weigh in with a couple of tender comments we might heed: when making love, the most important thing isn't the size of your organ, the duration of intercourse, the sex toys, the editorial from last month's *Cosmo* or *Playboy* on how to have multiple screaming orgasms ten times a night—it's timing. That's all. Make your move at exactly the right time and '*tis a point that can do everything'*.

As for Madame Montaigne, he says that like a child or a servant, 'I *was always superstitiously afraid of giving offence, and have ever had a great respect for her I loved.'* Of course, he *could* be referring to any of the other women he consorted with during his wild years, but I'd prefer to think he was speaking about *Madame*. For behind every great man is an even greater woman.

Chapter 22

Pain Never Hurt Anyone

'The world...thinks nothing profitable that is not painful; it has great suspicion of facility.' (Book 3, Chapter 13: 'Of Experience')

'I know one, who, when I question him what he knows, he presently calls for a book to shew me, and dares not venture to tell me so much, as that he has piles in his posteriors, till first he has consulted his dictionary, what piles and what posteriors are.' (Book 1, Chapter 24: 'Of Pedantry')

Montaigne, it seems, always took a lively interest in illness, even before his severe gastric problems lent a personal dimension to his writings on the subject. In his essay 'Of the Force of Imagination', he notes:

the very sight of another's pain materially pains me, and I often usurp the sensations of another person. A perpetual cough in another tickles my lungs and throat. I more unwillingly visit the sick in whom by love and duty I am interested, than those I care not for, to whom I less look. I take possession of the disease I am concerned at, and take it to myself.

Which is not a thousand miles away from 'J', the narrator of Jerome K. Jerome's *Three Men In a Boat*, as he pores through a medical dictionary:

I came to typhoid fever—read the symptoms—discovered that I had typhoid fever, must have had it for months without knowing it—wondered what else I had got; turned up St. Vitus's Dance—found, as I expected, that I had that too,—began to get interested in my case, and determined to sift it to the bottom, and so started alphabetically—read up ague, and learnt that I was sickening for it, and that the acute stage would commence in about another fortnight. Bright's disease, I was relieved to find, I had only in a modified form, and, so far as that was concerned, I might live for years. Cholera I had, with severe complications; and diphtheria I seemed to have been born with. I plodded conscientiously through the twenty-six letters, and the only malady I could conclude I had not got was housemaid's knee.I felt rather hurt about this at first; it seemed somehow to be a sort of slight. Why hadn't I got housemaid's knee?

Psychosomatic complaints are, in one doctor friend's parlance, 'mad peoples' diseases', in that we convince ourselves that we have them, even though we don't. And they can be 'cured' using placebos, which don't actually do anything. Which is the very opposite of what Stoics do when they're ill; they try to convince themselves that illness *is* all in the mind. Even if their leg's been torn off, they will try and make the best of a bad situation—after all, in the days before what my wife used to call 'heroic medicine', what else *could* they do?

The Stoic believed in 'Nature'—of which illness and death form an integral part. To be ill is natural; to die is natural. And if what you're experiencing is all part of Nature's plan, you should be indifferent or even content with your lot. There's a wonderful passage in which Montaigne relates the incredible and instantaneous relief he feels when passing a stone; why, he says, it's almost worthwhile suffering the pain just to feel its sudden departure. Which is Stoicism in a nutshell. Sometimes it's a bit nuts.

But modern heroic medicine has made it possible to live way beyond Nature's allotted span, and Stoicism can no longer hack it, particularly when medical science confuses ideas of 'being alive' with 'living.' The Renaissance Stoic could never have foreseen how developments in the field of medicine would render illness and pain not simply matters for resignation, to be philosophized away, but the occasion for a *battle* with Nature. *Against* Nature. Even if the drugs don't work and you're screaming in pain. Even if the drugs *do* work, and medicine is artificially prolonging your life. Even if you have forfeited all human dignity. Even if the only thing you want to do is die and your physicians can't let you for fear they'll be prosecuted. Even if you're *begging*.

For we've somehow managed to park ourselves in a philosophical cul-de-sac: we rightly agree that life is the most precious gift we have, and therefore, the law, in a staggering abuse of logic, has decreed that, in the majority of cases we must be kept alive as long as possible. Whatever the cost, human *and* financial. And, of course, the law is frequently buttressed in this matter by religion which, in many countries, both developed and undeveloped, hinders any possible reforms—or even flexibility—in those situations where science has overtaken Nature.

I think Montaigne would have been acutely puzzled by the many paradoxes generated by modern medicine—at least judging by this:

...in physic I very much honour that glorious name, its propositions, its promises, so useful for the service of mankind; but the ordinances it foists upon us, betwixt ourselves, I neither honour nor esteem.

Why, he would ask, prolong suffering needlessly? 'The wise man,' says Montaigne, is he that 'lives as long as he ought, not so long as he can.' So why, if patients are fully acquainted with their predicament, deny them the right to choose how their life is going to end? For a non-interventionist like Montaigne, the unholy conspiracy between medicine, religion and the law that robs the individual of his independence would be the focus for his righteous anger—'Whose body is it anyway?', would neatly encapsulate how he might view the matter. For, he would argue, my body belongs severally to me, to God and to Nature before those other institutions can claim it. And I would absolutely agree with him.

So if he were being treated for one of the more acute forms of cancer in a modern hospital, I'm pretty confident Montaigne would choose to let Nature take its course, even if he was given reasonable odds that he might be cured. I doubt, for example, he would have consented to chemotherapy; the contradiction that lies at the heart of the idea that you must first poison the body to cure it would, from a philosophical standpoint, strain reason to its breaking point and beyond. To what end is life being prolonged, would be the question he might immediately ask, before telling an incredulous hospital consultant the following:

We ought to grant free passage to diseases; I find they stay less with me, who let them alone; and I have lost some, reputed the most tenacious and obstinate, by their own decay, without help and without art, and contrary to its rules. Let us a little permit Nature to take her own way; she better understands her own affairs than we. But such an one died of it; and so shall you: if not of that disease, of another... they are sooner prevailed upon by courtesy than huffing. We must patiently suffer the laws of our condition; we are born to grow old, to grow weak, and to be sick, in despite of all medicine. 'Tis the first lesson the Mexicans teach their children; so soon as ever they are born they thus salute them: 'Thou art come into the world, child, to endure: endure, suffer, and say nothing.'

The trouble is, to decline medical help is, for the most part, viewed as stupid rather than noble or brave.[87] Court battles are regularly fought over the issue. We 'won't suffer the laws of our condition', yet, paradoxically, we *are* prepared to suffer the often devastating side effects of the treatments that are administered to cure or alleviate that condition.

And at this point, at least in my view, the modern world may have grown too complicated for Montaigne's philosophy, because we've long since left behind what he understood as Nature. Yes, we'll submit to the treatment, but not at *any* cost; yet No, we won't sit back, Stoic-like, if there's the chance of a cure or even a brief remission.

It's a tough call.

Because Nature has also conditioned us, as organisms, to cling on to life if we can. Whatever philosophy advises us. And that survival instinct will triumph over logic and reason just about every time, as Montaigne notes in his essay 'Of the Judging Of The Death Of Another':

When we judge of another's assurance in death, which, without doubt, is the most remarkable action of human life, we are to take heed of one thing, which is that men very hardly believe themselves to have arrived to that period. Few men come to die in the opinion that it is their latest hour; and there is nothing wherein the flattery of hope more deludes us; It never ceases to whisper in our ears, 'Others have been much sicker without dying; your condition is not so desperate as 'tis thought; and, at the worst, God has done other miracles.'

---

87. Look at Bob Marley—killed by a septic toe when he refused treatment because he reckoned Jah would see him right.

In other words, hope springs eternal—and not just in the patient. But there arrives a significant turning point in any kind of treatment, at which the patient either begins to recover or ceases to respond. In the latter case, the law of diminishing returns kicks in, and heroic medicine begins. The patient ceases to be a human being, endowed with intelligence, dignity and independence—and morphs into a biological organism that needs to be kept alive.

In a way, sophisticated medicine has made us revert, at least in part, to a more primitive conception of human Nature—that man is just an overdeveloped animal, no more than a collection of evolutionary progressions ruled by a complex system of chemical reactions, an animal that can be treated by hacking it about then sewing it back up, or pumping it full of other chemicals in a hospital full of hi-tech machines that go ping.

Five hundred years ago, however, the writers and philosophers of the Renaissance were fighting against that definition, which they would have considered insulting. OK, man was a worm before God, but he was far more advanced than any animal. He was way more than the sum of his biology. Mankind's unique capacity for reasoned thought would lead him out of ignorance, beyond the simple compulsions that govern the behaviour of animals. It would allow him to conquer illness, not simply by allowing his biology to get on with the job, but *reasoning* illness out of existence by denying it any significance. By removing the fear and superstition that attends it. By daily confronting its existence. By acknowledging that in the midst of life is death. Always.

A fond hope? An unrealistic ambition? Yes—but wonderfully quixotic. Staring in the face of death, it takes a pretty cool nerve, the strongest industrial grade philosophy, and/or faith in some kind of transcendent realm to accept the situation with any degree of calm or rationality. At least in my experience:

When you're watching the person you love slowly dying, knowing that they're beyond help, philosophy of any stripe can offer only scant consolation. The chasm between the reality of the situation and philosophy's attempts to place it in a broader perspective is too great to span. It's just too much to ask. The result is frustration and anger, not resignation. Philosophy seems trivial, platitudinous—not fit for purpose. Callous, even, in its cosy bower of unworldliness, in its insistence that in the great scheme of things, this doesn't matter. Life is temporary. Every day is borrowed. You're no different from anyone else, either now or in the past. We all have to face it some time, and now it's your turn. Or try religion, which at least holds out the prospect of continued existence somewhere beyond this life—even the possibility of a reunion if you've both kept a clean sheet with your chosen deity. Clichés. Coping mechanisms that can't cope.

Then witness the courage of your loved one. See how they fight. See how they endure the pain. See how they're trying to lessen your suffering by playing down their own. See how they want to protect you with what little strength they have left. See that they're not afraid to die. See that beautiful strength flare up in their eyes one last time—'I love you', they say.

See that strength slowly ebb away again. Agony. Wish you were in their place. Feel the injustice. Feel the anger. Feel it consume philosophy. Feel it consume religion. Feel philosophy and religion burn.

Feel the emptiness.

Still.

Chapter Twenty Three

Some Fantastic Place

I wrote that last essay in one burst three weeks ago on the fourth anniversary of my wife's tragically early death from cancer at the age of 48. I haven't changed a word of it, and have no intention of doing so. It is what it is—a record of sorts.

I was, and remain, pretty raw despite exploring all the avenues grief counselling can offer. My philosophy did burn (I have no religion), but it did gradually dribble back, many months later, penetrating the veils of numbness in bursts of angry self-recrimination. Like a true Stoic I told myself that to continue grieving was self-indulgent—masochistic even. I had nothing to feel guilty for—the doctors, our wonderful families and friends and I had engineered as painless and dignified a death as we could. And Chris was where she wanted to be—at home surrounded by those who loved her. I was (and am) very much aware that there are currently millions of families all over the planet sharing a similar burden, and, indeed, far worse ones. I'm so far from being unique I sometimes wonder I can allow myself these painful visitations. Yet I seem powerless to stop acting like Queen Victoria, whose grief for her husband lasted ludicrously beyond its sell-by date.

Anyway, before this turns into *Angela's* bloody *Ashes*, I'll stop—the world doesn't need yet another addition to the 'Painful Lives' catalogue. But the reason I've gone down this road can be traced directly back to my re-reading of the *Essays* prior to writing this book. Death is never very far from Montaigne's thoughts, and it's a theme that establishes itself almost immediately you open the Cotton translation.

In the Preface are several items of correspondence sent by the great man to friends, the Governor of Guienne—even King Henry IV of France. And in amongst those is the short note to Madame Montaigne mentioned in a previous essay, which prompted me to think about the power or otherwise of philosophy in tackling extreme emotional situations. Here's how he tries to console his spouse after their only child has died:

MY WIFE…you may recollect that the late M. de la Boétie, my brother and inseparable companion, gave me, on his death-bed, all his books and papers, which have remained ever since the most precious part of my effects. I do not wish to keep them niggardly to myself alone, nor do I deserve to have the exclusive use of them; so that I have resolved to communicate them to my friends; and because I have none, I believe, more particularly intimate than you, I send you the Consolatory Letter written by Plutarch to his Wife, translated by him into French; regretting much that fortune has made it so suitable a present you, and that, having had but one child, and that a daughter, long looked for, after four years of your married life it was your lot to lose her in the second year of her age.

But I leave to Plutarch the duty of comforting you, acquainting you with your duty herein, begging you to put your faith in him for my sake; for he will reveal to you my own ideas, and will express the matter far better than I should myself.

Hereupon, my wife, I commend myself very heartily to your good will, and pray God to have you in His keeping.

From Paris, this 10th September 1570.

Your good husband,

MICHEL DE MONTAIGNE

It's an extraordinary performance that I can't fathom at all. Is it loving, after the conventions of a Renaissance nobleman? Or utterly wrongheaded, notwithstanding its opening attempt at levity and tenderness.[88] 'Here', he says, 'read this book. It used to belong to my mate who's now dead, but console yourself with it in my absence. It's all in there, love. Ta ta.'[89]

It reminded me of that incredible moment in Shakespeare's *Titus Andronicus* when Marcus discovers his niece Lavinia raped, tongueless and handless in the forest, and instead of going to staunch her wounds and comfort her, he embarks on a stilted 46-line soliloquy packed with classical allusions, in which he helpfully notes that Lavinia's days with a needle and thread are over. It's entirely the wrong response. I know many women who would have told Montaigne what he could do with his book and his precious philosophy, and, indeed, where he could stick them.

Anyway, the text in question, Plutarch's *Consolatio ad Uxorem* deals with an identical situation to Montaigne's—the premature death of a young daughter. It's awkward mixture of love and formality, and, to these eyes at least, Mrs Plutarch (and by extension Mrs M) are made to work hard for their solace. Fortunately, at 3,000 words, the essay wouldn't have taken them long to read, but sometimes the philosophy can be

---

88. Quoted in that previous essay.

89. In fact, the letter as quoted here forms the preface to a collection of de la Boetie's work, accompanied by the *Consolation,* which Montaigne had privately published in about 1571.

maddeningly patronizing, and the concluding admonition is
lame, perhaps even a little desperate:

*For the laws forbid us to mourn for infants, holding it impiety to mourn
for those who have departed to a dispensation and a region too that is
better and more divine. And since this is harder to disbelieve than to
believe, but let us keep our outward conduct as the laws command,
and keep ourselves within yet freer from stain and purer and more
temperate.*

Philosophers sometimes appear spectacularly priggish to me:
'Oh, we don't want any of that emotion stuff, take it away', as if
it's somehow dirty and polluting to this lovely logical, rational
tower of cards they've constructed from the mess of day-to-day
living. Cool reason, not primal screaming is the route out of
grief. Which statement makes me want to tear their playhouse
down, room by room. But I'm not going to. Instead, I'm going
to try and work out why you might send a second-hand book
to a grieving woman you profess to love.

For a start, the 'Consolation' was a well-known literary
form—and there were loads of them written either as stand-
alone pieces or incorporated within longer works, so I could
begin the case for Montaigne's defence by noting that at least
he had literary precedent on his side for responding in the way
that he did.

Perhaps the most influential Consolation ever to appear is
Boethius's *Consolatio Philosophiae* which he wrote in jail, as he
faced execution on trumped-up charges of treason. Grieving
over his lot, he converses with the character of Lady Philosophy,
who informs him that everything good or bad is in the hands of
a divine Providence, which will see him right. She preaches on
the ultimate superiority of things of the mind, which she calls
our 'one true good'. And Boethius needed every scrap of consolation he could muster, as he was brutally clubbed to death

following an extended period of torture, during which a cord was twisted round his forehead so tightly that his eyes popped out of their sockets. Which only makes me hope that Lady Philosophy played a straight bat with Boethius, and something better really did await him on the other side. Unlike the suicide bomber who arrives in heaven, only to find the 24 virgins he's been promised as a reward for his self-sacrifice are all well into their 80s.

At least Boethius's book went on to be a bestseller: so influential was the *Consolatio*, that the text was severally translated from the Latin by King Alfred the Great (9th-century AD), Chaucer (14th) and Queen Elizabeth I (16th). And Alain de Botton borrowed the title for his attempt, published in 2000, to prove that philosophy could still prove a healing balm for troubled minds. Clearly, a lot of people have been seeking consolation down the ages.

The trouble is, those of us who live in cultures where ideas of transcendence (divine or otherwise) are in decline, are placing the entire burden of consolation on philosophy itself. Robbed of that central component, some of the reason-based philosophies (like Stoicism) are reduced to a mechanism that simply isn't equipped to deal with the kind of wayward irrationality unleashed by grief. Without a firm belief in the promise of ultimate salvation, philosophy appears, as I noted in the previous essay, to have been downgraded to the status of a collection of platitudes. Which is why consolations haven't consoled me.

At which point we have three choices: abandon ourselves to a) despair; b) religion; or c) draw solace that when you're dead you're dead, so you might as well focus on having a good time while you remain alive.

So which avenue does Montaigne take? As far as I can make

out, it's a combination of (b) and (c) inclining heavily towards the latter. Let's deal with religion first, an issue I've thus far been ducking, as I think Montaigne's views were complex and distinctly ambivalent.[90] Now, however, feels a good time to try and tease out some principles.

Correct me if I'm wrong, but Montaigne has been judged to be at his most religiously orthodox in the essay 'An *Apologia* For Raimond de Sebonde', in which he eloquently explains that Man, without an understanding of God, is no better than an animal.[91] Here's a sample:

The error of paganism and the ignorance of our sacred truth made the great soul of Plato, but great only in human greatness, fall yet into this other vicious mistake, 'that children and old men are most susceptible of religion,' as if it sprang and derived its reputation from our weakness. The knot that ought to bind the judgment and the will, that ought to restrain the soul and join it to the Creator, should be a knot that derives its foldings and strength, not from our considerations, from our reasons and passions, but from a divine and supernatural constraint, having but one form, one face, and one lustre, which is the authority of God and His divine grace.

That's pretty unequivocal. Even Montaigne's hero Plato who, let's not forget, he quotes more than anyone except Cicero, seems to get it badly wrong.

But then, we must remember that Montaigne is here commenting on the work of another writer—Raimond de Sebonde, who was himself heavily influenced by St Thomas Aquinas. The passion and clarity with which Montaigne expresses himself is

90. As things have turned out, we'll be examining option 'c' in the following essay.

91. The essay is sometimes abstracted from complete editions of the *Essays*; in others, it appears as Book 2 Chapter 12.

at a far remove from the more homespun, skeptical approach we've noted throughout the *Essays,* which makes me wonder what he's up to here. His motivations are straightforwardly expressed, but are far from being straightforward themselves.

We might begin by remarking that in classical tradition, an *Apologia* could be viewed as either a justification or an explanation (or both), the former indicating greater sympathy with the work or person in question than the latter, which is essentially a gloss. To justify something implies, to a greater or lesser degree, agreement or sympathy; a simple explanation offers no such attachment. Montaigne undertook to translate Sebonde's work into French for his dying father, and on one level at least, he treats this duty as an academic exercise: 'I found the imaginations of this author exceedingly fine, the contexture of his work well followed up, and his design full of piety', says Montaigne the scholar.

But how much do Sebonde's own rather rigid and doctrinal views chime with Montaigne the avowed skeptic's?

In Montaigne's view, Sebonde's purpose is 'to undertake, by human and natural reasons, to establish and make good against the atheists all the articles of the Christian religion: wherein, to speak the truth, he is so firm and so successful that I do not think it possible to do better upon that subject, and believe that he has been equalled by none.' Yet, Montaigne informs us, the work has met with two principle objections that he has been asked to clarify:

First, say the knockers, Sebonde overemphasizes divine wisdom. As humans, we don't have a direct line to God, so we try to explain faith by using human reason—a tool which Sebonde considers inferior and inappropriate. Montaigne argues, that yes, in a way he's right—we can't fully understand the divine—yet he adds that human reasoning could be put to no more noble use. In other words, there's no harm in trying:

[W]e must...accompany our faith with all the reason we have, but always with this reservation, not to fancy that it is upon us that it depends, nor that our arguments and endeavors can arrive at so supernatural and divine a knowledge. If it enter not into us by an extraordinary infusion; if it only enter, not only by arguments of reason, but, moreover, by human ways, it is not in us in its true dignity and splendour, and yet I am afraid we only have it by this way.

So we can't fully embrace Sebonde's lofty ideals, which, implies Montaigne, is a pity. I'm not sure exactly who Montaigne's 'we' refers to, but it looks as if he's saying that we're all in the same boat. So he's actually disagreeing with Sebonde. Pretty fundamentally.

Second objection: that Sebonde's arguments are weak. Montaigne counters these critics by turning their weapons back on themselves, paradoxically using human reason to justify something, divine knowledge, that he's just demonstrated exists outside reason's own sphere of operations. Alter the perspective slightly and we arrive at a second paradox: Montaigne using reason to destroy...reason:

Let us see, then, if man has in his power other reasons more forcible than those of Sebonde; that is to say, if it be in him to arrive at any certainty by argument and reason. For St. Augustine, disputing against these people, has good cause to reproach them with injustice, in that they maintain the parts of our belief to be false that our reason cannot establish; and, to show that a great many things may be and may have been, of which our nature could not found the reason and causes, he proposes to them certain known and indubitable experiences wherein men confess they have no insight; and this he does, as all other things, with a close and ingenious inquisition. We must do more than this, and make them know that, to convict the weakness of their reason, there is no necessity of culling out rare examples; and that it is so defective and

*so blind, that there is no so clear facility clear enough for it: that to it
the easy and the hard is all one; that all subjects equally, and nature in
general, disclaims its authority, and rejects its mediation.*

Oo-er. Now we come to the crunch question: does Montaigne
believe any or all of this, or is he engaged in a serious intellectual parlour game he is playing to win? The Sebonde essay
does a magnificent demolition job on mankind to the point
we should all be ashamed of ourselves. If we really are as bad
as he paints us, maybe we should do the honourable thing and
jack it all in.

But was Montaigne ever as witheringly misanthropic as this
essay makes out? Well, I'm afraid I don't know for sure…but I
don't think he could have been.

At the beginning of this book, I mentioned that many commentators explain away the *Apology* as Montaigne's low point,
his mid-life crisis, his long dark night of the soul; in 1576,
when he wrote it, it is often claimed he was undergoing some
sort of brainstorm. Perhaps Montaigne the skeptic had asked
too many questions to the point where his reason had slipped
anchor and his philosophy drifted out to sea. I'm pretty sure
the essay marked a turning point of sorts, as I'll discuss later
in the book; but although the ultimate destination's the same,
I would choose a different route to explain how Montaigne
arrived there…

Montaigne, we must remember, is not so much justifying the
ways of God to man, but the forceful arguments of Sebonde to
his critics: that is how he prefaces what follows. The essay is an
impressive bravura performance and a triumph of rhetoric—so
well written and convincing, in fact, that it's often been taken
at face value. Before he settled into the role of acting out the
philosophical counterpart to P.G. Wodehouse's eccentric Lord
Emsworth, Montaigne was possessed of a withering, rapier-

like intelligence, and there's no better display of it than in these 18,000 words.

BUT—I reckon it's an intellectual exercise in which Montaigne decided to let rip. Perhaps he was tired of the skeptical routine of seeing the other side of the argument and decided that for once, he was going to step out of character and play the hellfire preacher for a day. After all, he'd spent five years writing the early essays as Montaigne 'the apprehensive humanist'.[92] Why not try another approach? A radically different one? How about the Old Testament prophet?

Having reviewed what he'd written, Montaigne might have even have been surprised by how good he was at polemic. As good as his hero Cicero perhaps.

Whatever the motivation, the Sebonde excursion marked a sea change in Montaigne's approach to writing—as I'll argue in the following essay. And if indeed it was prompted by a crisis, it was one from which he emerged with renewed confidence and a clearer sense of purpose. For it was at this point, having ground mankind beneath his theological heel, he switches round and becomes our spokesman, almost our apologist in fact, justifying the ways of man to God.

A dyed-in-the-wool skeptic like Montaigne, however much he may have been depressed, could never take anything, even divine wisdom, at face value without questioning it. As he demonstrates both to us and himself in 'Of Giving The Lie', he is hard-wired for honesty and can take little on trust. Is divine wisdom *really* divine, he might ask. Or is divinity itself an intellectual strategy invented by man to justify what he cannot explain? A fascinating topic, but one which, unfortunately, lies beyond the scope of this book.

---

92. Donald Frame's apt description.

That said, I'm going to conclude this section of my essay with commentary that represents a further plunge into the ocean of wild subjectivity. It forms an overall impression rather than a particular observation, and I'm aware that it can easily be dismantled using a few apposite quotations—but here goes anyway, at the risk of being thought the Germaine Greer of Montaigne studies:

Montaigne strongly believed in the authority of the Catholic religion—most commentators allow for that. But reading the *Essays* as an uninterrupted sequence, I would conclude that much of that belief was a formality. There seem to me very few places where Montaigne gets terribly exercised by the idea of an afterlife, a heaven or indeed a God, other than to pay lip service to these ideas for the sake of propriety. These three ideas often appear in the text as metaphors as opposed to entities that exist outside the purposes of the arguments in which they are contained. I think if you were to press Montaigne on the matter, he might reply that at one point in the evolution of mankind's philosophy, religion did not exist and had to be invented. Often, I feel there's more of the anthropologist lurking in Montaigne than the man of religion. And his principles were also governed by pragmatism—at least outwardly:

It's been argued that until the trial of Galileo in 1633, the tenets of Skepticism and Humanism were still just about reconcilable with the Catholic faith. Even Montaigne's seeming preference for rationality over revelation had been addressed by the Flemish philosopher Justus Lipsius, and fashioned into a workable system. Montaigne even corresponded with him. So the interests of politics, philosophy and religion were, for a short period, delicately balanced. But this was largely irrelevant at a local level in France, which was being torn apart by religious schism.

From 1562 until 1598, the so-called 'Wars of Religion' were

being fought between Catholics and Protestants—eight mini civil wars that could easily have unleashed waves of reactionary reprisals on those whose views didn't fit the rapidly evolving (and wildly vacillating) *status quo*. And Montaigne was a prominent man, serving as Mayor of Bordeaux from 1581 to 1585; his head was well and truly above the parapet—doubly so, since he had published the *Essays* the year before, thus exposing many of his beliefs to general scrutiny.[93]

As we'll discover in the next essay, Montaigne didn't emerge unscathed from this period, but it's a tribute both to his diplomacy and political savvy that he owed his official position to an old-style Catholic (Catherine de Medici), yet was also courted by the future Henry IV—on his accession an avowedly Protestant monarch. Indeed, in an exchange of letters as his life neared its end, Montaigne praised Henry for his nous: 'You have acted very commendably in adapting yourself, in the matter of external forms, to your new fortunes,' he writes, 'but the preservation of your old affability and frankness in private intercourse is entitled to an equal share of praise.'[94]

Montaigne, like Henry, would have had to steer a difficult course between the warring factions in Bordeaux as he tried to keep the peace: pragmatism would have dictated that 'external forms' would need to evolve as the political situation changed. And whether he was a believer or not, that situation would have involved him in the ongoing religious debate. Publicly embracing Humanism or Skepticism would have been irrelevant, for these were religious wars fought and debated on religious

93. And this at a time when the Inquisition could disembowel and set fire to you just for looking at them funny.

94. Three years after that letter was written in January 1590, Henry was forced to renounce Protestantism and embrace the Catholic faith. In so doing, he prolonged his reign by 17 years. It was a pragmatic decision of which Montaigne, had he lived, would no doubt have approved: thirty-six years of war finally ended in 1598.

terms, not exclusively philosophical ones. So his public faith and private philosophy were most likely to be, shall we say, inconsistent with one another. Anything for a quiet life, perhaps. Or even a Renaissance equivalent of the Vicar of Bray.

So, to return to the alternatives I proposed earlier, I would claim that Montaigne, for all the religious bells and whistles that appear in his work, held to the belief that for us humans, our brains and our intelligence are all we've got. That needn't stop us aspiring to divinity, whatever that is: but we have to use the tools at our disposal to try and make sense of our lives, no matter how poor and inadequate those tools might be. Which is why he sent the book to his wife. He may well have considered it a sorry substitute for his presence, but I think he sincerely believed it might offer some consolation, however small.

I wonder if Mrs M accepted it in the spirit I'm claiming it was intended? Or did she too tell him where he could stick it?

Chapter Twenty Four

Montaigne's Final Essay

'If thou embracest not death, at least thou shakest hands with it once a month; whence thou hast more cause to hope that it will one day surprise thee without menace.' (Book 3, Chapter 13: 'Of Experience')

The last edition of the *Essays* published in Montaigne's lifetime appeared in 1588, four years before his passing. It included the newly written Book 3, which consisted of 13 additional meditations, of which the last 'On Experience' is a whopper— 25,000 words. The tone is noticeably less sprightly, bordering at times on the weary. But strength and resolution shine out from the very first sentences:

There is no desire more natural than that of knowledge. We try all ways that can lead us to it; where reason is wanting, we therein employ experience, which is a means much more weak and cheap; but truth is so great a thing that we ought not to disdain any mediation that will guide us to it.

It's impossible to tell whether this was chronologically the last piece he wrote, or whether he was aware it would be his last; but it does possess an air of finality, of drawing together some of the threads that run through his previous work. It's an absolute masterpiece—and in my student copy just about every sentence is underlined in pencil as being worthy of note. Yet it only warms to its theme about 5,000 words in, after he's got a rant about lawyers and doctors out of his system. So let's get it out of ours.

The first hobby-horse he addresses is one on which I too enjoy a gallop—how we interpret things. Or rather, how interpretation interrupts the sense of what has been said or written by complicating it. Montaigne draws his first examples from the law, and how more doesn't always mean better:

There is little relation betwixt our actions, which are in perpetual mutation, and fixed and immutable laws; the most to be desired are **those that are the most rare, the most simple and general**; *and I am even of opinion that we had better have none at all than to have them in so prodigious a number as we have.* [emboldening mine]

Montaigne knew whereof he spoke, having done his porridge in the legal profession—a calling which, to judge by his writings, he seems both temperamentally and philosophically unsuited. France, he declares, which has more laws than all other nations put together, is not only drowning in oceans of red tape; by following this path, it is degrading the very idea of what the 'truth' means. Truth consists of 'the most simple and general' route to anywhere—a sentiment echoed by the mighty Matthew Arnold in his 1869 collection of essays, *Culture and Anarchy*:

The great men of culture are those who have had a passion for diffusing, for making prevail, for carrying from one end of society to the other, the best knowledge, the best ideas of their time, who have laboured to divest knowledge of all that was harsh, uncouth, difficult, abstract, professional, exclusive; to humanise it, to make it efficient outside the clique of the cultivated and learned.

The truth is teased out from experience, and this process does not require oceans of exegesis. In any quest for the truth, you should end up with less material than you started with—not more, because you're throwing away everything that is unnecessarily obstructing the path to your final destination.

Both men longed for a kind of universal, cohesive knowledge, unencumbered by cant, rhetoric, jargon, obscurity—anything that comes between the true and original meaning and our subsequent understanding of it. In a statement not likely to be bandied about by literary critics, Montaigne observes:

...there's no book to be found, either human or divine, which the world busies itself about, whereof the difficulties are cleared by interpretation... There is more ado to interpret interpretations than to interpret things, and more books upon books than upon any other subject; we do nothing but comment upon one another.

True then, and ten thousand times truer now. It's no wonder that if you want to learn anything about a book, play or poem, it's usually a case of wading through a stagnant pond full of half-baked sociological/ anthropological/ psychological flotsam that entangles itself round your synapses and eventually drags you, suffocating, beneath its murky surface, taking your love of literature with it. It's called 'Literary Criticism'—a mongrel discipline that one of its practitioners unsmilingly defines thus:

[criticism]...is an attempt to understand the ontological, epistemic, axiological and praxic nature and implications and assumptions of the very phenomenon of 'literature' as a cultural formation and practice.

As bullshit bingo goes, that's pretty tame, entry-level stuff. How about this?

This article focuses upon the first of Shakespeare's Sonnets in order to analyse its generative position within the sequence and its interest in the reproduction of the individual. Whilst it questions the idealist subjectivity posited by Shakespeareans since the eighteenth century, the argument is also designed to resist the anti-aesthetic effects of recent historical-relativist criticism. Jacques Derrida's 'ethical' concern with the problematic singularity of both the individual and literature is thus invoked in an attempt to suggest how both might feature in a new turn to aesthetic criticism.

Now I've actually taught the *Sonnets* and, somewhat worryingly, I haven't a clue what this person's on about. I mean, not a single scintilla of comprehension. 'The reproduction of the individual'—does that refer to some form of hermaphroditic sexual intercourse? Or cloning? And if an individual's 'singularity' is 'problematic', surely he should seek psychiatric help? Or a good surgeon? But then, I showed this to a mate who's an English lecturer and he didn't bat an eyelid; in fact he was at a loss to think why I should be confused, because to him it was all completely transparent. These guys are speaking the same language as me, and individually, I understand all the words— only they don't mean anything.

In Lit Crit circles, it's a disease that seems to be spreading just about everywhere. Even to Australia, a country where unadorned speech has reached the status of an art form, yet where I've just found a journal dedicated to the 'performativity' of Shakespeare's plays. Interestingly, the Wikipedia entry for 'performativity' has one of those third-party caveats inserted at the top which reads, 'This article may be confusing or unclear to readers', and calling for it to be completely rewritten. On the money there, lads... here's a sample:

Others criticize Judith Butler for taking ethnomethodological symbolic interactionist sociological analyses of gender and merely reinventing them in the concept of performativity (Dunn 1997; Green 2007). For example, Green (2007) argues that the work of Kessler and McKenna (1978) and West and Zimmerman (1987) builds directly from Garfinkel (1967) and Goffman (1959) to deconstruct gender into moments of attribution and iteration in a continual social process of 'doing' masculinity and femininity in the performative interval. These latter works are premised on the notion that gender does not precede but, rather, follows from practice, instantiated in micro-interaction.

This *is* a joke, right?

Unfortunately, a quick glance at the accompanying discussion page indicates it isn't. Although *that's* pretty funny too. Someone has made the pertinent observation that the entry has clearly been written by someone in an institution of higher learning, yet someone who is wholly incapable of communicating what they have learned in language that anyone outside their immediate circle can understand. And probably being funded by the taxpayers of whatever nation this halfwit comes from.

Which brings us back to Montaigne's main beef with lawyers and their contracts. New specialist languages are being created which mangle sense and therefore truth. And in such a way that it takes highly trained (and highly paid) professionals to decode what's been written. As for you and I, we just sign the cheques.

In my early days as an independent radio producer, the BBC commissioned a series of programmes from me; as usual, the contract thudded onto my doormat a few weeks later, which, I noticed, had grown a lot fatter than the previous one. So I took the unprecedented step of actually reading it. It was quite a revelation, and it took me the best part of a week and a lot of phone calls to discover what I was signing away. Not only were they inciting me to commit a crime by granting rights to them in third-party material I didn't own, they'd inserted the following sub-clause (and here I'm paraphrasing into English): 'THE BBC reserves the right to broadcast

THE PROGRAMME in perpetuity by any means current or yet to be invented, throughout the universe or any universe yet to be discovered.' Which in plain English means: 'We Own Your Ass.' This raised the amusing possibility of the BBC's lawyers trying to sue a radio station broadcasting from another galaxy for copyright infringement. THE PROGRAMME in question was a reading of James Herriot's autobiographical tales of a vet's life in 1930s Yorkshire, which would, of course, go down a storm with aliens, particularly those memorable occasions when our hero gets his arm stuck up a cow's birth canal.

This isn't just covering your arse, or using a sledgehammer to crack a walnut: it's the equivalent of building a thirty-foot thick concrete wall complete with machine gun emplacements, tank traps, slavering attack dogs and patrolling stealth bombers carrying nuclear payloads to protect your garden shed from a five-year-old with a peashooter. And even then I bet those aliens would find a loophole in the wording. Then they could countersue—or simply destroy Earth with a death ray.

Montaigne is similarly skeptical of the ability of legalese to construct watertight defences. The truth, he says, is like quicksilver (mercury), in that it refuses to stay still. So trying to trap it by using words will simply make life more complicated for everyone—and you end up with jibberish. He quotes Quintilian's motto that 'Learning begets difficulties'. We should seek for unity in our studies, for learning, at base, is *synthesis*, a bringing together, and not the atomising of truth into infinity.

But taking the piss out of lawyers and academics is a bit unsporting: fish and barrels, elephants and banjos spring to mind—which is perhaps why Montaigne curtails his theme—which he seems to be enjoying, despite his frustration—and devotes the remainder of his final essay to teasing out a few basic tenets for a successful and carefree life. This lengthy pre-amble re: lawyers could perhaps usefully be summarized as 'Point One:

KEEP THINGS SIMPLE.'

There are five other Points, all of them similarly homespun and clearly the distillation of a lifetime's experience.[95] They might read as follows:

Point Two: KNOW YOURSELF;

Point Three: DON'T GET IN A RUT—BREAK RULES AND ROUTINES;

Point Four: BE ACCEPTING;

Point Five: LIVE HUMBLY, and;

Point Six: *CARPE DIEM.*

In a previous essay, I was discussing simplicity. Well, there you have it on a plate. Great big themes lived out in a domestic setting.

For in among these overarching principles, Montaigne shuffles about his daily business, sparing us no detail, however quotidian or intimate. The tone at this point is so confiding as to be almost confessional. It has been argued that because of Montaigne's 'imperious need to communicate,' and having long since lost his closest *confidant* (the poet Étienne de la Boétie), he began the *Essays* as his 'means of communication;' and that 'the reader takes the place of the dead friend.'[96] We, the audience, are now his friends—and as such, he will hold nothing back from us.

---

95. I hasten to add that these are nowhere stated in the text—they're just me violently précis-ing twenty-five thousand words.

96. A pertinent observation by one of Montaigne's translators, Donald M. Frame. More from him in a moment.

Nowhere is this assertion more demonstrable than at the close of the *Essays*. The tone is as beguiling as it is artless, and one feels somehow privileged to be trusted with these musings. It's as if we've become part of an inner circle, a cabal, whose instigator cares deeply for our spiritual well-being. Montaigne clearly feels time's wingèd chariot drawing near, and he's examining everything in the context of eternity. It's his last chance to set matters straight, to tell us what he's learned—not necessarily what he knows, but what he's learned, for knowledge moves relentlessly forward, and learning is a continual process. As he himself says:

All the fruit I have reaped from my learning serves only to make me sensible how much I have to learn.

And the *Essays* are the living embodiment of that humility. Montaigne's wisdom and is for the most part worn so lightly, he makes you forget you're reading one of the world's greatest books of philosophy. It's not a sermon, or a treatise, but a series of observations, recorded by a man clearly at peace with himself, yet rarely smug or self-satisfied.

The best way any of us could honour Montaigne is to be tolerant, understanding—and try our damnedest not to be stupid. That's how knowledge is put to best use. And although we will inevitably be frustrated in those ambitions until the day we die, it doesn't really matter. 'Our duty is to compose ourselves, not to compose books', he wrote, somewhat ironically for me and him, '[and] our great and glorious masterpiece is to live properly.' Well, we can but try. And perhaps, having read Montaigne, we'll hopefully make a better job of it than we otherwise would have done.

And there is one final lesson Montaigne can teach us greater than any of this: to value the life we have been given:

We are great fools.

*'He has passed his life in idleness,' say we: 'I have done
nothing to-day.'*

*What? have you not lived? that is not only the fundamental,
but the most illustrious, of your occupations.*

*'Had I been put to the management of great affairs, I should
have made it seen what I could do.'*

*Have you known how to meditate and manage your life?
Then you have performed the greatest work of all.*

Soon afterwards he starts discussing his bowels again.

Chapter Twenty Five

Postscript: Reasons To Be Cheerful

*My trade and art is to live; he that forbids me to speak according to my own sense, experience, and practice, may as well enjoin an architect not to speak of building according to his own knowledge, but according to that of his neighbour; according to the knowledge of another, and not according to his own. (***Book 2, Chapter 6: 'Practice Makes Perfect'***)*

All that remains for me to do is to perhaps make a few observations about what this prolonged re-acquaintance with Montaigne has meant to me.

But first I'm going to apologize: given that this book is about one sixth of the length of the collected *Essays*, I hope its selectiveness has not distorted or compromised the breadth of Montaigne's vision *too* much. It has been utterly frustrating beyond belief not to be able to include so much wonderful material, but it's all there in the *Essays* to enjoy.

Besides that…

At the end of many crappy films, the camera pans upwards from its immediate subject towards the heavens, in a cheap and easy attempt to confer some universal significance on what's gone before, or else to point to a hopeful future. In novels, characters climb to the top of a mountain or man-made landmark, and survey the scenery below. Which is exactly what I'm going to do now...

Reading Montaigne ultimately cheers me up, even when philosophy in a broader context doesn't seem up to the job. He reassures me, by his own example, that it is possible to lead a life largely free from despair, no matter what may happen. For although, throughout this book, I have focused almost exclusively on his sanity and philosophic composure, Montaigne's life was not an uninterrupted catalogue of earthly delights: the death of his best friend Étienne de la Boétie in 1563 was a trauma from which he never truly recovered; he lost five of his six children in infancy; his duties in the Bordeaux *Parlement* continually frustrated him; during a protracted period of civil unrest he was harassed by partisans, narrowly avoiding kidnap and even death; he was arrested in Paris in 1588; he and his family were condemned to six months of wandering when the plague struck his home town; and there was of course the chronic debilitating and hugely painful illness inherited from his father. Not much there to celebrate.

Yet amid this fairly continuous catalogue of woe, the *Essays* give no sense of a man gripped by despondency, but one who possesses an utterly enviable inner calm that is his protection against fortune's buffetings. It's this serenity that not only makes him attractive as a personality, but also conveys a compelling sense of natural authority: as he himself remarks in his usual puzzled tone, 'persons who had no manner of knowledge of me have put a very great confidence in me'. When briefly held captive by political extremists and in fear of his life, he is suddenly released by the leader of the brigands, who informs him that 'I owed my deliverance to my countenance and the liberty and boldness of my speech.' Similarly, when surprised in his own home by a gang of murderous thugs, Montaigne is spared by the ringleader who professes himself in awe of his 'countenance and frankness.' Finally, in 1581, he was elected Mayor of Bordeaux *in absentia* by four of the biggest movers and shakers in France—Catherine de' Medici, Henry III, Henry of Navarre, and Margaret of Valois—who weren't known to be particularly well-disposed towards one another. Yet the high esteem in which they individually held Montaigne managed to unite them into giving him the job without so much as an interview.

How could a man so ostensibly modest and unassuming pull this off? What's the secret of this quiet authority? If we could only bottle it...

I was once editing an interview with Pete Townshend of The Who, during which he described the first time he visited the HQ of his guru, the Meher Baba, in South Carolina. I can't remember his exact words, but he recalled that his fellow disciples, who were on the quiet side of boisterous but perfectly pleasant and welcoming, unsettled him. 'These were people,' he said, 'you definitely did *not* want to fuck with.' Only he couldn't say why. Townshend was at pains to point out that they weren't physically threatening—'they just had something about them.' Even from the perspective of twenty years, he still seemed to be not just in awe, but even a little cowed by the memory of these people and the almost palpable strength of their philosophy. Which for a rock star with Pete's ego is quite something.

I've lately begun to wonder if Montaigne wasn't possessed of that same singular presence—minus the creepiness, of course, which we can probably put down to some of Pete's many goblins. For beneath all the diffidence, understatement, reticence, disinterest, fair-mindedness, self-deprecation and bowel movements skulks a man with a cast-iron intellectual resolution—yet one who appears so casual, relaxed, modest and *laissez-faire* that he is the perfect role model for those of us whose moods are, shall we put it, less dependable, whose calm is more frequently ruffled, and whose philosophy is more... contingent.

In wanting to emulate Montaigne, some readers have convinced themselves they actually *are* him. Or perhaps more correctly, that he is just like them. I too have fallen, Zelig-like, into this category. According to Donald Frame, who produced an excellent translation of the *Essays* in 1958;

One of the mysteries of the Essays is how the portrait of Michel de Montaigne seems to become that of every man and thus of the reader. No one has explained this. [Ralph Waldo] *Emerson expressed it when he wrote of his first reading of Montaigne: 'It seemed to me as if I had myself written the book, in some former life, so sincerely it spoke to my thought and experience.'* [Blaise] *Pascal's comment is intriguing: 'It is not in Montaigne, but in myself, that I find all that I see in him .'*

Well, Donald, I'll take up your gauntlet and try to address the issue using my own experience as a guide.

To recap: If Montaigne *is* 'every man', what *is* it about him that we find so attractive? And what makes us see facets of ourselves in the portrait of 'Montaigne' we each assemble from our reading?

Part of the answer is, of course, contained in that second question; we feel we know Montaigne because, whether we realize it or not, we've all had a hand in creating him, just as we assemble our own versions of David Copperfield, Anna Karenina or Silas Marner when reading those texts. And because the *Essays* aren't a collection of dusty old saws but a vivid self-portrait, that's the easy part. The Montaigne most of us create, as I noted at the beginning of this book, is a bloke you'd like to buy a pint. Or several. Which indicates that he's at least likeable—and probably a decent sort of chap too. And we'd all like to be thought likeable and decent, and deserving of a pint.

But the second half of the answer is the tilt of the gaze upwards I noted at the start of this section: his message is life-enhancing, and he makes us feel that is not an impossible dream beyond our ability to grasp. He is not setting himself up as a guru whose followers creep us out, or, indeed has any followers at all beyond his readers (and those on social websites) [97]: his own philosophy is, 99% of the time, not parachuted in from some mysterious higher realm accessible only to the self-appointed few, it grows steadily and organically within himself, accreting round his personality and dispositions as he gets older, a process we can witness as we read. And so we build his vision together as we absorb the 20-plus year intellectual journey that the *Essays* represent. He does not tell us what to think; rather he *encourages* us to think, as the Amazon reviewer I quoted right at the start had already realized.

So, by way of conclusion, let's briefly look at the two generative components of that vision: Montaigne himself and Optimism: In Book 2 of the *Essays*, Chapters 17 and 18, entitled 'Of Presumption', and 'Of Giving The Lie' respectively, seem to mark a turning point in the text, and I think it's here, after a lot of noodling around in Book 1, Montaigne finally hits his stride and finds both his purpose and his voice. Donald Frame again:

The earliest chapters, written in 1572-74, are mainly short and relatively impersonal compilations of anecdotes with a rather brief commentary. In

---

97. Fact—in the last hour alone, 10 Montaigne quotes have been posted on Twitter from different correspondents all over the world.

some, however, Montaigne enlarged on certain problems that then beset him, such as death (Book 1: Chapter 20), pain (1: 14), solitude (1: 39), and inconsistency (2: 1). As he continued, the chapters became longer, looser in structure, more personal, more consistently on subjects of direct concern to himself.

Spot on. Frame continues by stating (accurately) that Montaigne's writing of his 'Apology For Raimond de Sebonde' (Book 2, Chapter 12) finally made his realize his true subject was Mankind; if humans were the worthless creatures of Sebonde's philosophy, it was high time they were rehabilitated. Yet he could only, with any honesty or clarity, speak for himself. So Montaigne set out to record as much wisdom as he could claim—while remaining painfully aware of his ignorance.

However, before he could assume the role of Everyman, he had to put himself through a job interview. So, he asks in 'Of Presumption', am I typical? Am I a worthy candidate to stand for the whole of Mankind? On balance, he thinks it would not be an act of gross presumption: he is not the lowest dregs of humanity, nor is he the noblest. Being average, therefore, he can truly epitomize the mode, the mean and the median of our species, the kind that is most numerous and therefore, it might be argued, the most representative. If he has any talent, he writes, it is for sound judgement and common sense, which will both come in handy.

Then, in 'Of Giving The Lie' he tests his capacity for accurate reportage and telling the truth. He passes this second test with flying colours.

With those two most important boxes ticked, off he goes. And from this point onwards, I don't think it's too fanciful to state that Montaigne grows in self-confidence; with his editorial line and purpose clearer, the *Essays* are no longer a simple *vade mecum* of received wisdom—they are endowed with profound originality.

Of course, having read the *Essays*, we would probably argue that Montaigne is far from average—in fact he's truly unique. But after applying a bit of sophistry, we can still think of him as Everyman—not so much the typical human being, but someone we would *like* to speak on our behalf if we were ever called on to justify our existence.

Now for that second generative component: Optimism. Another significant turning point had arrived in Book 1, Chapter 25 ('Of the Education of Children'), in which his conception of philosophy flips from negative to positive. A previous essay (Book 1, Chapter 19 'That To Study Philosophy Is To Learn To Die') takes its cue from Cicero, agreeing that all man-made wisdom and reasoning ultimately teaches us not to be afraid of death. In the later essay, he notes that, on the contrary, philosophy teaches us how to live well and happily. Somewhere in his mind while preparing the first edition, those two components fused and the second animating philosophy of the *Essays* was born, possibly without their author realizing it. By the time he's got to Chapter 12 of Book 3 'Of Physiognomy', he's ready to give his definitive statement—and leave Cicero far behind:

If we have not known how to live, 'tis injustice to teach us how to die, and make the end differ from all the rest; if we have known how to live firmly and quietly, we shall know how to die so too. They may boast as much as they please:

 Tota philosophorum vita commentatio mortis est;'

 ['The whole life of philosophers is the meditation of death.'

 —Cicero, Tusculan Disputations, ii. 30.]

but I fancy that, though it be the end, it is not the aim of life; 'tis its end, its extremity, but not, nevertheless, its object; it ought itself to be its own aim and design; its true study is to order, govern, and suffer itself. In the number of several other offices, that the general and principal chapter of Knowing how to live comprehends, is this article of Knowing how to die; and, did not our fears give it weight, one of the lightest too.

So knowing how to die is at best a mere subsection or postscript of a far greater theme—that of living. And so I feel we're entitled to modify T.S. Eliot's assertion that Montaigne had no philosophy at all, by saying that he created a wonderful stealth philosophy that Eliot simply didn't notice—in the absence of any systematic or ordered statements from the author, Eliot's preconceptions of what philosophy should be (erudite and difficult, like his own thinking) were destined to be frustrated.

Montaigne's, by contrast, is a philosophy that doesn't exclusively belong to academics or the super-educated. It involves, and indeed belongs to all of us. Indeed, as Ralph Waldo Emerson concluded, he had 'the genius to make the reader care for all that he cares for'. And that goes for *any* reader.

That's why he cheers me up. And it's also why we need him today more than ever: we don't need to get our opinions second-hand from anyone, because Montaigne gives us the tools and the confidence to think what we like, and the example, as I said earlier, to think *well*.

As to what Montaigne might think of living in the 21st-century... I think he would be highly amused, but far from surprised, at how little human folly has advanced in 500 years. A successful philosopher is never surprised.

Author's Note

Being given the chance to write this book has been something of a privilege: not only have I had the chance to re-acquaint myself with the great man; within the sanctuary of its covers, I've had the unspeakable luxury of not having to know things categorically and/or immediately.

So thanks to Simon Petherick, Tamsin Griffiths, Ian Pickard, Ryan Davies and everyone at Beautiful Books for the opportunity, help and support; all friends and family, sadly too numerous to mention individually (with the exceptions of Ernest Newrick and Victor Neuberg, grandfather and godfather respectively); Amanda Reynolds for her patience, understanding and suggestions; to everyone over the last 50 years who has made me think—teachers, lecturers, mates down the pub, work colleagues, broadcasters and writers—everyone. And of course: Fred and Betty Kent, the two best friends and mentors a lad could have wished for; and Christine—wish you were here.